SKYSCRAPER

SKYSCRAPER

The Politics and Power of Building New York City in the Twentieth Century

BENJAMIN FLOWERS

UNIVERSITY OF PENNSYLVANIA PRESS

PHILADELPHIA

Copyright © 2009 University of Pennsylvania Press

Published by
University of Pennsylvania Press
Philadelphia, Pennsylvania 19104-4112

Printed in the United States of America on acid-free paper

10 9 8 7 6 5 4 3 2 1

Library of Congress Cataloging-in-Publication Data

Flowers, Benjamin Sitton.
  Skyscraper: the politics and power of building New York City in the twentieth century / Benjamin Flowers.
      p.   cm.
  Includes bibliographical references and index.
  ISBN 978-0-8122-4184-6 (alk. paper)
  1. Skyscrapers—New York (State)—New York.   2. Architecture and society—New York (State)—New York—History—20th century.   3. New York (N.Y.)—Buildings, structures, etc.   I. Title.
NA6232.F66   2009
720'.483097471—dc22   2009004272

CONTENTS

INTRODUCTION

Narratives of the Built Environment:
Architecture, Ideology, and Skyscrapers

The tradition of all the dead generations weighs like a nightmare
on the brain of the living.
—Karl Marx

Landmarks, including many churches, had fallen to the dictator's bulldozers. In their
stead rose a forest of uniformly depressing apartment buildings. Beyond them, etched
against the frozen sky, was a steel gray forest of cranes that would have built yet
another layer of these ordered hives that had been Ceauşescu's vision of his gridded,
controlled world. The dictator's architect had been poised to erase the country's past
in order to transform it into a single cube of square cement in homage to their boss.
—Andrei Codrescu

In the mid-1980s my family moved to Bulgaria. My father worked for the State Department. At the time it was a hard-line Communist nation; few of the social or political reforms (or schisms) that took place in Yugoslavia, Poland, Hungary, or Czechoslovakia during the 1960s and 1970s took hold in Bulgaria, one of the closest allies of the Soviet Union. All Bulgarian children were required to learn Russian at school, and prominent sites all over the capital Sofia, where we lived, were named in honor of the Soviet Union (the "Hotel Moskva," "Rousski Boulevard," and the "Monument of Russian Liberators" still come to mind). Conservative analysts of the Eastern Bloc at that time noted that of all the East European ruling parties, the Bulgarian Communist Party (BCP) "demonstrated the most consistent loyalty to the Soviet Union."[1] It was rumored that Todor Zhivkov (who led the Bulgarian Communist Party for more than three decades and was in power longer than any other Soviet-bloc leader) once offered to make Bulgaria a part of the Soviet Union. An epigraph in a guidebook I still have to Sofia's cultural heritage notes (for those who did not know already): "The fascist hangmen tried to turn Sofia into a graveyard of revolutionaries, instead it became the pantheon of the revolution that triumphed." The shop where you bought your bread might be next to the House of Fighters Against Fascism and Capitalism.

Everything was political in Bulgaria. The Party, nationalism, and entertainment and arts commingled in everyday life. It was state policy that the broad fields of artistic endeavor serve revolutionary aims. While an official policy on cultural expression provides an immediate, obvious, and direct opportunity for dissent, resistance to the political authority of the state was no easy task. Under Zhivkov's leadership, members of the cultural intelligentsia were courted and rewarded by the state with an array of financial and personal privileges. Partaking, participating with the state apparatus repeatedly and over time, was a journey that left many, as one Bulgarian author noted, drained of their "distinctive creative identity."[2] The writer Georgi Markov made it more plain when he said: "They don't pay us to write, they pay us not to write."[3] If raising members of the cultural intelligentsia to the ranks of the elite didn't serve to cure them of their dissident fervor, there were, of course, other more permanent solutions. Markov, who left Bulgaria in 1969 and continued his dissident activities in England, discovered this when he was assassinated by the Bulgarian secret police in 1978.

Although state-sponsored television (the only kind) was broadcast for just a few hours a day (and even then was used mostly to provide updates on the latest five-year plan and news that the boot factory in Plovdiv had once again met and exceeded its annual production quota), the American cartoon *The Flintstones* was dubbed into Bulgarian and broadcast several nights a week. The cartoon was considered a depiction of American workers who, confined by the strictures of capitalism, labored in jobs that exploited them, their revolutionary instincts blunted by their desire for material rewards: a gargantuan brontosaurus steak, a new foot-powered car, or a night on the town at the bowling alley. Wilma and Betty, confined to the home by the gender divisions that helped sustain the capitalist labor market, were to be pitied. It was, all in all, not an entirely ridiculous interpretation.[4]

Amid this cultural battle between East and West (at a time when those stood in for capitalism and communism), Bulgarian architecture, rather than calling on the long and rich cultural heritage of a state with over a thousand years of history, was decidedly modern. International Style city planning was everywhere, with tall apartment blocks set among large green spaces. High-rises, the result not of density or high real estate costs but of the cultural weight attached to them, were employed for hotels, office towers, and luxury apartment buildings for the *nomenklatura*. Often positioned near major traffic arteries, these buildings were cast as testaments to the technological finesse of Bulgarian architects and engineers. Just as skyscrapers are seen as proxies for prosperity in the United States, so too were they in Bulgaria. Despite the phenomenal cultural, political, economic, and social differences between Bulgaria and the west, the rhetoric of modernism was surprisingly similar. History books celebrated Bulgaria's "new architecture . . . pure forms, glass and aluminum."[5] One such glass box tower located near our apartment was kept lit every night as a symbol of Bulgarian modernity, in spite of the fact that the surrounding neighborhood was pitch black due to chronic electricity shortages. Modern architecture was an index of the success of Communism, of the forward progress of Bulgarian history. One survey of the nation's architecture put it in a mouthful: "Modern Bulgarian architecture was born in the spirit of the 9th of September Uprising, after the defeat of capitalism and fascism and was and continues to be inspired by the drive for socialist construction."[6] What would pass for corporate modernism in New York was in Sofia the modernism of the Party. Context made all the difference in the world.

When a few years later we moved to Romania, I saw architecture similarly deployed for complex purposes. Nicolae Ceaușescu's architects and builders demolished hundreds of historic buildings, replacing them with monumental structures he thought were a testament to Romania's (and his) greatness. This process operated in fits and starts until the earthquake of 1977 provided a rationale for widespread demolition and rebuilding. It reached a crescendo in the final decade of Ceaușescu's regime; a 1989 report sponsored by the World Monuments Fund noted: "During the past six years large areas of old Bucharest have been destroyed almost in their entirety and rebuilt. . . . Simultaneously approximately 30 towns throughout the country have been razed and rebuilt according to new principles enacted by decree."[7] Bit by bit, building by building, the history that did not fit into the narrative of a revolutionary Romania was demolished and displaced by structures that ostensibly did. The centerpiece of this rebuilding effort was the Casa Poporului ("the House of the People"), a massive government headquarters with gold ceilings and 40-foot solid oak doors. The second largest building in the world (the first is the Pentagon), it was material evidence of the madness of the "Genius of the Carpathians," as Ceaușescu liked to be called. Churches, hospitals, and much more were destroyed to make way for this gargantuan, postmodern behemoth with its bizarre amalgamation of styles, along with housing for 50,000 families. Its construction occupied 100,000 workers, and the natural resources of the nation were plundered to adorn its interiors in fine woods, crystal, gold, and marble. Only the vehicles of Ceaușescu's motorcade were allowed on the Boulevard to the Victory of Socialism that led to the entrance. After the revolution, one popular pastime for Romanians was to drive up and down this road to nowhere.

The metro entrance gaped at our feet like a huge open mouth. We had read that the metro entrances of Bucharest were also entry points into Ceaușescu's maze of tunnels, a secret subterranean network constructed to outlast even nuclear war. . . . The underground network was reputed to be thousands of miles long, multilayered, a complicated nervous system whose exact shape and direction no one single person knew. Architects who had worked on portions of the system had been killed. When I told a poet friend that I could not think of anything similar in the modern world, he said: "I can . . . the Romanian mind after forty-five years of dictatorship."[8]

Marx wrote that the traditions of all the dead generations weigh like a nightmare on the brain of the living. In Bucharest it was not just the minds of the living that were weighed down: the city itself was haunted by the ceaseless tradition of demolition and building that fortified Ceauşescu's regime and gave it form. Just as the totality of the construction project was thought known to no single individual, the scope of destruction was difficult to know; the number of houses razed in Bucharest was "considered a state secret."[9] While Ceauşescu ruled, Romanians lamented, "We are dreams in the mind of a madman."[10]

Now Ceauşescu is dead, executed with his hated wife Elena in a grim courtyard of his own preferred design, but his built empire survives. Disassembling something so vast would mean dismantling the very commercial, industrial, and domestic infrastructure of the nation. Appropriated now to different groups and tasks (former palaces house the "new" ruling elite, composed mostly of aging former *nomenklatura*, apparatchiks, and Securitate thugs; the Casa Poporului houses offices of the two chambers of Parliament and a museum), these structures nevertheless carry the weight of history and pass on that burden. Nearly every block contains reminders of the tyrannical past, either in the form of the buildings, or in absences—the demolished churches, synagogues, houses, cafes, museums, and on and on. Ceauşescu and his architects butchered swaths of Bucharest, building in the clear-cut old quarter structures "whose only achievement," one Romanian architect summarized, "is the celebration of the power of having done so."[11] Even Baron von Haussmann and Napoleon III would have been impressed by the scale and scope of the undertaking.

My own understanding of the relationship between politics and architecture was profoundly shaped by the experience of living in societies where buildings spoke to all who passed by or entered, not just of aesthetics or history but of the very systems that governed their lives. Buildings were not symbols, they were forces—active participants—in the creation of the hegemony whose influence extended throughout every aspect of life. In this environment, one Romanian architectural historian put it, "It's quite frivolous to talk only about style or the details of that building, when you know that people were being killed because of that building."[12] Indeed, as Luminita Machedon and Ernie

Scoffham point out, of all the developments in Bucharest that "scar its soul," the built environment, "this last legacy—and all its connotations, the memories and the inhumanities that accompanied Ceaușescu's dictatorship from 1965 to 1989—is the hardest to bear, because it happened within most people's lifetime and because the buildings, the physical artifacts, will not go away." Buildings weigh on the brain of the living, and Ceaușescu was not the only one to understand this.

The buildings of New York are thousands of miles from Bucharest or Sofia, and they were shaped by a radically different society. The differences between the New York of the Great Depression and the city at the start of the twenty-first century alone are staggering. However, similar impulses exist in the forces that shaped the skylines here and there, then and now. Hilde Heynen writes, "It is my belief that modern architecture *has* the capacity to articulate in a very specific way the contradictions and ambiguities that modern life confronts us with."[13] While I am sure she was not referring to the seemingly contradictory embrace of modern architecture as a symbol of both capitalism and communism during the twentieth century, her point nonetheless resonates with that. Walking down Fifth Avenue today, one can hear the voices of those who say we are now residing in a non-ideological world, that the contest of the Cold War is over and we (or rather capitalism) won. Conservative commentators now describe ideology much as would orthodox Marxists from the other side of the Iron Curtain twenty years ago: as something standing in for the truth, a form of false consciousness. Capitalism then is no longer ideological but the truth of the way the world works; postmodern culture no longer labors under the weight of ideology, but is free to express true artistic desire. Alan Balfour, ruminating on the future of Berlin at the start of the twenty-first century, writes: "Now, relieved of the burdens and uniforms of ideologies, architecture has been freed to represent and enhance the myriad mysteries of existence."[14] But as Walter Benjamin cautions us: "for art's sake was scarcely ever to be taken literally; it was almost always a flag under which sailed a cargo that could not be declared because it still lacked a name."[15]

The three essays in this book each address a different skyscraper (or, in the last case, pair of skyscrapers): the Empire State Building, the Seagram Building, and the twin towers of the World Trade Center. These essays are not an attempt to write an exhaustive history. Any of these buildings could occupy a writer for a whole book, and indeed, each of the three is the subject of multiple monographs of varying lengths. This book is not a general history of the skyscraper in Manhattan; such a project is far vaster than the one undertaken here. Nor is it a survey on New York City in the twentieth century. Rather, these essays are narratives of the built environment. This project is modeled on previous works of architectural and urban history like Gwendolyn Wright's "interpretive essay" on housing in the United States that seeks to relate "various architectural and ideological modes"; Max Page's work highlighting the "fundamental tensions—both physical and cultural—at the heart of the urban experience"; and Carol Willis's treatment of skyscrapers as "vernaculars of capitalism."[16] Each of my narratives is an effort to examine the creation of a skyscraper as a form in space, and then the more abstract construction of each of these monumental buildings as malleable and often conflicting symbols for particular modes of urban habitation, differing political agendas, shifting cultural values, and disparate economic conditions. The architectural monument, Joseph Siry points out, "stands historiographically at the intersection of multiple narratives—architectural, technical, urban, cultural, and political—that reveal its meaning for its patrons, architects, and audiences."[17] My hope is that these skyscraper narratives flesh out the way monumental architecture resides at the rich intersection Siry describes.

Building is an expressive act, and the skyscraper is but one (albeit a phenomenal one) of the myriad expressive acts that form the urban landscape. Modern architecture in particular is an effort not just to define the contours of the present moment, but also to explain something about how the future should unfold. But these narratives are not fixed and stable. Buildings often outlast the particular context of their creation; skyscrapers age into eras when the ideas that motivated their creation have long since fallen out of favor. Making sense of the built environment around us depends on our ability to discern not just the symbols and forms that give it meaning at present, but also how, when, and why those forms arose in the first place and the values for which they were imagined to stand. Indeed, buildings are perhaps the most powerful and universal illustration of Faulkner's comment that "the past is never dead, it's not even past."[18]

In order to structure these narratives, I have afforded primacy to two overarching points of critical inquiry. The first is to explore the role of ideology in shaping the production and reception of the skyscraper. I am interested in how the skyscraper is deployed by the people who commissioned, financed, and built it to legitimize their political, economic, and social beliefs as well as their place in society. The clients for the Empire State Building, Seagram Building, and World Trade Center had specific agendas they hoped to further via architecture generally and the skyscraper specifically. This work studies those agendas as well as the reactions the trio of buildings elicited in the architectural and popular press. These buildings were and remain subjects of great interest among architects and critics and others outside those fields. I believe that exploring these competing voices, whether of patrons, architects, curators, builders, critics, or audience, offers a new understanding of the modern skyscraper. My second goal, following from that, is to examine the way wealth and power operate to reorganize the urban landscape. Exploring these two concerns will flesh out the relationship between the modern skyscraper and the broader cultural shifts that took place during the twentieth century.

As Neil Harris notes, such an approach affixes a "temporal dimension" to a building that is, "not simply an add-on." He argues that a temporal dimension is "fundamental" to a building's history as it takes into account "the individual resources of designer, builder, and patron," incorporates into the analysis "the work and business practices a building's space enclosed as well as the organizational culture it supported, [and] the popular as well as professional reception given to its appearance." Recording a building's life in such a fashion, Harris asserts, "constitutes both a challenge to writers of architectural history and a promise of a new way of relating to the heritage that surrounds us all."[19] My goal is to uncover the "temporal dimension[s]" of these buildings. Rather than elaborating on the already extensive body of formal criticism about the buildings, I focus on issues of patronage, construction, and reception.

Inevitably a project such as this must wrestle with the issue of selection. Why only three buildings? Why these three buildings? These questions vex the work of the historian of any time period. As Dorothy Habel notes in her study of Rome during the papacy of Pope Alexander VII, "The study of urban architecture breeds a certain tension: On the one hand there is the city itself as a built environment, and on the other there are the individual buildings that define the built environment."[20] It seems unquestionable to me that each of these three buildings is widely embraced as an icon of New York City. But more than that, each of these skyscrapers, though exceptional (whether in cost or height), also stands in for the building culture of its time. Perhaps other buildings reached greater aesthetic heights (certainly few hold the twin towers as models of formal stylistic achievement); perhaps other interventions into the urban landscape have held the historian's gaze more strongly in the past. So be it. The logic behind choosing these three skyscrapers depends not just on the characteristics of the individual skyscraper but on the potential for revealing new and previously unexplored connections, insights, and conditions when examined in concert with one another.

The Empire State Building, Seagram Building, and WTC represent multiple divergent uses of modern architecture. Located in the city that epitomizes the restless activity of the American marketplace, it seems inevitable that these buildings should stand in for the particular mode of capitalist organization of their time. As we shall see, the Empire State is a symbol of an era rooted in the values of an older producer economy— and its attendant definitions of Americanism—while the Seagram Building emerged from an expanding consumer culture that, during the Cold War, reworked the themes of Americanism and democracy the Empire State addressed decades earlier. Its somber exterior of repeated volumes is the appropriate analogue for a corporate entity that grew not by producing new products itself, but by purchasing other companies that did. The WTC, for its part, was a monumental capstone to the tremendous arc of the global U.S. economic expansion over the course of the twentieth century, with all its attendant social, political, and cultural conflicts. In the process of accommodating a gargantuan program designed to house an imagined global trading hub the twin towers reworked what Sandy Isenstadt calls modern architecture's "mandate of technological commensurability" to devastating heights.[21]

I chose the method of close examination for a variety of reasons. The first is that reactions to an individual building or exhibit offer clear examples of the struggles over architecture. As an architectural historian I am interested in the specific, particular details of history that can enlarge and enrich our understanding of building or exhibit, the architectural culture of which it is a product, and the time period in which it was produced. I want to take the opportunity to examine closely the many aspects—financial, aesthetic, or historical—that viewed critically allow us, in the words of one historian, to "penetrate the ideological significance of architectural form."[22]

Here I am indebted to the work of Eric Foner and his illustration of ideology as "the system of beliefs, values, fears, prejudices, reflexes, and commitments—in sum, the social consciousness—of a group, be it a class, a party, or a section."[23] Identifying the "ideological significance of architectural form" has vexed critics of multiple generations and viewpoints. Analyzing the expression or materialization of ideology in architecture requires a particular mode of inquiry. Unlike literature, where the expression of ideology can be narrative, or criticism, where it can be argumentative or discursive, ideological meaning in architecture employs spatial, historical, and experiential elements. These expressive elements, whether abstract, literal, metaphorical, or phenomenological, are often deployed in concert, adding to the layers of possible interpretation. At the same time, the predispositions of critics and historians leave them receptive to certain interpretations. Reviewing some of the critical tendencies of the past century, architectural historian Hilde Heynen describes how Walter Benjamin saw in modern architecture "the impetus . . . for the creation of a desperately needed 'new barbarism' that responds to the requirements of a new society, one that would no longer be based on mechanisms of exploitation and exclusion." Others, like Ernst Block and the critics associated with the school of Venice, "disclaim that architecture would be capable in one way or another of actually contributing to a project of emancipation and social progress." Somewhere between the two, Theodor Adorno thought architecture, like art, had a dual nature, "being socially fabricated as well as autonomous," and that this duality "generates a capacity for resistance and criticism."[24] My own tendency is to step outside the debates about whether architecture can express critical or revolutionary ideals, or serve the purposes of social emancipation. I do not wish to celebrate or condemn buildings from the standpoint of their ideological sincerity, strength, or weakness. I am interested in how modern architecture can express the positions of its clients or curators, and how different groups, informed by their ideological positions, interpret that same architecture.

Beyond a desire to explore the ideological significance of architectural form, these narratives trace the relationship between architecture and politics (broadly construed) during a century of great change. Clearly my analysis cannot exhaust the fullness of the relationship between building and politics, but it can add to the collected body of work on the subject, pointing to new sites of inquiry and new directions for study. A close study of these buildings illustrates the relationship between the practice of architecture and the economic conditions that shape building. It also reveals how architecture and building come into existence within the various trains of cultural thought at the time, and how these also play a role in determining form and the meaning assigned to it. Finally, each of the buildings was the result of the efforts of very determined architects, patrons, and investors, each of whom had a vision (generally preserved for history) of what architecture could contribute to the urban fabric.

In this I am in agreement with Sharon Zukin who writes: "We owe the clearest cultural map of structural change not to novelists or literary critics but to architects and designers."[25] Any study of modern architecture in the United States must acknowledge that architecture expresses the conditions of its creation. Far from being artifacts, however, buildings and the meaning we attach to them do not remain static. The agendas that were the impetus for the Empire State Building no longer define the building for contemporary audiences. Similarly, the Cold War context so crucial to understanding the Seagram Building today is for many merely a memory; while the form remains the same, new stories, myths, and interpretations have been layered onto Mies van der Rohe's classical geometries. Alice Friedman has written thoughtfully on the gender norms at the heart of the modern architecture's (often awkward) relationship with domesticity in the twentieth century.[26] As we will see, gender norms played a pivotal role in the Seagram Building's creation and reception, a role that was largely ignored until recently. The twin towers, now remembered as much as known, are vessels heavy with meaning they did not carry before their destruction. This tide of change itself is a topic worthy of attention, but before we can understand these changes, we must return to the eras in which these buildings were erected to examine the motivations behind them.

The history of modern architecture in the Unites States is a complex subject. Its development in the United States was neither wholly independent of political and economic influences nor wholly dependent on them. Rather, modern architecture developed, in the words of Nancy Stieber, "as a semiautonomous factor within a dynamic theater of social relations."[27] The goal of my research is to describe how architecture—as a form of aesthetic expression and as a social practice—was transformed in the rich and varied American context (economic, cultural, and political) over the course of the twentieth century. This transformation occurred within historically contingent opportunities and constraints, and while the final products of that transformation, the buildings themselves, are well known, the tensions between opportunity and constraint that shaped them are not. "Those tensions," to quote Nancy Stieber again, "are what the historian can and must try to describe."[28]

One effort to do just that is Annabel Jane Wharton's study of the relationship between politics, architecture, and the Cold War in the construction of Hilton Hotels. Wharton describes how executives and designers at Hilton believed that modern architecture was one of the "most convincing demonstrations of the vitality of American culture."[29] Conrad Hilton, founder of the corporation, insisted that modern architecture was a weapon the United States must deploy in its battle with communism: "We mean these hotels as a challenge—not to the peoples who have so cordially challenged us into their midst—but to the way of life preached by the Communist world."[30] After World War II, in an era when, according to Henry-Russell Hitchcock, "American architecture has come to occupy a position of special prominence in the world,"[31] it is crucial, as Wharton notes, to understand its role in the construction of "American identity and self-representation." My research is an effort to understand these concerns at a different site, remembering her caveat that politics are embedded in architecture, and that the effects of this "continue when you aren't looking."[32]

PART I

The Empire State Building:
The Setback Skyscraper,
the Great Depression,
and American Modernism

1

Building, Money, and Power

The Medal of Honor for 1931 of the New York Chapter of the American Institute of Architects has been awarded to R. H. Shreve, William F. Lamb and Arthur Loomis Harmon, designers of the Empire State Building. . . . The noble simplicity of this structure makes it an inspiring landmark in our city.

—Announcement in *Architectural Record*, 1932

Why build the Empire State Building? Why build the tallest building in the world? Much of what we know about the Empire State Building centers on its size, which admittedly is difficult to communicate through words alone. Approaching the building on foot in Manhattan from a distance is probably the only way to take in the enormity of it. The phenomenal human effort required to construct the building becomes much clearer when you stand at its base and cast your glance skyward in a vain effort to see the top. The famous mooring mast, the most recognizable feature of the building, is only visible from a distance; up close it is hidden by the massive shaft which supports it. The base of the building, running the length of Fifth Avenue between Thirty-Third and Thirty-Fourth Streets (and consuming nearly half the block between Fifth and Broadway), is seldom recorded in photographs published in architectural histories or guidebooks, leaving first time visitors to the building unprepared for the size of the Empire State's footprint. Its enormity was surely even more striking when it was completed in 1931 in the midst of the Great Depression.

Historians and architects offer a variety of answers to the question of why we live among skyscrapers and why they look as they do. Louis Sullivan matter-of-factly described the skyscraper as the result of "social conditions." Sullivan's primary concern

Figure 1. The Empire State Building, 1934. Courtesy of the Library of Congress.

with the skyscraper was not how it came to be but how it would come to express "those higher forms of sensibility and culture that rest on the lower and fiercer passions." The question for Sullivan boiled down to this: "How shall we proclaim from the dizzy height of this strange, weird, modern housetop the peaceful evangel of sentiment, of beauty, the cult of higher life?"[1] Others view the ascending heights of tall buildings as an aesthetic response to increasing technological innovation and suggest that, while usually unburdened by piety, skyscrapers, like the spires of cathedrals and churches, nevertheless express a desire to ascend to the heavens. An alternate explanation treats advances in technology as a factor in the race for the sky, but posits that the driving force behind ever-taller buildings lies elsewhere: "Man may once have been inspired to ascend toward heaven, God, whatever, by building high; but in the end it was not divine thoughts but money, ambition, and the desire for power that created the skyscraper."[2] Yet in the 1920s, as one architectural historian notes, "the distinctions between commerce, culture, and civic life narrowed."[3] One result was that the form of the tall building could carry some or all of the symbolic heft of commerce, church, and civic values. Without doubt, this mix influenced the creation of the Empire State Building. In such a scenario the tall building can serve more than a single agenda while remaining, in the words of architect Cass Gilbert, "a machine that makes the land pay."[4]

For these reasons the Empire State Building must be understood as more than a business venture. It was, as we shall see, a building intended to celebrate a new America, built by men (both clients and construction workers) who were themselves new Americans. In the 1920s and 1930s the United States was divided politically and culturally between older, rural traditions and emerging modern urban ones. The construction of the Empire State Building, fueled by the wealth and power of clients who were the children of immigrants rather than the scions of old New York society, served to add status and legitimacy not just to the men who built it, but to a vision of a pluralist, modern, urban America. With its economical design and its general lack of reference to historical styles, the building embodied an architecture freed from many of the aesthetic restraints of the past. It was a building appropriate to a city upon which "the stamp of modernity was early put on," as William Taylor notes, "by a succession of photographers and other graphic artists who were sensitive to the visual character that the city was assuming and who saw in these new shapes and forms a vision of the future."[5] Capital from around the United States and the globe coursed through the institutions of New York. Likewise labor poured into the city from places far and wide. These combined with vast material resources—steel, stone, glass and more—in the creation of the skyscraper. For the clients of the Empire State the building was more than an investment; its creation and its subsequent fame offered opportunities for negotiating changing cultural and political norms in a quest to transform themselves from outsiders to insiders in American society.

A number of aspects of the Empire State Building make it well suited for such a task. First and foremost it is a skyscraper, a building type that, as Robert A. M. Stern notes, "placed America in the forefront of architecture . . . the nation was at last more than a cultural colony of Europe."[6] Yet Stern's accolades pale in comparison to those of critics in the 1920s like Fiske Kimball, who argued that the skyscraper symbolized American architecture and was regarded "not merely as one of the wonders of the history of art but as one of the crowns of human endeavor."[7] Others in that decade were no less effusive; Edward Avery Park wrote that the skyscraper "is an expression of our unheeding youthful vitality, the genius of the day. By ingenuity and courage we have set down in one spot a great measure of our strength and made it fit and beautiful. It is our very own effort."[8] Perhaps more important, as Deborah Pokinski points out, the skyscrapers of this period, responding to the restrictions of the landmark comprehensive 1916 New York City Zoning Resolution as well as the needs of clients, "were the most conspicuous architectural development of the twenties, discussed and lauded by conservatives and progressives alike throughout the decade."[9] Indeed, Pokinski notes, while many critics since have been content to write off the 1920s as a "dark age" that preceded the arrival of modern architecture from Europe (in the form of a Museum of Modern Art exhibit discussed later), the setback skyscraper of the 1920s (such as the Empire State Building) "became the prototype for a new American skyscraper style."[10]

More than appearance makes the Empire State Building an icon of the era of its creation. The personal stories of its clients slotted neatly into a populist narrative of self-determination and opportunity. While at first it seems incongruous to regard the world's tallest building as an emblem of populist thought or rhetoric, it is important to remember that it was built due in large part to the efforts of John Raskob, an Irish Catholic self-made millionaire, a man whose life story epitomized the ideal of a classless American capitalist democracy where grit, talent, and determination—not ancestry—paved the road of opportunity. Raskob, the son of immigrants, was an outsider in the elite world of big business in New York. His ability to accrue wealth and political influence was cast in newspaper articles as a testament to the possibilities that awaited other new Americans in a country defined by pluralism and opportunity for all. It is no surprise to find that Raskob regarded himself in such a light and that he dispensed sage financial and social advice in an article in 1929 titled "Everybody Ought to Be Rich."[11] He was joined in his efforts to build the Empire State by Alfred Emmanuel Smith, former four-time governor of New York, Democratic presidential candidate, and the best known Irish American politician of his time. Raskob cast his financial success as a testament to the boundless opportunities of the American marketplace; Smith's career was for many an index of the rising political power of urban immigrant communities. Finally, Raskob's quest to build tall was buttressed by the wealth of Pierre S. du Pont, Raskob's longtime business partner, and also one of the wealthiest men in the United States at that time. Pierre du Pont kept a low profile, but his involvement nevertheless complicated the public's response to the Empire State Building.

More than the personal stories of Raskob and Smith gave this skyscraper its association with populism, that strain of American thought with, as Richard Slotkin notes, faith "in economic individualism" and a desire for "a broad diffusion of opportunity to 'rise in the world.'"[12] The Empire State Building was designed to accommodate small and medium-sized independent businesses rather than large corporate clients. It is a building whose program offers a plethora of modest offices and an efficient use of space to serve the needs of a capitalist democracy rooted in small, independent producers. Indeed, the building's distance from Wall Street prevented close association with the large banks and trusts whose influence in American society was a source of significant political contention in the 1930s. Even today the views of tenants in the Empire State Building reflect these populist values. Jack Brod, a dealer in metals and jewels, moved into the building when it opened in 1931 and still occupied his small, cluttered offices on the sixty-seventh floor in 2000. When asked about the landmark battle by Donald Trump to buy the building in the late 1990s, Brod spoke with pride of his small part in preventing "the big wheels" from taking over the Empire State Building. Donald Trump, he said, "was full of crap."[13]

The construction of the Empire State Building was guided as much by the political and economic interests of its patrons as by the aesthetic interests of the architects who designed it. The "hegemonic ambitions of New York's urbanists," David Scobey notes, merit consideration as "they sought programmatically to embed their class authority in the fabric of the built environment."[14] At the center of the group were two men whose ethnicity and religion made them outsiders in American society. By building the Empire State Building in a style that was, as Deborah Pokinski writes, "convincingly modern and conspicuously American," these men placed themselves at the top (and center) of a new, modern, urban, society.[15] The honors that accrued to the building, such as the AIA Medal of Honor, also accrued to its clients.

Unfortunately, most historical and architectural studies emphasize the Empire State Building's technological advances and feats of engineering but underplay the complexity of the impulses at the heart of its construction and the rich variety of responses the building engendered.[16] Robert A. M. Stern, in his history of architecture in New York City, while detailing the changes in the plan and form of the Empire State, attributes these solely to the architects, mentioning only in passing that the building was backed by "investors."[17] Similarly, while Dell Upton correctly describes the "widely admired massing of the Empire State Building" as "derived from the calculus of lot coverage, rental values, [and] building costs," he gives no explanation for why and how people chose to invest capital in buildings rather than equally (or more) remunerative investments.[18]

Carol Willis fruitfully explores the interplay between architecture and finance, describing how "form follows finance," yet her research contrasts the subjective aesthetic concerns of architects and designers with the (in her view) objective and rational interests of builders, businessmen (renters), and financiers.[19] In this formulation economics are the "chief determinant of form."[20] As a result, Willis distinguishes aspects of a building's planning and construction that are "entirely financial, not architectural."[21] Whether a clear division could ever be drawn between the financial and architectural elements of the building process is a question open to debate. Certainly imposing this distinction on a building such as the Empire State Building raises as many questions as it answers. In the end Willis, in creating a dichotomy between "subjective" aesthetics and "objective" economic demands, misses the chance to engage the ideological nature of capitalism itself. This is an oversight worth correcting, as speculative real estate ventures such as the Empire State Building are never exclusively objective or rational projects.

Building the "monument to American hubris in the Roaring Twenties" required financial muscle, political connections, and the right friends.[22] It required, in other words, power. The construction of skyscrapers is intended to provide a physical manifestation to that power, a memorial to power for all to see. But beyond memorializing power, skyscrapers enact the power of their patrons to alter the skyline of a city, to change the daily routine of city residents, to enable certain paths through the city and block others. Skyscrapers change the pedestrian patterns around them, the path of wind as it flows through the city, sunlight and shadow. They present a vision of a particular kind of ordered urban existence. While their construction is clearly a financial undertaking, it is also so much more.

The Outsider Clients

> I am sure that you will agree that John [Raskob] should be set up on a pedestal for his patience in working out this splendid investment against serious odds. The pedestal of his monument is the Empire State Building itself.[23]

Personality and personal history influence architecture. The exploration of the personality and sensibility of a particular architect, as other critics and historians have pointed out, is widely embraced by architects themselves since the "distinctive personae" created in the process were usually as "well known to the public as their architecture."[24] In the case of the Empire State Building, however, to understand the broader cultural significance of modern architecture—here particularly its appropriation by clients seeking legitimacy in American society—one must understand the history of those "outsider" clients. The men who built the Empire State Building had fame, wealth, and political power. Legitimacy in the eyes of society, was that elusive element that neither fame, nor wealth, nor political power had yet truly provided them. To understand the motivations of the clients, we must understand their backgrounds, their place in American society, and their ambitions. These histories in turn help us make sense of the range of reactions the building elicited on its completion and throughout the 1930s.

With the exception of their own palatial estates, neither Raskob nor du Pont had previously been involved in building projects. As governor Al Smith had supervised

Figure 2. Estate of John Raskob, Claymont, Delaware. Courtesy of the Hagley Museum and Library, 70.200.02931.

Figure 3. Longwood Gardens, the former weekend home of Pierre S. du Pont, near Kennett Square, Pennsylvania. Courtesy of the Hagley Museum and Library, 70.200.07485.

sizable bond issues to fund hospitals, prisons (including Sing Sing), and other facilities, but he had no experience supervising speculative real estate investments and certainly was not versed in selling commercial office space.[25] Barons of New York real estate these three were not, and it showed.

In 1929 when they proposed their project, they chose a location outside the existing business district and poorly served by public transportation. The Empire State Building far exceeded its "economic height" (the height that would produce the maximum return on investment). The commercial real estate market was already nearing saturation and in less than a year the stock market would collapse and the United States would enter the longest and severest depression in its history. According to the principles of investment then and now, it was a serious gamble. Other investments would certainly have made a safer home for the dollars of du Pont and Raskob, and Al Smith could have found easier jobs than filling the vast empty floors with tenants.

Figure 4. Conservatory, Longwood Gardens. Courtesy of the Hagley Museum and Library, 70.200.06863.

John Raskob

John J. Raskob was born in 1879 into a large, working-class Catholic family. His father was a cigar maker of Alsatian descent, his mother Irish.[26] In classic Horatio Alger fashion, the rags into which Raskob was born could hardly predict the riches he would enjoy later in life. Pierre du Pont hired Raskob in August 1900 as a bookkeeper; he had a "sharp, quick, ingenious mind that was especially good at the manipulation of figures" and was soon helping Pierre with his various financial schemes.[27] The two became friends, and perhaps no one was ever closer to du Pont than Raskob (to the dismay of some in the du Pont family, who dubbed him "Raskal").[28] So close were the two that Raskob referred to du Pont (only nine years his senior) as "Daddy" (as did Pierre's siblings). The relationship was no mere business partnership but a lifelong friendship between two men with an intense devotion to one another. Pierre du Pont never had children of his own, but in the words of one historian Raskob served as du Pont's "devoted and grateful son."[29] A letter to Pierre thanking him for the loan of funds used to purchase Du Pont stock expresses the extent of Raskob's filial devotion:

> Dear Daddy,
>
> It is hard for me to express myself in words under ordinary circumstances and it seems impossible to properly do so when my heart, always so full of love and affection for you, is filled to overflowing with the thought that you too really care so much for one who at times, I fear, has been very unruly and sorely tried your patience. . . .
>
> . . . With me there has not been the slightest opportunity to fail because you just wouldn't let me and the magnified credit you always give me is really a reflection for you and your work in a mirror you have succeeded in polishing after a great deal of hard work. Remember, Daddy, it is always possible to ruin mirrors through breaking them, and aren't you afraid of spoiling me through your continued praise? . . .
>
> Now I am going to build another monument by keeping your gift as a fund separately invested to grow and be used in the future in some way that will ever make me think of you in my endeavors to handle it in a way that I think will make my Daddy love me more if that is possible.[30]

Their lifelong bond was one in which accumulation of wealth and exchange of affection were inexorably linked. In later years, each would describe the Empire State Building as a monument to the other.

When Pierre du Pont became chairman of the board of General Motors in 1915, he saw to it that Raskob was also brought onto the board.[31] Raskob's major tasks at GM revolved around his skill at complex financial transactions; as chair of the Finances Committee he was responsible for many of the financial innovations of the company.[32] Over the next two decades Raskob and du Pont oversaw the transformation of GM from a corporation on the verge of bankruptcy to the largest manufacturing company in the world. For them, whether corporations or buildings, size mattered.

Raskob and du Pont also became well-known political figures. By the late 1920s Raskob, then best known as a financial wizard, had an increasing interest in politics. Then as now, politicians and the business elite traveled in the same circles and Raskob's control of large sums of Du Pont and GM capital made him a powerful and popular figure among the heads of banking institutions and other leaders of New York society. However, Raskob's political interests were also unusual in that he was interested in national rather than local Irish politics. (Anti-Catholic bias was still a prominent feature of American life, and at the national level, neither the Republican nor the Democratic party had

Figure 5. Pierre S. du Pont and John J. Raskob, 1937. Courtesy of the Library of Congress.

given Catholics positions of leadership.)[33] His two central political concerns, not surprisingly, mirrored those of Pierre du Pont. Both opposed Prohibition and increased
government regulation of industry generally. In 1927 Raskob and du Pont joined the
Association Against the Prohibition Amendment with the goal of increasing its membership and lobbying powers in the various state legislatures.[34] Soon afterward, by

virtue of his network of business and social connections in New York and his willingness to participate in public appearances, Raskob became the association's best-known spokesperson.[35]

In the political climate of the late 1920s, an "articulate 'wet'" like Raskob "attracted the attention of leading Democrats in New York."[36] At the same time his newfound interest in the repeal of Prohibition was drawing him, a Republican until then, closer to the Democratic party. By 1927 Raskob had been introduced to Governor Al Smith, and according to Alfred Chandler:

> Smith and Raskob immediately took a liking to each other. Both were devout
> Roman Catholics as well as "wets." Each considered the other a man of humble
> origin who had "made good" in his field. Moreover, Raskob's wealth and his
> business reputation (the press enjoyed extolling him as one of the financial
> wizards of the age) made him especially welcome as a recruit to an organization
> that was devising plans to challenge the party of business and prosperity.[37]

Concerns that Raskob's association with du Pont and GM, or his personal fortune of $100 million, might be in conflict with the political trajectory of the Democratic party in the coming years seem to have been subsumed by the political expediency of having a popular "wet" associated with the party.[38] The Great Depression would change much of that. In 1928, however, when Al Smith wrapped up the Democratic nomination for president he tapped Raskob to be his campaign manager and chair the Democratic National Committee. With du Pont's blessing Raskob accepted the offer. Raskob used his influential position on Wall Street to champion Smith's candidacy as one friendly to big business, saying, "Alfred E. Smith as President would give the country a constructive business administration. Business, big or little, has nothing to fear from Governor Smith." The statement was reprinted by a correspondent for Dow, Jones, and Co. on the company's ticker and within an hour GM stock rose by 3.5 points.[39]

Pierre du Pont

The first son of eleven children born to Lammot du Pont and Mary Belin, Pierre S. du Pont (1870–1954) was as quiet and introspective as a child as he was in his adult years. The DuPont Company,[40] which Pierre would one day head, controlled some 90 percent of the U.S. gunpowder market and DuPont gunpowder was sold around the globe.[41] Under Pierre's direction, the family business would expand into chemicals and plastics, accrue profits at a phenomenal pace, and become the model for the modern American corporation. While DuPont was largely a family-run company, Pierre had a calculating and ruthless mind for business, one disinclined to allow family relationships to interfere with business. In 1902, "amidst the great merger mania of the early Progressive Era," Pierre and two cousins (T. Coleman "Coly" du Pont and Alfred I. du Pont) "capitalized on the death of chief executive Eugene du Pont to seize control of the family corporation."[42] The three cousins now controlled a company with assets worth between $12 and $14 million, including the world's largest black powder mill, in Mooar, Iowa.[43] By 1915, with the help of Raskob and through a series of stock buyouts and aggressive court actions, Pierre had wrested sole control of the business from his cousins, largely against their will. As one historian of American business describes it, Pierre's singular dedication to his corporate interests made him "the single most influential executive in not one but two of the nation's largest and most powerful business corporations during the most critical periods of their existence."[44]

Due certainly in part to the fact that business came first, Pierre did not marry until he was forty-five. In keeping with a du Pont custom favoring marriage between cousins to preserve family wealth and to "be sure of honesty of soul and purity of blood," he married Alice Belin, a maternal cousin.[45] They had no children.

Pierre, free from the obligations of family, focused on building the DuPont empire, one that was under regular scrutiny from the government. As early as 1907, congressional hearings about DuPont monopolies in the chemical and munitions industries raised the specter of anti-trust suits. Federal antipathy toward the family and its business was not eased by their wealth (company assets in 1914 were $308 million) or their secretive corporate practices.[46] During World War I, for instance, "Du Pont refused to provide the Secretary of War with information on the company's foreign munitions contractors." Similarly, requests for technical trade information were not acceded to until after the U.S. entered World War I and placed major orders for TNT with the company.[47]

The Great War was good business for the DuPont company. Net earnings on munitions were $5.6 million in 1914 and $82 million in 1916; in 1918, even after a fall in powder prices, the company netted $47 million.[48] Pierre diversified corporate holdings, moving into chemical production and paving the way for continued corporate growth.[49] By 1919 he wanted to step down from leading the family business and retire to his gardens at his 200-acre estate, Longwood.[50] As his responsibilities at DuPont lessened, he soon replaced them with new ones in the process of reengineering the General Motors Corporation. His tenure at GM with John J. Raskob was characteristic of the "managerial revolution that swept American corporations after 1900" and added to the already enormous wealth of the du Pont family.[51] Pierre retired from active involvement with the day-to-day management of GM in 1928, and shortly thereafter became a primary investor in Empire State, Inc.

Although the family business brought the du Ponts great wealth, it was not without risk. Explosions at the powder mills were not uncommon; a deadly one involving nitroglycerine ended Pierre's childhood. When his father was killed at the family's Repauno Chemical Company (which produced dynamite), Pierre, at fourteen, told his mother "I'm the man of the family now."[52] His younger brothers and sisters from that point on called him "Dad." "Years later," one biographer notes, "he would be called the 'father of the modern corporation.'"[53]

Al Smith

If John J. Raskob was the "industrial imperialist" and Pierre S. du Pont the progenitor of "industrial federalism," then Alfred Emanuel Smith, at the end of his career, was in many regards the industrialist's politician.[54] Yet, according to one historian, Al Smith also was the politician who more than anyone else of his time "did more to demand that the new generation of immigrants be included as Americans."[55] This is not surprising, given his origins as a working-class Irish Catholic boy from the Fourth Ward (near the Brooklyn Bridge and bordering on the Bowery) who left school at age fourteen.

Smith began his political career as a Tammany Hall Democrat, and while he lobbied for numerous reform causes and considered himself an ally of "the little man," he would, in time, come to oppose Franklin Roosevelt's presidency, join the wealthy and very conservative American Liberty League, and attack the policies of the New Deal.[56] The story of Smith's career, as a politician and later as a public figure, is a complicated one. After all, although Smith was a Tammany politico through and through he knew the laws and regulations of the state of New York as well as or better than any of his contemporaries. His time in the various political offices he occupied was spent making numerous back room deals, but he also was moved to undertake reforms for the cause of, in his words, the "rabble from the city," and "the little guy." Like Raskob, Smith was a newcomer to American politics and big business. As one historian puts it, "In every fiber of his being, Al Smith personified the new American."[57] While Smith's political legacy today has faded, when he died on October 4, 1944, one eulogizer was moved to pronounce "no event since the death of Abraham Lincoln, fourscore years before, stirred so deeply the sympathy and reverence of the people of our country."[58]

Born December 30, 1873, in a tenement on the Lower East Side, Al Smith came to be the "leading Irish-American politician of his era," and remained, until the election of John F. Kennedy, the best-known Catholic politician in the United States.[59] His parents, Alfred Smith, Sr., a Civil War veteran who worked as a mover, and Catherine Mulvihill, at various times an umbrella maker, seamstress, and shopkeeper, were the chil-

Figure 6. Tenement at 174 South Street on the East Side where Al Smith was born. Courtesy of the Library of Congress.

dren of immigrants. While Smith's family were not the poorest in the Fourth Ward in those years, they were far from well off. Smith's father died when he was twelve and his mother's health began deteriorating soon afterward, in all likelihood due to the long hours and poor conditions under which she labored at the umbrella factory. Smith quit school at fourteen and spent the next several years working as a newsboy, shipping clerk, at the Fulton Street Fish Market, and finally as a laborer at the Davidson Steam Pump Works in Brooklyn. He met Catherine Dunn, a daughter of Irish immigrants in the Bronx, in 1894, and married her in 1900 after a long courtship. They had five children together.

Tom ("Big Tom") Foley, the Fourth Ward Tammany boss, launched Smith on his political career. Smith's ability to execute "contracts" (passing money or information between players in the Tammany machine) made him a favorite of Foley, and in 1903 he was rewarded with a nomination for state assembly.[60] He easily defeated his Republican opponent, with the support of Tammany Hall and 75 percent of all votes cast.[61] Smith's loyalty to those who had provided him with such opportunities was commensurately fierce: "In the assembly Al did as he was told, voting the Tammany line."[62]

In 1905 Smith's career changed course when his friend James Wadsworth was named speaker of the Assembly. Through him Smith obtained committee appointments and went from a low level figure in the Tammany machine to real political power in the Assembly.[63] Whatever educational deficit he may have had, Smith more than made up for with his relentless study of the procedures and rules that governed the operation of the Assembly. By 1909 he was considered one of the most powerful Democrats in the Assembly, and according to one Republican, "the most dangerous man in the state to tangle with because he knew more about state government and its actual operation than any other man."[64]

Smith's years in the legislature gained him a reputation as a reformer and friend of the downtrodden. This legacy rests largely on his legislative efforts following the horrific Triangle Shirtwaist fire of March 25, 1911. That fire, which broke out late in the afternoon, killed 146 sweatshop workers, mostly young immigrant Jewish women and girls, in less than fifteen minutes.[65] The emergency exits had been locked by the employers to prevent workers from taking unauthorized breaks and the deficient fire escape collapsed when fleeing workers attempted to use it. The exits that were not locked opened inward, and the crush of workers attempting to flee the building made opening them nearly impossible. Some women tried to climb down the elevator cables and fell to their death. Others, their hair and dresses on fire, jumped from the windows and roof to their death. Their bodies hit with tremendous force, in some cases breaking through the sidewalk and falling into the subway below. Some who jumped were impaled on the wrought-iron fence that ran along one side of the building. The fire department's life nets were useless, as they could not withstand the force of bodies that fell from nearly ten stories. The factory owners were never convicted of any crime. It remains the worst industrial fire in the history of New York.[66]

Widespread outrage over the fire and tremendous loss of life led to the creation of the Factory Investigating Commission (FIC), which Smith vice-chaired. Charged with the task of investigating safety and working conditions in city factories, the FIC encountered "some of the most wretched work environments in the nation's history."[67] Men, women, and children labored under conditions that robbed them of just recompense, dignity and health, and humanity. One child, asked by FIC investigators how long he had worked at a cigarette rolling factory, replied, "Ever since I was."[68] These findings propelled the 1913 passage of numerous reforms at both the municipal and state level. Smith's involvement with such measures as the 1913 workplace safety and fire safety laws aligned him with the progressive, reformist wing of American politics. Yet he was still a Tammany Hall man, and his political actions outside the FIC reflected this.[69]

In 1915, after a brief stint as speaker of the Assembly, Smith was nominated for sheriff of New York County, a comfortable political reward for his years of hard work within the Tammany Machine, and was elected by a broad margin.[70] Largely without political clout, the real value of Smith's new position was financial; his salary went from $1,500 per year to $12,000. Furthermore, the sheriff kept half of all monies he collected and, as the chief duties were to collect money and property from debtor businesses and individuals, this was no small bonus. All in all Smith was probably earning around $50,000 a year.[71]

Two years later Smith ran for president of the Board of Aldermen, the (distant) number two position in the city after mayor, on the Democratic ticket. In 1918, a year later, he ran for governor, winning narrowly in a campaign truncated by the influenza epidemic that swept the nation and the globe. He received the endorsement of President Woodrow Wilson and Franklin Roosevelt (then secretary of the navy), and positive coverage in the newspapers of William Randolph Hearst; he courted the votes of union members and newly enfranchised women.[72]

His victory, while sweet, was short. In 1920 he lost his reelection campaign against Republican Nathan Miller, a former corporate attorney. It was the first election Smith had ever lost. Undaunted, he regained the governor's mansion in 1922 and was re-elected twice. As governor Al Smith brought little-known Yale graduate Robert Moses into his inner circle of advisers. It was Smith's tutelage that led to Moses becoming, as his biographer Robert Caro describes it, the man "who shaped New York."[73] It is one of those curious twists of history and place that Moses started his career under Smith and ended it many decades later paving the way for the World Trade Center. While governor in 1924 Smith ran unsuccessfully for the Democratic nomination for president; he succeeded in 1928.[74]

After spending a great part of his career appealing to the specific concerns of his New York constituency, on entering the national political stage Smith shifted his rhetoric and strategies rightward. Whereas his earlier work with the FIC in the wake of the Triangle fire had left him skeptical of industrialists and their claims that any industrial reform would ruin the American economy; now he made one of the richest industrial leaders in America his campaign manager and head of the Democratic National Committee. After appointing Raskob, he noted "I believe that it is good political strategy to let businessmen of the country know that one of the country's most important industrial leaders has confidence in the Democratic Party as well as in its platform and in me."[75] While Smith supporters hyperbolically called Raskob's appointment "the boldest and most courageous thing in the history of American politics," supporters of the progressive wing of the Democratic Party feared that the "era of Raskobism" would turn the party into a near-GOP.[76]

The 1928 presidential campaign pitted Alfred Emmanuel Smith—an urban politician, son of the Lower East Side, and proud Catholic—against Herbert Hoover—wealthy, midwestern, and Protestant. In his speech at the convention nominating Smith, Franklin Roosevelt had called him the "Happy Warrior," but the campaign of 1928, riven by the issue of prohibition and sullied by racial, anti-Catholic, anti-immigrant bigotry, left the Democratic nominee a warrior in a divided army.[77] One historian looking at the 1928 campaign wrote: "Al Smith, as a Catholic, a wet, an out-and-out urbanite, was a different type of candidate from those who had come before him . . . his candidacy was seen by many of his contemporaries as a litmus test of American toleration."[78] The campaign did little to burnish the image of American tolerance.[79] Smith was attacked as a politician of "rum, romanism, and ruin," and the language turned far dirtier as time progressed. Cross burnings frequently greeted Smith as his campaign moved through the South. The *Baltimore Sun* reported that Smith proposed changes in immigration law that would "mean unloosing on us a horde of immigrants from such races as have already been proved hardest to assimilate."[80] Similarly, in the *Christian Advocate*, Bishop Edwin Mouzon claimed the nomination of Smith signaled "the uprise of the unassimilated elements in our great cities against the ideals of our American fathers . . . Smith himself is utterly un-American."[81]

If Al Smith had been under the impression that his four terms as governor of New York meant that he was no longer an outsider in American politics, that notion was thoroughly disabused in 1928. He lost to Herbert Hoover in a monumental landslide. Hoover claimed 444 votes in the electoral college to Smith's 87 and won the popular vote by a margin of over 7 million. Smith lost traditional Democratic strongholds like Texas, Florida, Oklahoma, Virginia, North Carolina, and Kentucky, and in fact failed to win any state outside the South except Massachusetts and Rhode Island. He won New

York City (buoyed by the endorsement of Babe Ruth), but lost the state where he had been elected governor four times. It was one of Smith's few political defeats, but it was a resounding one, and it ended his career as an elected politician.[82]

On August 29, 1929, less than a year after his defeat at the polls, Smith announced plans for the construction of the Empire State Building.

Figure 7. Babe Ruth wearing a campaign pin supporting Al Smith, 1928. Reprinted by permission from Transcendental Graphics, Getty Images Sport Collection © Getty Images.

After he took on responsibilities as the public face of the Empire State Building, Smith's politics continued their rightward trajectory. In 1932 he challenged Roosevelt for the Democratic nomination and lost. It was a bitter defeat. Two years later Smith, "his emotions roiling, set aside his heritage and joined up with an organization remembered most of all for its wealth and for its blind, ineffective reactionaryism: the American Liberty League."[83] In the words of John Raskob, former DNC chair who now opposed the actions of his party, the League would "protect society from the sufferings which it is bound to endure if we allow communist elements to lead the people to believe that all businessmen are crooks."[84] The membership of the League was composed of presumably likeminded men of business, including Pierre and several other du Ponts, Wall Street financier Edward Hutton, Alfred P. Sloan of GM, and Sewell Avery of Montgomery Ward. Smith served on the executive committee, which often met in his office in the Empire State Building.

The league never had a membership that much exceeded 75,000, and its political impact was probably restricted to boosting Roosevelt's image as an ally of the common people against the vested interests. The Liberty League was clearly out of step with the times, and represented the views of a small, wealthy minority. Al Smith had always been a politician who appealed to the working poor, but now he was lobbying for the interests of the rich.[85] Roosevelt, clearly the more astute politician, made good use of the Liberty League's animosity toward him, telling a cheering crowd at Madison Square Garden in 1936 that members of the League "are unanimous in their hatred of me and I welcome their hatred."[86]

In an era when populist thought continued to resonate with Americans struggling with the effects of the Great Depression, the biographies of John Raskob and Al Smith were charged with meaning. Both were working-class boys who had attained respect, political influence, and social prominence. Overcoming the hurdles placed in their path in an era of intense anti-Catholicism, both were widely regarded as self-made men. John Raskob, son of a cigar maker, became one of the country's best-known industrialists and patron of the world's most famous building. Al Smith's career began in the Fulton Fish Market and closed with him in charge of the tallest building in the world. Popular opinion often overlooked that Raskob had gotten rich with the help of one of the nation's wealthiest industrialists and that Smith's career was in part the result of the efforts of one of the most powerful political machines in American history. At the same time, as the 1930s progressed, both men became increasingly intolerant of popular New Deal policies and engaged in political associations, in particular the American Liberty League, that allied them with very conservative trends.[87] Many could be forgiven for believing that when Al Smith moved his office from the governor's mansion to the Empire State Building his political allegiances underwent a significant shift.

Figure 8. Al Smith with his realtor's license. Courtesy of the Library of Congress.

Indeed, Smith's association with the Empire State Building marked a pivotal point in his career. But just as the Empire State Building was a defining element of Smith's public life, so too was the building shaped by his association with it. In newspapers throughout New York and the country, the Empire State was often referred to as "the house that Al Smith built." In barber shops and bars, where different standards of decorum applied, it was also known as "Big Al's last erection." The fame of the politician shaped public reaction to the building, and in turn the politician's reputation changed as well. It was difficult to define Smith's association with the Empire State as an extension of his political efforts to "fight for the little guy." Now he was on the side of the rich and powerful, the men many blamed for causing the Depression. Such a transformation could not take place without public notice. When asked by Raskob to join the Liberty League, playwright Elmer Rice responded: "To the hungry, the maimed, the disinherited of this land of ours, your phrases about liberty and freedom must seem as empty as the Empire State Building."[88]

To say that Pierre du Pont and John Raskob were motivated by profit to build the

Empire State Building is to get part of the story. Profit between these two men, after all, was about much more than money. Raskob thought of making money as a way to please his "Daddy," a way to make Pierre love Raskob even more. Pierre, who never had children of his own, seemed to relish Raskob's success, much as a father might that of his child. When Raskob seized on the idea of building the Empire State, it is not hard to believe that Pierre went along out of a desire to please Raskob. Of course, in the past Pierre had profited handsomely from funding Raskob's many ventures, but it is likely that Pierre thought of love in the same monetary terms as Raskob. While throughout his life Pierre demonstrated that in the pursuit of profit he was willing to take ruthless action against his own family, he never acted with such cold calculation toward Raskob.

In addition, both men throughout their lives made clear their desire to become figures of influence in American society. Raskob's tenure as chairman of the DNC, Pierre and Raskob's involvement with the Liberty League (largely funded with du Pont money), both men's stance on the need to repeal Prohibition clearly indicates not only their desire to express their opinions on issues of the day, but their willingness to spend money to add influence to their words. These actions sometimes raised the hackles of

Figure 9. Raskob testifying to Congress about his contributions to anti-prohibition causes, 1930. Courtesy of the Library of Congress.

the establishment, as when Raskob was grilled by Congress while chair of the DNC about his contributions to anti-prohibition causes. Desire for power is clearly central to the logic of both men's involvement with the Empire State Building. Recall that one historian, describing the break between du Pont and Franklin Roosevelt in the mid-1930s, wrote that the New Deal "had come to threaten something far more crucial to the family than profits—power."[89]

Clearly the creation of Empire State Building (in spite of the populist personal stories of two of its three clients) evokes progressive ideology with its emphasis on a "corporate economy and a managerial politics."[90] John Raskob and Pierre du Pont oversaw the transformation of DuPont and General Motors into two of the largest corporations in the United States, and in GM's case, the world. In the process, du Pont and Raskob established the managerial, financial, and organizational standards for the modern corporation, following the progressive vision of "the steady transformation of small individual concerns into large economic and political institutions—small farms into industrial farms, shops into factories and factories into corporate complexes."[91] This "steady transformation" played an important role in the construction of the Empire State Building. Some of the longest exchanges of correspondence in Pierre du Pont's files are those that address which suppliers would be awarded contracts for the Empire State Building. Time and again companies in which du Pont or Raskob had significant holdings or the du Pont family had interests in, had their goods and services chosen for the world's tallest building. As just one example, in mid-April 1930, du Pont received a letter from W. D. Gray, president of the Cardiff Green Marble Company, informing him that the quarry the company owned in Cardiff, Maryland, was one of two in the United States that produced green or verde antique marble. The letter informed Pierre that Cardiff Marble "is chiefly owned by Eugene du Pont and Mrs. Anne du Pont Peyton."[92] On the same day Pierre wrote to both Al Smith and Shreve, Lamb & Harmon: "I am taking the liberty of introducing W. D. Gray, representing the Cardiff Green Marble Company. The quarry he represents is owned by one of my relatives, who has called my attention to the quality of this marble. . . . Anything you can do for Mr. Gray will be much appreciated."[93] Two months later, after some twelve memos, letters, and telegrams between the different parties, green Cardiff marble was chosen in lieu of the originally planned light imported marble for all eighty-five stories (except the more ornate main floor).[94]

Pierre sent similar entreaties to Smith, Raskob, and the architects about a number of other businesses, General Bronze Corporation and Chase Brass and Copper Company among others, and they were subsequently awarded contracts for the Empire State Building. The skyscraper was not just a new form of architecture; it was a new frontier for economic investment and the production of wealth. Writing on the significance of the frontier in American history, Frederick Jackson Turner noted that "American social development has been continually beginning over again on the frontier. This perennial rebirth, this fluidity of American life, this expansion westward with its new opportunities, this continuous touch with the simplicity of primitive society, furnish the forces dominating American character."[95] Progressive ideology looked for new frontiers of economic growth to compensate for the end of westward expansion. The Empire State Building would not just remake the skyline; it would cast the trajectory of American economic and social growth not westward but skyward. Radical new architectural forms replaced the western frontier as generative forces. The skyscraper proffered a landscape disposed to support the needs of a modern, corporate, and capitalist republic.

The architectural style and form these clients chose mingled elements and cultural motifs to suggest that the construction of skyscrapers was part of a broader goal of civic improvement. In the 1920s and 1930s many regarded skyscrapers as "emblems of greed and unbridled competition."[96] Pierre du Pont's involvement with the Empire State Building took place during a time when Huey Long was fond of attacking "the du Ponts, the Vanderbilts, the Astors," as "pigs swilling in the trough of luxury."[97] Further negative publicity came in the form of congressional hearings on the U.S. entry into World War I and the role of lobbying by the munitions industry (which had made the Du Pont Company and family very wealthy) in that decision. Instigated by Senator Gerald Nye, the hearings, Alan Brinkley notes, seemed to confirm the worst criticisms against the Pierre du Pont by figures such as Long and Father Coughlin.[98] These attacks did not pass without notice at the Empire State Building. A letter to Pierre from Robert Brown, vice-president of Empire State, Inc., written at the time of the congressional investigations, notes "I am firmly convinced that aside from a few followers of Father Coughlin the general sentiment of the population is favorable and those of us who know you resent most heartily the attempt of the Nye Committee to make you appear malefactors."[99]

The clients for the Empire State Building sought to define not only their skyscraper, but the world of business itself, as a civic benefit. To do so, they chose to build in a form that while modern could nevertheless sustain associations that would ennoble the activity that took place within it. Of course, this effort required both the careful deployment of aesthetics and a thoughtfully marshaled publicity program. With great care and effort both client and architect helped invest the Empire State Building (the world's tallest and greatest skyscraper) with an aura of civic virtue that transformed it from a place of mundane white-collar activity into a cathedral of commerce.

This cathedral of commerce, built at a scale heretofore only imagined, was an effort by Raskob, Smith, and du Pont to build New York City (in particular Manhattan) as they thought it should be. The Empire State Building was an urban microcosm. The commute of white-collar workers on and off the island of Manhattan was replicated by the movement of such workers in and out of the Empire State Building. The blue-collar laborers who maintained, cleaned, and serviced the building were a smaller version of the army of labor that did the same for Manhattan. The day-to-day operation of the building regulated relations between the labor that worked there, the small business owners who rented space in it, and the mighty industrialist who collected the rent and paid the wages. The power of the patron was not just the power to raise the building in the first place, but the power to manage the economic and social world the building contained. The power to build is more than the power to change the skyline, it is the power to order the daily life of those who inhabit a building.

2

Setback Skyscrapers and American Architectural Development

The Site, Speculative Ventures, and Manhattan History

The history of Manhattan since the mid-nineteenth century is a chronicle of the finite supply of land, rising real estate prices, and the role of these two forces in shaping the form and skyline of the island.[1] Mona Domosh describes New York at the close of the nineteenth century as already the "ultimate material expression of a capitalist city," and notes that "its mercantile and financial elite class continued a never-ending search for outlets for conspicuous consumption."[2] As it is for the whole of Manhattan, so too is it for 350 Fifth Avenue.[3] To understand a building as something more than an object in space, we must come to grips with the historical legacy of its site. What sorts of social habitation took place there? How does architectural creation respond to this history? What agendas were enacted on the landscape not just by construction, but by the destruction that in a dense urban condition inevitably must come first? It is even worth knowing simply how a parcel of urban land is maintained over time. If the Empire State Building's lot had been sold off in pieces, or in any other way divided, the skyscraper we know today would never have been built.

Located between Thirty-Third and Thirty-fourth Streets, the lot the Empire State Building occupies was, in the early nineteenth century, farmland on the edge of the city. A family's wealth kept the lot intact, inherited by one relative after another for decades until it was sold, first to a relative of Pierre du Pont and then to the builders of the Empire State Building. William Backhouse Astor purchased the lot, which at the time of purchase ran from Madison Avenue at Thirty-Second Street to Sixth Avenue at Thirty-Sixth, in 1827 for $20,500.[4] His decision was far from arbitrary. His father, John Jacob Astor, became the wealthiest man in the United States by buying inexpensive property at the edge of development in New York and waiting for the growth of the city to multiply the value of the land.[5] In the 1850s William Backhouse Astor's daughter-in-law Caroline Schermerhorn Astor chose to move from Lafayette Place and build a house on the lot at the southwest corner of Fifth Avenue and Thirty-Fourth Street. She and her husband occupied a free-standing brownstone of grand but undistinguished proportions; her cousin John Jacob Astor III also built a home on the site. Despite the fact that the area was still largely farmland, the social presence of the Astors was more than enough to make it the center of high society for years to come.[6] At her home Caroline Astor organized balls, dinner parties, and other such forms of entertainment for the city's self-appointed elite. It was there that the "four hundred" came to be, named after the number of guests her ballroom served comfortably.[7]

By 1870 the character of Fifth Avenue around the Astor homes had changed. In place of the homes of the wealthy, forms of commercial spaces from stores to hotels had proliferated.[8] Between 1890 and 1897 two hotels rose on the site of former Astor residences, the Waldorf and the Astoria. The two eventually merged, becoming the famed Waldorf-Astoria.[9] The hotel was the largest in the city, with more than a thousand rooms. It was organized and equipped to satisfy the whims of the rich and famous who stayed for a night or stopped in for dinner and a drink. Its marble lobby floor, dotted with palms, was called "Peacock Alley," and it attracted a regular retinue of men and women anxious to see and be seen there.[10]

Just as the presence of the Astor clan attracted the rich to build their houses along Fifth Avenue, the presence of the Waldorf-Astoria "attracted major retail establishments to it, and the demand for business and office space continued unabated. This sweep of trade up the avenue was irresistible."[11] This influx of commercial development was exactly what many of the wealthy inhabitants of Fifth Avenue had moved there years earlier to escape. The construction of mansions in sizes ranging from grand to overwhelming was, according to Mona Domosh, "characteristic of a city where social standing needed to be constantly reconfirmed by displays of wealth, one of the most direct forms being housing."[12] After all, "these upper-class enclaves constituted the first homogeneous neighborhoods in the city, as Protestant, native-born, wealthy New Yorkers sought to flee what was increasingly a commercialized downtown inhabited by recent immigrants."[13] Once those mansions were surrounded by commercial businesses and the traffic from all walks of life they brought with them, the class cachet of a neighborhood declined.

In 1918 Coleman du Pont, Pierre's cousin, bought the leases for the Waldorf-Astoria. Coleman had decided to become a New York real estate mogul using the money from Pierre's buyout of his interests in the Du Pont Company.[14] The hotel continued to prosper, and in 1925 Coleman purchased the land on which the hotel sat from the Astors. Coleman du Pont had already made a splash in the New York real estate world

Figure 10. The Waldorf-Astoria. Reprinted by permission from the Museum of the City of New York/Byron Collection, Hulton Archive © Getty Images.

in 1915 when he financed the construction of the Equitable Building. The massive size of the building, rising straight up from the edges of its lot, in turn inspired the passage of the 1916 zoning plan, which used streetwall height restrictions, setback ordinances, and lot coverage standards that became a model for zoning standards across the nation.

By the late 1920s the political and social landscape of the nation and New York had changed and the Waldorf-Astoria was no longer the epicenter of elite society in the city. With that came an attendant decline in profits. The passage of Prohibition, the Eighteenth Amendment to the Constitution, was the final nail in the coffin for the hotel. The large and extravagant spaces of the Waldorf-Astoria, absent the lure of alcohol, went empty.

In a real estate market that was churning out new buildings at a rate unequaled in the city's history many property owners saw no reason to hold onto a building whose profits were declining. As historian Max Page notes, the "list of what was destroyed, what was built and destroyed again in this era, is stunning. Individual monuments of American architecture and engineering fell regularly, often only a few years after being built."[15] The effort to extract ever greater rates of return on capital investments, nurtured by easy credit and liberal zoning regulations, propelled the growth of New York by 38 million square feet of office space in the boom decade of the 1920s.[16]

In this bull market the Waldorf-Astoria presented a rare opportunity to any potential buyer: the chance to control a full-block site. Since 1925 office space in Manhattan had been built at a frenetic pace. Both speculators and capital were in abundant supply. What was in short supply was the opportunity to redevelop city lots of the size occupied by the Waldorf-Astoria. Developers trying to purchase entire blocks were faced with costly and time-consuming negotiations with building owners holding out for the highest offer. Developers like Irwin Chanin (who built the modestly named Chanin Building) lamented, "it is seldom, except when some old and large holding comes on the market, that an operation involving an entire block of property is at all possible. This is due mainly to the fact that the last property owner always holds out for the ultimate dollar, for which he cannot be blamed under the present system."[17] Developers faced with such conditions often built on irregularly shaped lots. A speculative building works best—that is to say earns the most profit—when its design accommodates the real estate market above all else. All this made the Waldorf-Astoria worth buying only to tear down.

Thus, even before the first steel beam was in place, the Empire State Building was exceptional because of the size of its lot. Indeed, the hunt for a large enough lot was decades later a factor in deciding the location of both the Seagram Building and the World Trade Center. The destruction of the Waldorf-Astoria and the plans to raise the Empire State in its place, furthermore, signaled an important change in the character of Fifth Avenue. Over the course of the twentieth century, Fifth Avenue "spun through cycles of construction and destruction at a rate unmatched in the city."[18] As Max Page notes, "If we are to locate and understand . . . the primary engine of Manhattan's continuous transformation—it is to Fifth Avenue, the 'spine of Gotham,' we must look."[19] For earlier critics like Henry James, developments on Fifth Avenue stood in for larger trends; if the Avenue was now "a monster of the mere market," so was the rest of the city.[20]

Architect and developer Floyd Brown, who had recently completed a skyscraper at a profit of $1,000,000, was prepared in 1928 to pay $14,000,000 for the Waldorf-Astoria, the highest real estate price recorded that year in New York City.[21] He put down $100,000 in earnest money along with $900,000 from the Chatham Phenix National Bank and Trust Company[22] to make his first mortgage payment. Then, in what was fairly standard practice for the time, he publicized his intentions to build a fifty-story 2,000,000-square-foot mixed-use building designed by Shreve & Lamb Associates. The design, flat-topped, composed of multiple setbacks and heavy massings, was large but otherwise not memorable. Nonetheless, it was Brown's hope that the renderings of the building, published in December in the *Real Estate Record and Builders' Guide*, would attract potential investors who would enable him to meet his next mortgage payment of $1.5 million.[23] Unfortunately for Brown, investors failed to flock to his proposal and he defaulted on his mortgage.

The construction of the Empire State Building represented a shift in the neighborhood economy from one based on provision of leisure and entertainment to one dependent on small businesses and entrepreneurs in the world's tallest office building. It would transform Fifth Avenue from a "millionaire's mile" of big name families to one populated largely by anonymous businessmen. Once home to the aristocratic grandeur of the Astors—and their retinue of the rich, royal, and famous, the 400—the Avenue was now the locus of the more mundane and modest world of middle-class, bourgeois capitalism. Even the name change was suggestive: unlike the Waldorf-Astoria, the Empire State Building didn't name its patrons. Rather than memorializing the wealth of the men who built it, the Empire State honored its place of residence. In place of "Peacock Alley" came the less extravagant two- or three-room office. In place of an opulent and ornamented hotel there would be a soaring tower, whose sleek façade pointed to the future, to a city of towers. Where the Waldorf-Astoria unquestionably celebrated the wealth of the elite scions of New York society, the Empire State Building—itself a symbol of great wealth—would memorialize the ingenuity and productivity of engineers, architects, and builders. They would raise a tower to hold thousands of white-collar workers. In the late 1920s it seemed as if their numbers might grow forever.

Louis G. Kaufman, president of Chatham Phenix Bank, knew the site had great potential for development. Pierre S. du Pont and John Raskob served with Kaufman on the board of directors of General Motors and the three were friendly, so in 1929 Kaufman contacted Raskob about becoming a part of the redevelopment of the Waldorf-Astoria.[24] After some preliminary discussion, Raskob sent Kaufman a letter dated August 28, 1929, outlining some of his thoughts on diving into the speculative real estate market. Written in a tone of address among familiars ("Dear Lou," it began), the letter outlined Raskob's willingness to supply, with Pierre du Pont, $5,000,000 in start-up cash for the project. Furthermore, the letter made clear Raskob's intention to revise Brown's original building plans. Instead of a fifty-story 2,000,000-square-foot building, Raskob proposed a 34,000,000-cubic-foot building of an undetermined height. According to Raksob erecting such a building, and buying the land underneath it, "would give a total cost of about $50,000,000."[25]

Raskob was vague about the particular use he imagined for a building of that size (office, loft, mixed-use, etc.) and did not mention style or design other than to point out that once funding was secured and the Waldorf-Astoria was demolished architects would be chosen to "prepare plans for a new building as expeditiously as possible."[26] He did outline the pay and benefits for the job of president that Al Smith would assume. The specific details revolved around financing for the building. Raskob closed his letter by noting, however, "I appreciate the opportunity you have given us . . . in the privilege of being associated with you and your group in the doing of something big and really worthwhile. I am sure it will be the most outstanding thing in New York and a credit to the city and the state as well as those associated with it."

Kaufman's reply to Raskob ("Dear John") notes that "we have had numerous calls from important downtown people" about the "Waldorf proposition," and closes with, "If this undertaking brings us closer together, it will remind me of the good, old, early days of General Motors, and I do not know of anything more pleasing than to have an active association with you, Mr. DuPont [sic] and the Governor."[27] The "good, old, early days" of GM had been very good indeed, making all three men very rich. Clearly Kaufman hoped this next project would do the same.

Kaufman organized a syndicate to join Raskob and du Pont as investors in the project, and together they assumed control of the property development corporation Waldorf-Astoria Office Building, Inc., which, on September 5, 1929, was renamed Empire State, Incorporated.[28] Late in the afternoon at the offices of Chatham Phenix Bank four days later, at a "Special meeting of directors," the Board of the Corporation unanimously appointed Al Smith president and Robert C. Brown (a vice-president at Met Life) treasurer and vice-president. John J. Raskob and Louis G. Kaufman were added to the board of directors and made members of the executive committee of the board, as was Smith. In addition, it was resolved that the president, vice-president, treasurer, and secretary (Fred L. Chapman) were now "authorized to obtain subscriptions for the remainder of the authorized unissued shares" of Empire State, Inc., at the rate of $5 for each share of common stock (99,990 unissued) and $95 for each share of First Series Preferred Stock

(99,990 unissued).[29] The organizational and financial management practices of the modern corporation were adopted for the construction of the world's tallest building.

A day later, September 10, 1929, Brown, in his capacity as vice-president of Empire State, Inc., sent a letter to Pierre outlining the corporation's offer to sell Pierre 25,000 shares of common stock and 25,000 of preferred stock for a total cost of $2,500,000. In addition Pierre's acceptance of the proposal would "constitute a contribution, to and for the benefit of the Corporation, by you as aforesaid of 25 percent of the Common Stock of the Corporation so subscribed for by you, and a release by you of all right, title and interest in and to such 25 percent of Common Stock."[30] Of this, 20 percent would go toward securing financing for the Corporation and 5 percent toward securing the "services of a chief executive" (in this case, paying Al Smith's $50,000 per year salary).[31] In essence Pierre would be giving Empire State, Inc., $31,250 (25 percent of his $125,000 common stock investment) for the right to buy into the development of the Empire State Building. Pierre accepted immediately.

Arrangements for financing and construction continued at a steady clip, and on September 20, 1929, the board of directors met again. Three crucial votes were on the agenda. The first concerned hiring the builder, Starrett Brothers, Incorporated.[32] The second was how much to pay (up to a ceiling of $675,000) for "the Astor property immediately adjoining on the West the real estate belonging to this Corporation and known as the old Waldorf-Astoria site." The third was whether to hire Shreve, Lamb & Harmon as architects. All three motions passed unanimously. In addition, Smith reported that the Corporation had received permission from the Mutual Life Insurance Company to begin demolishing the Waldorf-Astoria Building.[33] On the same day Empire State, Inc., signed an agreement with Shreve, Lamb & Harmon for $570,000 ("with reimbursements as hereinafter provided") for architectural and engineering services. The agreement notes that the proposed building "may be a 30-story building and may include an 80-story tower, and may contain approximately 34,000,000 cubic feet of volume (but it is understood that the size and character of the proposed building has not yet been determined)."[34]

In less than a month Raskob, du Pont, and Smith had gone from discussing the idea of a speculative real estate venture to forming a development corporation, securing the rights to the Waldorf-Astoria site, hiring a team of architects and a builder, and obtaining permission to demolish the mammoth hotel. This breakneck pace suggests that little time was available to ponder questions about the design and style of the building; in fact, most of the discussion on paper about the project to this point was financial. Throughout the second half of the nineteenth century development in New York City had been "controlled by real estate speculators, not public officials or planners."[35] The destruction of the Waldorf-Astoria and the plans to build the Empire State Building in its place in the first half of the twentieth century were driven in part by that same speculative fervor. But in addition to the urge to rake in profits, the speculators behind the Empire State were driven to remake the skyline of New York City.

The Architects

The architects of the Empire State Building are little remembered today. Fame in this case accrued to the building and not the architects.[36] The firm responsible for the design, Shreve, Lamb & Harmon, is absent from most surveys of significant architects of the twentieth century. Yet R. H. Shreve, William Lamb, and Arthur Loomis Harmon had excellent architectural pedigrees. Shreve received his degree from the school of architecture at Cornell, where he also served on the faculty after graduation. Lamb and Harmon both received degrees from Columbia's school of architecture.

R. H. Shreve and William Lamb met at the New York firm of Carrere & Hastings (Shreve joined in 1906, Lamb in 1911). In 1920 the firm became Carrere & Hastings, Shreve & Lamb.[37] Five years later Shreve and Lamb started their own firm, Shreve & Lamb.

Floyd Brown had hired Shreve & Lamb to prepare an initial fifty-story scheme. When his deal collapsed, Raskob retained the firm on behalf of Empire State, Inc. Raskob first met Shreve & Lamb in 1928, when the firm designed the General Motors Building (Columbus Circle between Fifty-Seventh and Fifty-Eighth Streets). That building was characterized by some critics as having a "directness of expression evident in few commercial buildings."[38] Raskob apparently approved of such directness of expression, as well as the firm's ability to handle large projects efficiently. Shreve & Lamb had already begun the initial designs for the Empire State when Arthur Loomis Harmon was invited by Shreve to join the firm. Harmon had worked previously as a designer for McKim, Mead & White and was an associate at Wallis & Goodwie for a brief stint before running his own firm for nearly twenty years. Shreve & Lamb became Shreve, Lamb & Harmon.

The firm had a reputation for the on-time and on-budget production of attractive, serviceable, and, critically, profitable buildings. In stark contrast to their contemporary Frank Lloyd Wright (or Ludwig Mies van der Rohe in the postwar era), the members of this firm regarded architecture as a business, not an art form. According to Lamb, "The day that an architect could sit before his drawing board and make pretty sketches of decidedly uneconomic monuments to himself has gone." Lamb had a general disregard for architects who produced "pretty sketches," and championed one who possessed an "intense earnestness to make practical necessities the armature upon which he molds the form of his idea."[39] His partners agreed. Shreve, describing the factors that shaped the design process for the Empire State in the pages of *Architectural Forum*, focused on programmatic concerns: "A fixed budget, no space more than twenty-eight feet from window to corridor, as many stories of such space as possible, an exterior of limestone, and completion date of May 1, 1931, which meant a year and six months from the beginning of the sketches."[40]

Such a view of architecture made the firm appealing to the businesses it served. More than just an opinion, it was the way the firm operated: there was a clearly defined and organized division of labor. Design concerns were handled separately from administrative and operational elements. Architects and other employees were divided into work groups charged with managing a single process in the design and construction of the building from beginning to end. In a foreshadowing of a trend that would radically rearrange the skilled workforce of the United States, aspects of planning and construction were subcontracted to experts in other fields as necessary. Finally, the contracts detailed flat fees rather than the American Institute of Architects 6 percent standard charge, a practice that reassured developers and investors that the firm would work as efficiently as possible. The Fordist and Taylorist regimes that defined the construction of the Empire State Building as a vertical assembly line (with labor operations broken down to the smallest component part) were likewise to be found at the very start of the design and planning for the building. Shreve, Lamb & Harmon was much in tune with the business climate of the time. In their propensity for treating architecture as a business (albeit one with concerns for beauty and proportion), the architects were well suited to work with John Raskob and Pierre du Pont. This in turn, seems to have made the firm less attractive to historians and critics. Yet, although Shreve, Lamb & Harmon failed to produce another building that captivated New York to the extent of the Empire State (who could?), the firm merits recognition for merging in such a spectacular fashion the twin concerns of design and profit.

The Setback Skyscraper

> Business rules the world today, and as long as business can best be served
> where many offices are concentrated in one small area, in buildings designed
> as machines . . . business architecture will be supreme.[41]

The completion of the Empire State Building, writes Deborah Pokinski, marked the "triumph of modernist attitudes" in the United States.[42] It was also another example, perhaps the greatest, of what architecture critic Sheldon Cheney labeled the supremacy of "business architecture" in the skyline of New York. More important, the Empire State Building, where modern design responded to the demands of business, was a monumental conclusion to a particular trend in skyscraper design in the United States, one that

Figure 11. The Empire State Building, 1931. Courtesy of the Hagley Museum and Library, 70.200.06054.

at once suggested an emerging modern American architectural sensibility and linked it to the demands of the marketplace.

In New York City tall office building architecture in general and the design of the Empire State Building in particular were shaped by two important factors: the requirements of the 1916 New York City Building Zoning Resolution and explosive growth in the commercial real estate market in Manhattan. The aesthetic response architects developed to these forces was the setback skyscraper. The 1916 ordinance, generated during the pre-World War I building boom and the massive air- and light-obliterating buildings produced then (like the Equitable Building), dictated height limits. It left two loopholes allowing for buildings exceeding those limits: setbacks could rise above the cornice line if they followed a predetermined angle of "sky exposure" set from the middle of the street, and for towers that occupied no more than 25 percent of the lot, the only restriction on height were the limits of technology and the client's bankroll.

The effects of these regulations were powerfully interpreted by architect and draftsman Hugh Ferris in 1922 in a series of drawings in a *New York Times* article.[43] These renderings illustrated the transformation of a single lot occupying a city block from the maximum building allowed by the zoning envelope to a finished setback structure with a fully developed façade and form that took into account the need for light, air, elevators, and other necessities of commercial construction. The setback skyscraper Ferris designed was, as Pokinski writes, "massively three-dimensional . . . imbued with an awesome drama," and suggestive of "buttresses chiseled out of solid rock rising majestically to support a soaring central tower."[44] The "imposing elegance" of the final result helped establish a new standard for beauty and style, based on form, that was widely influential on "business architecture." As architecture critic Douglas Haskell noted at the time, "Movies and the cheap theater may still burst with plaster-of-Paris and gilt for the populace; but the headquarters of large national firms will outdo one another in the effort to proclaim dignity, conservatism, and a suave elegance."[45] Talbot Hamlin, another contemporary architecture critic, agreed, describing Ferris's renderings as "a magic wand to set the American city architecture free from its nightmare . . . buildings became interesting in outline and silhouette as well as in detail. . . . No longer was the high building apparently built by the mile and cut off to order, but it was composed break upon break, buttress on buttress." "The possibilities of poetry entered in."[46]

Poetic possibilities in this case were also decidedly modern ones, as setback skyscrapers were considered both entirely American and modern: "a zoning law, has given architects a chance to create beautiful and appropriate buildings, not Greek temples nor medieval cathedrals, but something modern, born of a new spirit . . . which is tensely of today."[47] As these buildings carried little ornamentation, and sought to express what Ferris called the "underlying truth" of building, they were a "significant aspect of the development of modern American architecture" and "a nascent American modern style."[48] This emerging modern style, free from the symbols of an older, exclusionary American culture, would have appealed to Raskob and Smith.

Of course it took more than developments in form and style to make the setback skyscraper, as one critic put it, "the building that symbolizes the times"; it also took the construction of an unprecedented number of office buildings.[49] In the second half of the 1920s, the amount of office space in New York City increased by 92 percent; buildings completed after the stock market crash increased the total by another 56 percent. The prominence of new construction in the city's skyline (and therefore an aspect of the predominance of the setback style) can be attributed to the new zoning law that encouraged the assembly of ever larger lots to secure larger rates of return. Thus, as W. A. Starrett (whose firm built the Empire State Building) noted, "more than twice as many buildings have been torn down annually in Manhattan in recent years as have been erected, largely due to the fact that one new building usually occupies the site from two to a dozen old ones."[50] Older buildings of other styles and forms, now no longer able to turn as much profit as newer ones, were torn down and replaced.

When completed the Empire State Building was the "era's ultimate skyscraper," and it took great advantage of the compositional elements that made the setback form so dramatic: good proportions, a soaring central tower, and careful detailing, all on a steel frame.[51] While some argue that setback skyscrapers "did not express the skeleton frame," Talbot Hamlin wrote that the building has "that feeling of delicacy which is peculiarly the spirit of steel construction."[52] Furthermore, in his assessment of the prizewinning buildings of 1931, Hamlin stated that the Empire State Building, winner of the Gold Medal Award of the Architectural League of New York, was one of the few to "stand out from the mass as exceptional." He applauded the tower above all, especially for its use of "masonry, but obviously as a skin, not as a support." The "proportions of the setbacks are fine," he continued; "there is strength and dignity in them." The use of metal in the façade also met with his approval for "the manner in which they pick up the color of the sky, or flash back the brilliance of the sun, as though the whole tower itself were hung on a framework of light itself." In sum the building revealed a "deeper quality, an authentic beauty that is a new note, a new creation."[53]

It is interesting to note that Hamlin's assessment of the building ignores its world record height; in this he was not alone. In his appraisal of the building in his "Skyline" column in the *New Yorker*, T-Square (the pseudonym of architecture critic George Sheppard Chappell) wrote: "That it is the world's highest is purely incidental. . . . In spite of Frank Lloyd Wright's characteristically sweeping statement that our modern skyscrapers are all the same, we claim that this one is distinctively different, its difference and distinction lying in the extreme sensitiveness of its entire design."[54]

The design of the building, applauded for its "efforts to rationalize the tall building's urbanistic presence," also revealed, in Lamb's words, the architects' "intense earnestness to make practical necessities the armature" on which the form of the building was molded.[55] This point speaks to the trend of the time that Raymond Hood described: "the architect designing a big building today is more like a Henry Ford than a Michelangelo."[56] In fact, there was a division of labor among the architects, builders, and owners working "in committee to develop the building's program" that reinforced Hood's allusion to Fordism.[57] H. I. Brock, writing in the *New York Times*, also noted this change: "The architect who was only concerned with the façade in the days when the front to the street was all there was of urban architecture has small space in the modern scheme." No firm's work in this era better illustrates this trend than Shreve, Lamb & Harmon. Their adaptation to the economic and cultural demands of the time, however, failed to garner them lasting recognition in architectural history.

3

Capital Nightmares

Nowhere had America's Great Depression struck harder than in America's greatest
city. New York in 1932 was half-completed skyscrapers, work on them long since
halted for the lack of funds, that glared down on the city from glassless windows.
It was housewives scavenging for vegetables under pushcarts. It was crowds
gathering at garbage dumps in Riverside Park and swarming onto them every time
a new load was deposited, digging through the piles with sticks or hands in hopes
of finding bits of food. New York was the soup kitchens operated from the back
of army trucks in Times Square. It was the men, some of them wearing Chesterfield
coats and homburgs, who lined up at the soup kitchens with drooping shoulders and
eyes that never looked up from the sidewalk. New York was the breadline, "the worm
that walks like a man."

—Robert Caro

Collapse, Depression, and Corruption

In 1929, on the eve of the Great Depression, the board of Empire State, Incorporated,
was in the midst of the frenzied preparations for the construction of their skyscraper.
These seven men, Al Smith, John Raskob, Pierre du Pont, Ellis P. Earle, Louis G. Kaufman, Michael Friedsam, and August Heckscher, were busy that fall. They had already
purchased the Waldorf-Astoria, hired builders and architects, demolished the old hotel, applied for the necessary mortgages, and begun bankrolling the project. The board
then commissioned H. Hamilton Weber (Renting Supervisor of the New York Central
Building) to prepare a real estate survey to predict annual rental income for a proposed

building of 34,000,000 cubic feet. Weber provided an appraisal detailing an "estimated schedule of rental income" and "an approximate set-up of operating expenses." The letter is dated October 21, just eight days before Black Tuesday inaugurated the Great Depression. Weber cautioned that he was "quite reluctant to make any assertions whatsoever concerning operatin [sic] costs at this time," in particular because realistic figures "can only be obtained by a very thorough study, which will require more than the two week's time that I have had, and also more detailed information." In essence, Weber characterized the operating figures he offered as nothing more "than a practical man's guess."[1]

Nevertheless, Weber continued: "For the estimate of rental income, this, *of course*, is possible to obtain to a greater degree of accuracy inasmuch as we have ample knowledge of what to expect in the way of rentals." He pointed out that he based his estimate on "the fact that we will have an outstanding building of the highest character, but that there will be a certain amount of inducement required to form the 'necessity urge' in establishing this district in the minds of the clientele to which we hope to appeal." He predicted an annual rental income of $7,961,580.

Weber's memo closed with the caveat that in "submitting this [report], may I state that I have not taken into consideration the apparent result which may accrue from the character of ownership and certain other features of the building, preferring to let this take care of itself." If seven million in rent could be counted on before taking into account the cachet the association of Raskob, du Pont, and Smith would add to the building, or the fame that would accrue to it as the tallest building in the world, then the future looked bright indeed. Weber expected that the building would have a high occupancy rate, with the prediction "of the building being 90 percent to 100 percent rented."

This optimism was shortly put to the test. The financial collapse that inaugurated the Great Depression took place at the end of October 1929. Plans for the Empire State Building were not put on hold, however, and the process of assembling capital for the building continued. It seems impossible to imagine that, by the time construction began, anyone thought the building could return seven million in rent or achieve an occupancy rate anything like 90 percent; yet if there was any doubt about the wisdom of moving forward with the world's tallest office building, it was not expressed in the meeting minutes, memos, or letters of the various members of the board of directors. Pierre du Pont visited the White House and, along with President Hoover, reassured the public that the state of the American economy was sound. In the short term this absence of doubt would prove a mixed blessing, as the effects of the Depression would paradoxically make the construction of the Empire State far cheaper than originally planned, while at the same time effectively eliminating the possibility of the building returning a profit to its investors.

Figure 12. Pierre S. du Pont and Alfred P. Sloan at the White House to confer with President Hoover about the state of the economy, 1929. Courtesy of the Library of Congress.

Although the Great Depression is considered by most economists and historians, in John Kenneth Galbraith's words, the "great modern case of boom and collapse," agreement over its causes and effects often ends there.[2] Nevertheless it remains the "defining moment"[3] in the development of the American economy; even though the United States has undergone financial panics and recessions since then, "none have had the legacy of the panic of 1929."[4] Probably no other event in American history had as great an impact on the public reception of the Empire State Building as did the Great Depression. Certainly at no other time did the national economy exercise such a tremendously negative influence on the finances of the building. During the Depression years, the Empire State Building was defined by forces outside the control of even Raskob, du Pont, and Smith.

The clients of the Empire State Building sought to marshal whatever advantage their wealth and influence might afford them. The rules of real estate in New York required business sense, and also the capacity for finesse. The latter buttressed the former and helped determine which elements of the building code, for instance, would be enforced and which could be sidestepped. As Robert Caro notes, "the hands which city inspectors held out, palms up, could not easily be doubled into hard fists of regulation."[5] Then as now, real estate investment is most profitable when augmented with the right connections and information disseminated among the select few rather than the deserving many. It is a market that operates on, as one economist recently labeled it, "asymmetrical information."[6]

Shortly after excavation for the foundations of the building was completed, the architects and patrons of the Empire State Building used their connections and their finesse on the office of Mayor Jimmy "Beau James" Walker to secure favorable changes in the building code of New York City. These reduced the steel bill (which generally accounts for 15 to 20 percent of the cost of a skyscraper) by $500,000, a significant sum at any time, but especially during the Great Depression. The code, which had not been revised since the turn of the century, required structural steel to carry no more than 16,000 pounds per square inch. In 1928 the Merchants' Association of New York had proposed increasing the load maximum to 18,000 pounds per square inch (the standard in many other large cities at the time). The new standard had already been approved by the American Institute of Steel Construction and the American Society of Civil Engineers, yet when a bill enabling the change in the code came across Mayor Walker's desk, he vetoed it. Walker announced that he would not alter the building code line by line, but rather favored a complete revision. Such an overhaul was not forthcoming.

The proposal languished until 1930, when the Board of Aldermen was lobbied to adopt the proposal and six other changes to the building code to stimulate construction and lower unemployment. An ordinance was passed calling for change in the code. Mayor Walker approached the Merchants' Association of New York and asked them to set up a committee to study the proposed changes. R. H. Shreve, the point man for Shreve, Lamb & Harmon on the planning for the Empire State, conveniently happened to serve on that committee, so the proposal for the increased load on structural steel was pushed to the forefront once again. While Shreve was working the legislative end, Smith and other members of Empire State, Inc., were "politicking—perhaps with more urgency—in private" with Beau James. In the end, despite his insistence on not altering the code bit by bit, in March 1930 Mayor Walker "signed into law the revision on steel." A day later the steel frame of the Empire State Building was being raised.[7]

Labor and Construction

Just twenty months elapsed between the time Shreve, Lamb & Harmon were hired and the day the building opened for business, May 1, 1931. In that short space of time, Carol Willis writes,

> the Victorian pile of the Waldorf-Astoria Hotel was demolished, the foundations and the grillages were dug and set, the steel columns and beams, some 57,000 tons, were fabricated and milled to precise specifications, ten million common bricks were laid, more than 62,000 cubic yards of concrete were poured, 6,400 windows were set, and sixty-seven elevators were installed in seven miles of shafts. At peak activity, 3,500 workers were employed on site, and the frame rose more than a story a day. No comparable structure has since matched that rate of ascent.[8]

As the builder for the Empire State said, "Never before in the history of building had there been . . . a design so magnificently adapted to speed in construction."[9]

In essence, the construction of the Empire State in less than two years demanded the creation of a vertical assembly line. The managerial regulations of Taylorism and Fordism that revolutionized industrial production in the early twentieth century had a decisive impact on the labor force at the Empire State Building. Workers involved in every kind of construction, whether riveters, masons, carpenters, or electricians, had their tasks divided into strict component elements. Every stage of construction was divided and subdivided in an effort to minimize extraneous motion and effort and maximize efficiency and productivity. The workplace itself was transformed to extract the maximum result from every worker's time at the site. Cafeterias were installed at various levels so that workers would not lose time traveling up and down the building, much less to and from the worksite, for their meals. Similarly, latrines and medical aid stations were placed at regular intervals throughout the building. It was the builders' goal that workers would ride the elevators once in the morning when they arrived and once at the end of the day when they left.

An assembly line is most effective when it can be arranged without the need to double back on itself. Albert Kahn's magnificent and monumental industrial buildings in Detroit and its suburbs housed exceptionally efficient assembly lines. The task at the Empire State Building demanded an even higher order of efficiency: the assembly line was constantly in motion upward. Workspaces were the product of the workers' own labor, and the final product of the assembly line itself. Once the building was complete, the assembly line disappeared. Pay rose in concert with height (and inevitably risk), with riveters earning nearly twice as much as unskilled workers. The hoisting engineers, who labored closest and most often to the top of the building, were also at the top of the pay scale, and took home over three times what unskilled labor did.

Labor, the critical commodity in the construction process, built the Empire State Building at a pace heretofore unknown. The tremendous physical endeavor this feat required was recorded by the photographer Lewis Hine.[10] At the request of Empire State, Inc., Hine, assisted by his son, spent six months in 1930 photographing the men who built the Empire State Building. Hine was fifty-five years old at the time; the physical effort required to lug his 4 x 5 Graflex around high on the scaffolding in the summer must have worn on him. Hine was a curious choice (it is believed R. H. Shreve, Hine's neighbor, suggested him to the board for the job).[11] He was undoubtedly well known and regarded as a fine documentary photographer, but his politics were well to the left of Raskob's and Smith's and were hardly unknown. Nearly two decades earlier his photographs had been published in Scott Nearing's exposé of poverty and capitalist exploitation, *Poverty and Riches: A Study of the Industrial Regime.*[12] Hine's work was also featured in Charles Frederick Miller's earlier study of poverty among black residents of Washington, D.C.[13] His photographs for both books revealed his keen eye for finding and recording human misery and no trace of negative judgment toward those it recorded. Hine had no obvious sympathy or admiration for bankers and builders, nor was he routinely hired to document the construction of notable buildings.

Nevertheless, he was hired, and a letter from the secretary of Empire State, Inc., informed the heads of the construction site that Hine "is to be admitted to all Empire State property."[14] Hine took more than 1,000 exposures in his six months, an incredible number using a camera where each negative had to be loaded individually. The photographs were celebrations of the skills of tradesmen, records of the physical dangers of skyscraper construction, and homage to a vision of heroic labor. They were widely published during Hine's lifetime and are collectors' items today.[15] Oddly, they were not used by Empire State, Inc., in publicizing the building. It may have been that Hine's focus on the working men did not suit the public relations needs of an office building. Hine, when asked about his determined focus on steel workers, bolt bosses, derrick boys, and the others who labored in cutoffs and caps, rather on than architects or engineers, said simply, "Skyscrapers don't build themselves."[16]

Fiscal Meltdown

The Empire State Building became a New York City landmark essentially the moment it was finished (if not before). It was also immediately something else: a financial failure. In the midst of a national nightmare of capital attrition, this skyscraper was a towering manifestation of the evisceration of profit. The original numbers for the first year of the building's operation, reprinted by various architectural historians, tell a story of hemorrhaging capital. Indeed, according to financial records written in 1932, in its first fiscal year of operation the Empire State Building collected just over one million dollars in rent. Admission fees to the observation tower coupled with souvenir sales and restaurant receipts nearly equaled rental income, at more than $900,000. The building was operating at a deficit of more than $3,500,000. Adjusted for inflation, that would represent in 2008 a loss of about $53 million.[17] "The year just closed," the first fiscal year report to the stockholders of Empire State, Inc., noted, "has been one of the most difficult that owners of real estate have had to face in many years."[18]

This was actually an understatement. The operating numbers for the first fiscal year were restated the following year, and these showed that Empire State, Inc., had assumed over $300,000 in leases for the first fiscal year, with the result that net rental income was in fact below $700,000.[19] This meant that tower income exceeded rental income by nearly 20 percent. The building was far more profitable as a tourist attraction than as an office building. (The adjusted numbers for the first year of operation seem to have fallen under the radar of other histories of the building, as they are not mentioned elsewhere.) Smith closed his report ominously: "I have endeavored to lay before you the results of the past year; I have no prophecy to offer for the ensuing year."[20] While today the building earns a handsome profit in rent, until after World War II it never operated in the black. As the world's largest speculative building it was a spectacular failure.

The second year of operation brought little change from the first; as Al Smith noted, "the fiscal year 1932 was even worse in all respects than that of 1931." While Smith had cut wages of all building employees (except his own) and finagled a reduction in the building's assessed value from $40,000,000 to $34,000,000, reducing yearly taxes by a quarter million dollars, the Empire State Building was still operating at a tremendous loss. It didn't help, as Smith pointed out, that "We still have with us the Landlord who will name any price in his frantic effort to hold an old lease or secure a new tenant," probably a reference to Rockefeller Center.[21] As Robert Stern has written, John D. Rockefeller "used extraordinarily aggressive tactics to lure other tenants, taking up their old leases, offering bargain rents, and paying moving costs."[22] Rockefeller's behavior took its toll on owners of other office buildings as their tenants were lured away by such tactics or demanded rent reductions to stay. August Heckscher, Empire State Inc., board member and real estate mogul in his own right, went so far as to take Rockefeller to court, calling him "a Modern Frankenstein."[23] He was not alone in his negative assessment of the tactics employed by Rockefeller secure rental income. *Architectural Forum* published an article on Rockefeller Center tellingly titled "A Phenomenon of Exploitation."[24]

Rockefeller Center was also a topic of discussion in the fiscal report for the following year. Smith noted that while rental income at the Empire State Building for the year had "not been one to fill us with pleasure or even any degree of satisfaction," that "omitting the Rockefeller Center development, whose practices and prices we have not attempted to imitate," rentals for the year at the building had been near or on par with their other principal competitors.[25] While rentals at the Empire State may have been competitive, and while Smith opened his report to the stockholders by noting "there seems to be a rift in the dark cloud of depression and the spirit of anxiety and hopelessness that pervaded such a large part of out populace is now being replaced by hopefulness," this could not disguise the fact that the building was still losing money.[26] Ever the politician, Smith linked "optimism . . . tempered with a large share of caution" among prospective tenants to "some fear of what the national administration may decide."[27] Smith's opinions about the Roosevelt administration were probably colored by his experiences in 1932 when he sought the Democratic presidential nomination and was humiliatingly defeated by Roosevelt. By 1934 his antipathy toward Roosevelt and the programs of the New Deal was pronounced enough that the financial failure of the Empire State Building was seen as evidence not of an unwise investment but rather of bad federal policies emerging from Washington.

In 1933 on movie screens across the country a giant ape threatened the Empire State Building. In the real world, plummeting income was the source of terror. Profit remained very elusive for the Empire State throughout the 1930s, and composing the annual reports to stockholders in these years must have tested Smith's endurance as one bad year followed another. In 1935 Smith wrote that "the recent renting season for the fiscal year ending April 30th, 1935, has been the least productive of any since we opened the building. Owners of office buildings and real estate brokers are in accord in pronouncing it the poorest since 1920."[28] A year later, in 1936, Smith's report declared, "It

Figure 13. King Kong atop the Empire State Building. His celluloid trip to the observation tower mirrored that of thousands of other visitors who were the major source of profit for the building in its early years. Reprinted by permission from the Hulton Archive © Getty Images.

is the consensus of the best brokers that this season was the worst in years."[29] By 1938 the situation was so bad that Smith had run out of words to describe to stockholders how dire the situation was and was forced to quote his previous yearly reports: "In my annual report for the fiscal year 1934–1935 I made the statement that owners of office buildings and real estate brokers were in accord in pronouncing it the poorest rental year since 1920. This past year has been even worse."[30] No amount of effort, it seemed, could secure more tenants and income for the building. However, Smith's efforts to boost the bottom line by reducing the building's operating expenses were much more successful. His ability to manipulate the costs associated with owning and operating a building of this size once again highlights how different the Empire State was from other speculative buildings, and how much the rules of the real estate market fluctuate depending on the principals involved.

Throughout the 1930s, Al Smith was engaged in regular and consistent negotiations with the Metropolitan Life Insurance Company in an effort to reduce the financial burdens faced by Empire State, Inc. During the second year of operation, Smith secured a reduction in the interest on the first mortgage from 5½ percent to 5 percent, and an agreement allowing payment of only 2 percent interest for the next two years with no added interest on the deferred 3 percent. During that same time Smith also re-ceived an assurance from Met Life that it would not foreclose on the building, at least prior to March 1, 1935.[31] The following year Smith arranged to extend this agreement for a third year, and "prevailed on the Metropolitan Life Insurance Co. to permit us to carry $15,750,000 of fire insurance against 21,600,000 previously carried." In 1935, 1936, and 1937, the 2 percent for 5 percent swap was extended yet again. It was becoming clear that the last thing Met Life wanted was to foreclose on the "Empty State" and assume responsibility for the headache in managing the place that currently fell to Smith. Sell-ing the building would be impossible, filling it with tenants was not something at which Met Life could expect more success than Al Smith, and boarding it up to save on main-tenance costs would be a public relations nightmare. So, well aware that Met Life would rather take something than nothing, Smith continued to negotiate last-minute deals to keep the building afloat.

A similar strategy characterized Smith's dealings with the city tax assessors. Taxes, like mortgage payments, were one of the larger fixed capital costs of operating the build-ing, and a great deal of effort was expended on their reduction. From the moment the building opened Smith was engaged in efforts to have its assessed value (and thus the property tax) reduced. In the first year alone he succeeded in lowering the value of the building by $2,000,000; the following years saw further reductions in the range of four to six million dollars a year. Between 1931 and 1936 the building's assessment dropped from $42,000,000 to $27,750,000, a decline of more than 30 percent. The building was now worth less (according to the city's assessors) than the cost of its construction. Given the average commercial property tax rate of 2.7 percent for these years, this provided for an impressive reduction in annual tax expenditures for Empire State, Inc.[32]

Undoubtedly the Empire State Building was an economic force in New York City, one large enough to throw its weight around with both bankers and tax collectors. The scope of the building's influence did not end there, however, as its 102 stories of steel and stone, and the men responsible for their construction, also exerted formidable po-litical influence. Throughout the 1930s, as detailed in various stockholder reports, in-ternal memos, and letters between Smith, Raskob, and du Pont, the officers of Empire State, Inc., lobbied at both the municipal and state level against a variety of bills that would have increased the financial obligations of the corporation. The officers, in Smith's words, "successfully opposed the passage of a bill before the Board of Aldermen" that would have taxed "under sidewalk vault space," saving the building some $25,000 in annual taxes. Other efforts included protesting, "successfully, against the passage of a bill in the New York State Senate—the Assembly having passed the bill—which would have taxed us $27,500 per year, being 2% on the interest paid on our first mortgage."[33] Al Smith's experience with the Assembly and his political savvy bolstered lobbying to

Figure 14. The Empire State Building at night, 1937. Floor after floor sits dark, empty, and profitless. Courtesy of the Library of Congress.

defeat various "pieces of legislation . . . offered in the Board of Aldermen and in the State Legislature the passage of which would have added to your tax burden." Although Smith couldn't manipulate the economy, he still knew how to win the odd political battle. Those burdensome pieces of legislation, he wrote in his report to shareholders, "were successfully opposed."[34] In addition to his own efforts, in 1935 Smith organized the officers of Empire State, Inc., in "association with other owners," to work as a group against forms of legislation "adverse to real estate" such as forbidding building owners to sell electrical current to their tenants.[35]

In spite of the tax breaks, the surprising flexibility of Met Life, the legislative efforts, and the combined influence of Al Smith, Raskob, and du Pont, the Empire State would not turn a profit until after World War II. Misfortune attracted misfortune, and in 1945 a B-25 bomber crashed into the building. While the sturdy tower survived remarkably well, the event and publicity around it did little to help the bottom line. When Al Smith died in 1944, a few months after his wife, the building was still in the red; he would not live to see it become the profitable and popular icon it is today. Pierre du Pont had resigned from the Board of Empire State, Inc. in 1938, and his involvement with the operations of the building largely ground to a halt—although he was still sent his complimentary year-round pass to the observatory for years after his resignation.[36] After John Raskob's death, his heirs seemed far less attached to the building and sold it in 1951. It seems that without the need to achieve legitimation through building, the heirs were happy to take their profits from the building's sale and move on to other investments. Not surprisingly, however, the new buyers, led by Harry Helmsley and Leonard Wien, saw their purchase of the Empire State Building as proof that they had arrived at the upper echelons of the New York real estate business. Helmsley, like Raskob, was a self-made man, and buying this skyscraper was a way to claim his right to be regarded as one of the city's biggest wheels. Each successive group of owners in turn have spoken of how ownership of the Empire State Building carries a symbolic heft no other building can support.

Raskob and du Pont made their initial investment in the Empire State Building during an enormous building boom in New York City. By the end of the 1920s office space alone in Manhattan almost doubled.[37] The pace of construction was frenetic, and the height and size of the buildings rose as well. Three or four years earlier most new high rise buildings "averaged between thirty and forty stories, but by the end of the decade, most new buildings were forty to forty-five stories."[38] Wave after wave of investment capital swept through the city, searching out new investment opportunities and offering easy credit to those who wanted to build. In such an environment it must have seemed that demand for new office space would continue to grow and that real estate remained a solid investment. Four days after Smith announced that Empire State Inc.,

Figure 15. Photo-diagram illustrating impact of B-25 bomber. Courtesy of the Library of Congress.

had received permission to begin demolition of the Waldorf-Astoria, crews were dismantling the mammoth hotel. When the market crashed the commitment to build was already in place. Raskob, du Pont, Smith, and the architects, and builders raised the world's tallest building in a time of increasing economic uncertainty.

The Empire State Building was, in the words of one of its builders, the capstone of a decade of "frenzy" and "imagination." It was completed in the first year of a decade of poverty and turmoil. The Depression would dramatically alter the future of this great building, and more importantly, alter the way in which the general population looked at architecture and grand building projects. The architectural profession would face a decade in which building activity declined, leaving architects across the nation without work. But if building was suddenly on the wane, debates about what would be built when prosperity returned were increasingly popular. Museum exhibitions and professional journals were hosts to a variety of manifestos and arguments about what the future of architecture would bring. The story of the Empire State Building during the Great Depression becomes a story about the struggle to define architecture's role in society, about whether architects were visionary thinkers or servants of the marketplace, about whether architecture would offer solutions to the problems facing society, or whether it would serve the interests of the wealthy and the elite. Politics and architecture were inseparable.

The skyscraper is not just a tall building; it is a material expression of a set of relations, of the course chartered by capital through the urban landscape. A host of networks are called upon in the creation of a structure so vast. The contours of the power circulating among those networks give shape to the individual skyscraper and the form of the skyline.

4

The Politics of American Architecture in the 1930s

The story of the Empire State Building is truly an epitome of all that has preceded . . .
it tells all the spirit, the imaginative and technical daring, and even some of the frenzy,
that animated the decade of which it was the culmination.

—Paul Starrett

The Empire State Building is without doubt, to use a memorable phrase coined by Cass Gilbert, "a machine that makes the land pay," and therefore it must be understood not as a final destination for capital but rather as a location for it to undergo, as Immanuel Wallerstein calls it, self-expansion.[1] This fact, however, need not obscure the reality that politics played a key role in the building's creation and operation, and that politics affected whether people in New York and across the nation saw the Empire State as a great proof of American prosperity and ingenuity, or an empty monument to a passing era, or worse an indictment of the capitalist economy from which it sprang.

In turn, as Katherine Solomonson has observed, the design and reception of skyscrapers in the early twentieth century, while influenced by balance sheets and profit margins, was nonetheless informed by "questions concerning beauty and civic values."[2] Her comments echo Raskob's description of the Empire State Building as a project that would be a "credit to the city and state."[3] Seventy years after Raskob and du Pont's gamble was opened to the public, it remains, in the words of one newspaper article, "a beacon . . . an old friend," one to which city residents are "increasingly attached."[4] The sense that the Empire State Building possesses a civic value greater or more profound than other buildings means that long after it lost the title of the tallest building in New York, New Yorkers nonetheless think of the building as "a reflection of who we [are]."[5]

Figure 16. Empire State Building, 2007. © Peter Aaron/Esto.

Today the Empire State Building stands in not only for New York City, but for a particular kind of active, bustling, and dense urbanism. The thousands of people who line up daily to visit the building testify to its status as a beautiful site and a civic treasure. In the 1930s, however, there was far less consensus about whether the building addressed the "questions concerning beauty and civic values" that Solomonson mentions.

Certainly, when dealing with the banks or tax assessors, Smith and his fellow officers of Empire State, Inc., tried to define the building very precisely as one that was beautiful and addressed civic values. In a letter to the Board of Commissioners of the Department of Taxes and Assessments, Al Smith made his case for a reduction in taxes by making, among other points, the statement that "We [the owners of the Empire State Building] are exhausting every effort . . . to prevent the failure of this great enterprise which would be a great blow, not only to the owners, but to the City of New York."[6] Furthermore, Smith argued, without the implementation of some form of tax relief for "towering office buildings . . . the erection of beautiful buildings, such as the Empire State Building and Rockefeller Center, both of which do much to beautify the city and make it a mecca for the traveling public, will cease." As additional evidence of the good will and civic responsibility of the owners, Smith pointed out that "We have, without rental, placed sections of the building at the disposal of the Emergency Unemployment Relief Committee, the New York Tuberculosis and Health Association, the Association for Improving the Condition of the Poor, the Cancer Society, American Red Cross, the New York State Commission for the Blind and others and have endeavored in numerous other ways to be of public benefit."

In a touch of hyperbole, Smith went on to point out that those who built grand developments like the Empire State were in effect performing a public service, noting, "We have built the most magnificent building in the world which is an honor to the city and the nation. We have replaced old structures the assessed valuation of which was about one-half the assessed valuation we are asking. We have increased the land value of the entire neighborhood and we have anchored that value for years to come." Foreign dignitaries visited the building regularly, and it was, Smith thought, "unthinkable that your honorable body after due consideration will not grant" the tax relief Empire State, Inc., petitioned. Reading those words today, one has to wonder whether Smith's use of the language of beauty and civic responsibility was genuine or a cynical effort to window-dress a plea for a tax break for the owners of the Empire State. They were, after all, some of the wealthiest individuals in the nation.[7]

Numerous newspaper articles and advertisements at the time of the building's opening praised it in terms of its beauty and its importance to the life of the city. A great many of these were collected into a clippings book for Pierre du Pont by the public relations firm Publicity Associates, which was headed by Belle Moskowitz, a former close adviser to

Figure 17. Al Smith taking the Duke of Windsor on a tour of the Empire State Building, 1941. Reprinted by permission from Keystone, Hulton Archive © Getty Images.

Al Smith. A column in the *New York Times* on opening proclaimed "All must feel also that the Empire State Building is a monumental proof of hopefulness. Those who planned and erected it and found the funds for it must have been firm in the belief that the future of New York is assured. . . . Thus today's celebrations are thought of as having a significance which extends far beyond the corner of Fifth Avenue and Thirty-Fourth Street, and catches up the whole city, with all its diverse elements, yet with common hopes, into its inspiring sweep."[8] Here aesthetics, profit on speculation, and civic duty are nearly one, as the construction of a skyscraper is applauded because it will inform others that the economy and society are fundamentally sound. The construction of the Empire State Building was evidence that the Great Depression could not, would not, last.

Other news articles reinforced this impression by discussing the history of the site on which the mighty skyscraper was built. The *New York Sun* wrote that the Empire State Building "should persuade the wise to buy and keep good real estate": the building that occupies "less than an acre stands on part of the Thompson farm of twenty acres, bought in 1799 for $2,500. The part of an acre on which the magnificent building stands is worth more than $10,000,000."[9] Stories in the *New York Times* likewise repeated this tale as evidence that real estate investments were sound, as the history of Manhattan time and time again showed how one could profit from the appreciation of property.[10]

Among the other civic benefits of the building was that its great height offered those at the top the chance to gain a new perspective on the day-to-day dramas of life on the streets below. Heywood Broun described just such a scenario in his May 2 column (May 2 was the day the building opened to the general public). Commenting on the soapbox debates between a group of communists, socialists, and members of the Veterans of Foreign Wars on the street below, he wrote: "Everybody with a desire to grow philosophical should spend half an hour each week on this high platform. . . . At that distance policies, either political or economic, blended into the extraordinary sameness of humankind."[11] Broun suggests the Empire State Building might serve as a place of political reconciliation through its offer of an entirely new perspective on the world, one where people are conditioned to regard differences as less important that our "extraordinary sameness." What better example of civic duty could there be than this? Years later, in 1959, a curious variation of this scenario played out when Nikita Khrushchev and his wife visited the Empire State Building. Where once the "Empty State" was a symbol of capitalism's weakness, it was now expected to serve honorably in the Cold War confrontation between East and West.

A wide variety of businesses, from clothing stores to hotels to apartment buildings were also eager early on to connect their products with the Empire State Building. The results, which often seem a bit camp, nonetheless reflect the immediate adoption of the building as a positive symbol of New York in general and Fifth Avenue in particular. Most

Figure 18. Nikita Khrushchev and his wife at the Empire State Building, 1959. Reprinted by permission from Al Fenn, Time & Life Pictures Collection © Getty Images.

advertisements made use of the building's great size to comment in some fashion on the product being marketed. One particularly interesting example published in the *Wall Street Journal* was for Sarnoff & Co., a nearby clothing retailer. The ad prominently displayed the top floors and mooring mast of the Empire State Building; the copy read: "Hail!—Empire State! What an aspiration you are to ever strive for greater heights! In our modest way, we, too, aim for greater achievement. We welcome our thousands of new neighbors in the Empire State and cordially invite them to test our claim of leadership in *Low Prices for Fifth Avenue Fashions*."[12]

Just as the newspapers cast the building as an index of improved economic conditions, the vast majority of advertisements that featured the Empire State also made claims about its economic and social significance. London Terrace, a West Side apartment complex that claimed to be the largest apartment building in the world, ran a series of ads "Welcoming" the skyscraper to the neighborhood. In this series every effort was made to intertwine the Empire State Building, the economy, and even patriotism with the promotion of apartment sales. A typical example read: "It is significant of America's ultimate progress that in a time of economic depression *two such magnificent buildings* should be conceived . . . built . . . and brought to completion! Our faith in the future of America is justified."[13] The Hotel New Yorker also ran a "welcome" ad that prominently featured the Empire State's mooring mast and that offered this salutation: "Big neighbor—we predict that you will find business very good in this modern locality. *We* have found business 'great!' May *you* enjoy success equal to that of Hotel New Yorker!"[14]

These advertisements and news reports sought to cast the Empire State Building (not to mention business generally) as a civic benefit. There were, however, other voices raised in response to the building. Two cartoons from wildly different sources, the *New Yorker* and the leftist *New Masses*, offer a glimpse of the negative opinions the building elicited in its early years. Despite their obvious differences in outlook, both nevertheless criticize the Empire State Building for failing to consider or address social concerns.

The *New Yorker* illustration is by Reginald Marsh, the American painter and illustrator who is best remembered for his works depicting New York society and life in the 1930s and 1940s. Published in January 1932, it depicts a city park, darkened by the shadows of the Empire State Building, where a number of evidently unemployed (and possibly homeless) men have congregated. The sky in this charcoal rendering is filled with ominous-looking clouds and the caption beneath reads: "Where men accumulate and wealth decays."[15]

Here is the most famous tall office building in the world drawn in a dark and foreboding fashion, one that does not celebrate its aesthetic achievements, great height, or engineering. The Empire State Building is drawn as if it has no windows, reducing it to a sort of towering tomb or vault, perhaps a cenotaph for the cities devastated by the Great Depression. The apparent emptiness of the building is reinforced by the wording of the caption, which suggests that parks and other public spaces are where men accumulate, not office towers. As a place where "wealth decays," it is treated not as a site of productive labor, but as a tomb for rotting capital. Far from creating wealth, it is slowly eating away at the money it took to build it. It performs no civic duty.

The analogy of the Empire State Building as a tomb is taken even farther in the illustration from the *New Masses*. This cartoon shows the building in outline, rising into a dark, thunderhead-filled sky. Set among a sea of anonymous squat structures, the building is filled with the contorted bodies of dead workers, their corpses rising to the top story, where its famous mooring mast has been replaced by the Grim Reaper. The caption reads: "42 men killed constructing the new Empire State Building . . . 'the building was completed on time.'"[16] Decaying capital here has been replaced by decaying flesh, and the building is a monument to death. Rather than condemning the building as a waste of money or a physical burden on the city, as the *New Yorker* had, the *New Masses* criticized it for exploiting labor in the most violent way imaginable, until it could labor no more. The image presents a vision of labor alienated not only from its own product, in this case the Empire State Building, but from life itself: as these forty-two men died in order for the building to be "completed on time."

The *New Yorker* treated the Empire State Building as an example of a particular kind of excessive capitalism, hopefully left behind as the nation recovered from the hangover of the speculative bubble so recently burst. The *New Masses* used the Empire State Building to criticize capitalism itself. Given what we know of the Empire State Building, how its patrons were the driving forces behind some of the largest and wealthiest industries in the nation, how it was an exemplar of the types of financial arrangements that typified the market in that era, how it became a victim of its own ingenuity and excess, such a critique has its merits. No site better illustrates the creative destruction that drives capitalism than this one, once home to the Waldorf-Astoria, torn down because it could not turn *enough* profit and replaced with a building that took full advantage of new technologies and a host of political and economic connections and yet could turn *no* profit. The creative destruction at the heart of the system, the *New Masses* cartoon seems to suggest, was now devouring itself, destroying its ability to fulfill its primary function—to make more money. That this process simultaneously destroyed the lives of workers made it all the more useful as propaganda for those who advocated an end to the current economic order. The *New Masses* may also have known that the men behind the Empire State Building's construction secured promises "from all the dealers furnishing lumber to the Corporation to the effect that none of it came from Russia."[17] Raskob and du Pont had no intention of sending their capitalist dollars to the socialist Soviet Union.

As far as can be documented, forty-two men were not killed during the construction of the Empire State Building. Records from Starrett Brothers and Eken, the builders, show that six workers and one passerby, a woman, were killed during the eighteen months of construction. In fact the builders often attempted to publicize their efforts to improve workplace safety at the Empire State, and there seems no reason to doubt that they did make such efforts. Yet, in spite of this, in the 1930s people were more than willing to believe that the Empire State Building was the death of many who worked on it. Some thought, or at least claimed, as did Edmund Wilson, that more than 100 workers had been killed during construction of the building. Starrett Brothers and Eken's notes on the construction claim, "A malicious propaganda in the form of rumors and subtle press articles became widespread during the construction period. The impression created was that adequate protection of human life was entirely disregarded."[18]

While such impressions may not accurately characterize workplace safety at the Empire State, they do suggest that many Americans in the 1930s were ready to believe the worst about those responsible for raising such tremendous structures. Given the climate of the Great Depression, it is certainly possible to attribute this to the general antipathy towards big money and big business among those who were living lean at the time. Certainly men like Pierre du Pont were not exactly widely popular at any point in their careers, Depression or no Depression. But the builder's notes offer a different thesis:

> These press articles which appeared in various sections of the country, were undoubtedly inspired by political animosity, inasmuch as they charged by innuendo that a nationally prominent politician who was at the head of the enterprise, was responsible for having the public agencies suppress all information regarding the number of workmen killed on the building. These character assassins, who became so expert in villification [sic] during the Presidential campaign of 1928, would try to make a gullible public believe (especially in the hinterland) that a man like former Governor, Alfred E. Smith would sponsor such a condition and then suppress the true facts from being known.[19]

Al Smith was a son of the working class. His reform efforts in the wake of the Triangle Shirtwaist Factory Fire as the vice-chair of the Factory Investigation Committee suggest that he was unlikely to cover up the deaths of workers at the Empire State Building. However, Smith's association with the skyscraper marked a change in his political views, and, as we saw earlier, the public's view of Smith changed as well. After all, the skyscraper in the 1930s often served as the preeminent symbol of capitalist excess and exploitation. Nothing so clearly illustrated how society could serve the wishes of the wealthy and ignore the needs of the masses than an empty skyscraper like the Empire State Building. In his book (first published serially in the pages of the *New Masses*) titled *Capital in Lithographs*, artist Hugo Gellert wrote, "*Das Kapital* is our guide. Like the X-ray it discloses the depths below the surface. It is my hope that in this abbreviated form the immortal words of Karl Marx will become accessible to the Masses."[20] Time and time again, Gellert uses the skyscraper as a symbol of capitalism's most exploitative aspects. The illustration used to explain "The Origin of the Industrial Capitalist" shows a mustachioed man in a three-piece suit wearing a top hat and smoking a cigar towering over a city skyline. In his right hand he holds a bag of money which he rests on the top of a skyscraper. Blood (presumably the blood of workers) leaks from the bottom of the bag and runs down the sides of the building. The same skyline of skyscrapers, this time with a naked, emaciated child wandering among them, is employed later to illustrate the "Law of Capitalist Accumulation" and its effects on "the working class." For many critics on the left, the skyscraper served as a repository for the destructive elements of capitalism. It was a form that spoke to them of exploitation and abuse, of the efforts of the bourgeoisie to remake the world in their own image. And so, in spite of their differences, critics left and right agreed (knowingly or not) that whatever else the skyscraper stood for, it was a clear and unmistakable expression of the power of capitalism to remake the landscape.

The sheer size of the skyscraper made the form particularly ripe for debate over its social, political, and economic merits. But it was not just the exceptional form in architecture that was debated, often ferociously, in the 1930s. The trend away from Beaux-Arts traditions in design, away from revivalism of various classical styles, and the rise of modernism in a variety of forms all contributed to a sense of new possibilities. Just a year after the completion of the Empire State Building, the seminal 1932 Modern Architecture: International Exhibition opened at the Museum of Modern Art. Although it ran for only a few weeks, the exhibition and its accompanying text garnered a fair amount of attention in both the popular press and architectural journals. The exhibit and book assume a central place in most narratives of twentieth-century American modern architecture. The modern architecture MoMA chose to display was as much a reaction against the American modernism of the Empire State Building as an embrace of the architecture on display.

Assessments of the impact of the Modern Architecture: International Exhibition often characterize it as one more stop on the path toward depoliticization and formalization that modernism, and particularly the international style, underwent as it crossed the Atlantic from Europe to the United States. In part, this depiction has been bolstered by writers whose exploration of the exhibit is based largely in the discussions about modern architecture taking place in architectural journals. And indeed, the discourse about modern architecture found in *Pencil Points, American Architect,* and *Architectural Record,* among others, tended to be oriented to discussions of style and design more as formal concerns rather than as social or political ones. However, there were voices in competition with these that sought to offer an alternative definition of modern architecture in general and the MoMA exhibit in particular. These are worth examining because they illuminate certain corners of the discourse around architecture as the United States moved from the setback modernism of the Empire State Building to the international style modernism of the postwar era.

The Museum of Modern Art, the Exhibit, and the International Style

The Museum of Modern Art was founded in 1929 by a trio of women, Mrs. John D. Rockefeller, Jr. (formerly Abby Green Aldrich), Miss Lizzie P. Bliss, and Mrs. Cornelius J. Sullivan (Mary Quinn Sullivan). They were, in Russell Lynes's words, "women of spirit, vigor, adventurousness, and, not unimportantly, of commanding wealth."[21] In May 1929 "The ladies," as they would eventually be referred to by museum staff and trustees, invited A.

Conger Goodyear, a Yale graduate, World War I colonel, and wealthy businessman, to take on a leading role in establishing the museum. By November that same year the museum had put on its first show, an exhibit of paintings on loan by Cézanne, Gauguin, Seurat, and van Gogh. Conger hired a young art history scholar at Wellesley College, Alfred Hamilton Barr, Jr., as director of the new museum. It was a providential hire for Barr, then a twenty-seven-year-old associate professor; the leap to museum director was significant in terms of both responsibility and pay. He accepted the directorship saying "This is something I could give my life to—unstintedly."[22] Barr's dedication to modern art was indeed energetic, but it was also rigorously formal, and this formal vision dictated the immediate future of the young museum. Years later, the museum's director would describe Barr as "that dedicated and courageous scholar who is generally recognized as one of the world's greatest authorities on modern art."[23]

The young museum had no building of its own at the time, so Sullivan and Barr began a search for quarters. By mid-July 1929 they had ten locations under consideration. With the advice of a real estate broker who managed many of the Rockefeller interests, they settled on the Heckscher Building, at Fifth Avenue and Fifty-Seventh Street. In one of those curious twists that illustrate how small the circles of elite culture in New York City often are, the building was owned by none other than August Heckscher, a board member of Empire State, Inc. In just a few years, Heckscher would be involved with two seminal events in architectural history in the twentieth century: the construction of the world's tallest building and an exhibition of modern architecture that would introduce the "International Style" to American audiences. The Museum of Modern Art rented roughly 4,600 square feet on the twelfth floor for $12,000 a year. As the museum became more popular, the stream of visitors soon overwhelmed the capacity of the elevators, causing great delays for guests and tenants alike. The situation was increasingly unsatisfactory for MoMA and became so bad that Heckscher threatened to evict the museum three times during the years it was in his building. Barr began looking for alternative quarters.

The 1932 season would be the last at the Museum of Modern Art's first location. In the midst of the political and economic turbulence of the Great Depression, the museum put on the show Modern Architecture: International Exhibition, the final exhibit in the Heckscher building. In a memo to MoMA trustees, Philip Johnson, who organized the exhibit with Henry-Russell Hitchcock, wrote: "America has for a long time sought a definite and practicable program for housing people in the lowest wage-earning class." A show of modern architecture, Johnson proposed, would display "solutions to this problem arrived at by European and American experts."[24] It was important, Johnson added, that the United States be exposed to this "new mode of building which fits so decidedly our methods of standardized construction, our economics, and our life." A different sentiment was expressed by Barr, who made the case for the exhibit by attacking American architects ("modernistic impresarios") and their skyscrapers: "We are asked to take seriously the architectural taste of real estate speculators, renting agents, and mortgage brokers!"[25] In stating his disdain for letting speculative investors or bank practices guide architectural innovation, Barr established a hierarchy of taste that placed his (and the Museum's) educated and scholarly judgments far above those of the crude (and presumably undistinguished) values of the market. Undoubtedly, Barr's antipathy was directed toward setback skyscrapers like the Empire State Building. The exhibit (referred to in internal museum documents simply as Exhibition 15) ran from February 10 to March 23, 1932. Nearly 33,000 people attended during its six-week run. Hitchcock and Johnson's *The International Style: Architecture Since 1922* was published at the same time.[26]

The exhibit featured the photographs, models, and drawings of nine selected participants (Frank Lloyd Wright, Walter Gropius, Jacques Le Corbusier, J. J. P. Oud, Ludwig Mies van der Rohe, Raymond Hood, Howe & Lescaze, Richard J. Neutra, and the Bowman Brothers), as well as short biographies of each. A section on housing organized by Lewis Mumford with Clarence Stein, Henry Wright, and Catherine Bauer rounded out the show. In his foreword to the catalog of the exhibit, Alfred Barr declared, "Expositions and exhibitions have perhaps changed the character of American architecture of the last forty years more than any other factor."[27] Clearly, Barr expected MoMA's effort to follow in the tradition of seminal exhibits he went on to cite: the Columbian Exposition of 1893, the Tribune Tower Competition of 1922, and the Paris Exposition of Decorative Arts in 1925. Barr also introduced the term "International Style" into the language of American architecture, for better or worse.

The exhibit's impact on building was constrained first by the Great Depression, and then by the materials shortages of World War II. In the postwar era, however, the International Style found favor among many architects and city planners across the United States. The formal and stylistic elements described by Hitchcock and Johnson were widely accepted, while the social and political aspects were either ignored or adapted significantly to suit the demands of the marketplace.

The exhibit and companion text continue to have a pronounced impact on American architecture. Franz Schulze cites them as "seminal events in the history of twentieth-century architecture," and Edward Durell Stone said the exhibit "did for architecture what the famous Armory Show had done for painting."[28] Exhibition 15 is famous not only for introducing U.S. audiences to a particular vision of modern architecture, but for offering a vision that was largely formal and apolitical. M. Christine Boyer writes of the exhibit that "Hitchcock and Johnson pushed the American architect to stress formal style over social functions." Robert A. M. Stern, following their lead, summarizes the exhibit as having established that the "hallmark of the radical new work was aesthetic minimalism." Along similar lines, Kenneth Frampton notes that the complex heterogeneity of the International Style was far "removed from the exclusively formal motivations" Henry-Russell Hitchcock and Philip Johnson attributed to it. An article about Philip Johnson in the *New Criterion* some fifty-plus years after the exhibit lists as its primary legacy Johnson's introduction of the terms "curtain wall" and "structural integrity" into "the vocabulary of American architecture."[29]

The Spectrum of Responses to Exhibition 15

Reviews of the Modern Architecture: International Exhibition were published in a number of venues. The breadth of responses to the show, and the variety of sources where they were published, serves as an index to the discussion of architecture in the era. Debates about the appropriate intersection of politics and architecture (or revolution and architecture) were becoming increasingly widespread during the 1930s. Throughout the decade there was robust debate about the form U.S. cities would take when the country emerged from the Great Depression and building resumed. These years were not a decade of intense building activity, but they saw intense intellectual activity about the process and purposes of building. A great many structures and cityscapes were sketched on paper, and the skylines of American cities after World War II and in the flush years of the 1950s were without doubt influenced by the imaginative work of the 1930s.

In his "Sky Line" column in the *New Yorker*, Lewis Mumford took the opportunity to praise Exhibition 15 by excoriating the architectural practices that had dominated the 1920s. He wrote: "this exhibition will, I trust, scandalize those who have taken seriously the notion that the skyscrapers produced by the New York City setback ordinances and the reckless gambling of our bankers were the chief boast of modern architecture."[30] Mumford's disdain for letting speculative investment practices guide architectural innovation led him to conclude that the "best buildings in New York at the moment are the models and photographs that Mr. Philip Johnson has arranged with such clarity and intelligence." The setback skyscraper was decisively not the sort of building Mumford felt should be championed.

Mumford's review emphasized that modernism entailed "forms of architecture which integrate both the practical and the ideal elements in modern civilization . . . relating air, sunlight, space, gardens, outlook, social intercourse, economic activity, in such a fashion as to form a concrete whole." For Mumford "modern architecture, in its organic sense, is a way of feeling, seeing, acting, living," and thus connected a shift in architectural design with a shift in world view.[31] Commenting that "American buildings, with all their affectations of modernity, are chaotic and incomplete," Mumford concluded, "Nothing like this fundamental unity [displayed by Exhibition 15] has existed since the Middle Ages." This unity between the idea of an improved social order and the design through which to achieve it (or, perhaps the designs in which to live out the new order) was for Mumford the great victory of the MoMA exhibition and the remedy to the disorder of American cities.

Mumford, who was involved in the "Housing" section of the exhibit, was perhaps less than objective in his review. Nevertheless, it is interesting to see how much attention other reviewers gave to the formal, stylistic elements of Exhibition 15, ignoring the social, economic, and political aspects of the show Mumford found so appealing. A review in the *American Magazine of Art* characterized the point of the show as "the machine, which for good or evil, has been continuously reshaping our economic and social views is now, rather abruptly, taking up architecture, and in the process there will be some necessary readjustments of our aesthetic beliefs."[32] Aside from commenting in vague terms about the connection between industrialization and architecture, the review noted the "avowed purpose" of the show was the display of design that was "essentially modern in its attitude toward life." The details of this "essentially modern" attitude are never laid out, nor are the effects of the machine on architecture ever made explicit. Instead, the review takes pains to treat architectural innovation in abstract (and somewhat antisocial) terms, pointing out that "Nothing is more man-made than architectural style and yet no man nor group of men can consciously create it. No mortal ever assisted at the mystery of its birth." Architecture, in this view, exists in a world separate from and superior to the everyday, and so it is "at once stimulated and sickened by money," and this is proof that "architecture, even in its most materialistic forms, partakes of the quality of art, whose alliance with Midas is, at best, a marriage of convenience."

If some reviews attempted to subsume the social elements of Exhibition 15 beneath language that spoke of architecture for art's sake, others employed the same language of style and form to attack the architecture on display, and by extension, the social agendas associated with it. William Williams, writing in *Pencil Points*, commented that the exhibited designs were so "international" as to be "intergeneric": "the only way to tell what a building is nowadays in this modern style is to snoop around and find out what is going on in it . . . if hundreds of kids are wandering around inside," then "it might be a school, or it might be a plant for the scientific production of unemotional bipedal automatons. But then again it might just be an asylum for juvenile delinquents— youngsters suspected of liking flowers and harboring affection for their parents!"[33] The designs, in addition to victimizing children and resembling in one case "the Tower of Babel," were a pointed reminder, in Williams's words, that "Art has become nowadays largely a matter of ideas," and that it was questionable whether "the average man is ready to accept the intellectualism which is producing the modern style . . . for he looks upon it dubiously, as a reflection of the disorderly mind and degenerate morals."

Williams's critique of modern architecture as reflective of disordered minds and degenerate morals raises (one assumes unwittingly) the specter of the National Socialists in Germany, who also associated modernism with degeneracy and insanity. Later that year, as reported in the pages of *Architectural Record*, they would close the Dessau Bauhaus, denouncing it "as a source of what the Hitlerites called 'kultur Bolshevism' and the spirit of modernism as against old German traditions."[34] Williams was not alone in his concerns. A similar connection between mental health and modernism was made in the pages of the *American Architect* by William Orr Ludlow, FAIA, who, beneath a photo of Gerrit Rietveld's Schroder House, posed the question: "Livable? What would be the psychological effect of living in a house such as this?"[35] Ludlow never answered his own question—perhaps living in such a house would turn one into a "bipedal automaton."

The *New York Times* described the guiding principle of the show as "nothing more nor less than the paramount importance of being different from every familiar and approved other architectural style."[36] Rather than seeing the rejection of previous architectural styles as part of a broader critical social and political agenda, this review defined difference as a pursuit of architects searching for an individual style. The review concluded that the new architectural language on display at MoMA was "at best an 'international' makeshift, like pigeon [sic] English."[37]

As William Curtis has noted, the development of modern architecture was "a revolution in social purpose as well as architectural forms."[38] The *New York Times* complained, however, that in the show "a church and a factory are easy to confuse," and that the houses resembled "airy bird cages." For his part, though, Lewis Mumford thought that "in these houses one beholds the virtues that had crept into architecture through the backdoor in the design of factories, grain elevators, bridges, power dams, subway stations. . . . Why should one seek archaic methods of escape from forms which so obviously lent themselves to use and enjoyment?"[39]

A second review in the *New York Times* was more sympathetic. Edward Alden Jewell, house art critic for the *Times*, applauded "how intelligently" problems of materials, construction, and function were addressed by the works displayed at the exhibit.[40] Catherine Bauer, who was involved in putting together the housing section with Mumford, wrote in *Creative Art* that the show offered more "intrinsic matter to judgement than any league or hodge-podge has presented to American eyes."[41] In the *Nation*, Douglas Haskell applauded the designs, but suggested they would appeal largely to the elite, to "the aristocrat of modern taste." Haskell also expressed his doubts about the thesis put forward by Johnson and Hitchcock that the architecture on display constituted a "style" rather than a built response to a set of social, economic, and political needs.[42]

The title of Talbot Hamlin's review in *American Architect*, "The International Style Lacks the Essence of Great Architecture," summarizes his view of the show.[43]

In the end all this debate points clearly to the fact that modernism was contested terrain in the 1930s. It did not arrive on U.S. shores neutralized of its progressive or radical heritage. Rather, it underwent a process of transformation, one that was responsive to its context. A critical position that refuses to acknowledge any relationship between architecture and politics is itself a political position. The debate whether architecture was properly informed by politics or instead should be a high art tradition operating at a remove from such considerations continued throughout that decade and into the next.

The *New Masses* and the Political Reception of Exhibition 15

Architects debated these issues not just in journals of architecture, but also in magazines of politics, in particular the *New Masses*. The direct successor of two earlier magazines of radical politics and art, *The Masses* and *The Liberator*, the *New Masses* was published from 1926 to 1948.[44] Based in New York, and the dominant radical publication of its time, it labored to be the independent cultural organ of both workers and revolutionary intellectuals across the nation. As its editor Mike Gold put it, the *New Masses* would "not be a magazine of Communism, or Moscow, but a magazine of American experiment."[45] This mix meant that the cover of the magazine might feature the hammer and sickle one month and Abraham Lincoln the next.

The *New Masses* was committed to supporting the struggle of workers for "bread and roses, too," and as such was home to lively writing that sought to explore the totality of the lived experience of labor in the United States. Articles addressed topics such as art, architecture, and urbanism from the perspective of advancing the cause of working people, refusing to separate the worlds of culture from those of economics and politics. As one U.S. Army Intelligence report in 1932 put it, "The Metropolitan Area of New York City in the natural centre and fountain-head of all radical and subversive activities in the United States." In addition to New York having a large "foreign population," the report noted the role of journals such as the *New Masses* in the spread of subversive ideas in the city: "The situation is made more acute by the large number of so-called intelligentsia in the fields of journalism . . . who through their prominence and widely distributed followings can get a hearing in the press and before the public." All these elements in concert made "New York a veritable sess-pool [sic] of indigestible foreign elements."[46]

A "loud and colorful journal with fairly advanced Marxist ideas about both literature and politics," the *New Masses* published, among others, the work of Langston

Hughes, Richard Wright, Myrna Page (its Russian correspondent in the mid-1930s, who would later write *Moscow Yankee*), James Agee, Meridel Le Sueur, and the graphics of Hugo Gellert and William Gropper.[47] By the mid-1930s, when the magazine became a weekly, it had a circulation of about 25,000, and its pages included advertisements not just for radical magazines and newspapers like *The Communist, Labour Monthly, Daily Worker,* and *Labor Unity,* but also for the arts journal *Hound and Horn.* The mix of culture and politics in the *New Masses* was such that readers might find an ad for "The New LENIN Head (for wall mounting; ivory or bronze finish)" from the Workers Book Store (50 East Thirteenth Street, New York City) on one page, and an ad for a performance of the Martha Graham Dance Troupe on the next. While it was always closely associated with the Communist Party, and in its final years the editorial stance was increasingly sectarian, as historian Paul Buhle notes, its literary critics "lavished praise upon Sinclair Lewis, Sherwood Anderson, Eugene O'Neill and others who had opened new imaginative territory in their exploration of machine age America."[48]

In 1932 the journal found an exhibit of architecture that addressed the same concerns in the Museum of Modern Art, an institution that would at first seem to have little in common with the *New Masses.* The *New Masses* was scrappy, committed to revolutionary democracy, and sought to use the frank, direct language of everyday life; MoMA was a bastion of wealth, privilege, and cultural aristocracy. Its founders and directors were culled from the very elite and powerful New Yorkers whose political and cultural hegemony the left in the 1930s sought to challenge. Nevertheless the politics of modernism were actively in contest at the time and the Museum exhibit, if not the interpretation MoMA sought to give modern architecture, was applauded in the *New Masses.*

The review of the show in the *New Masses* lauded not only the aesthetic innovations of the modern architecture on display at MoMA but also its political significance. The first line of the review, written by young art historian Meyer Schapiro under the pseudonym John Kwait, stated: "The recent exhibition of architecture at the Museum of Modern Art (New York) is surely the most important in its history." The reviewer conceded that earlier shows of "French painting were artistically better"; however, "They cannot have the same social importance. The buildings [on display] are more than designs or spectacles; they are a social program and a necessary part of a new society. The intentions of the most advanced architects imply a social revolution."[49]

The review makes it clear that, regardless of the reception of Hitchcock and Johnson's presentation of modern architecture as largely a formal aesthetic development devoid of social concerns, U.S. audiences could decide for themselves the political implications of modern architecture.[50] In Schapiro's words, these "bolder architects anticipate the style of a Socialist Republic." Indeed, the *New Masses* sought to claim the central project of modern architecture for the left. In her study of communitarian and socialist architecture in the United States, Dolores Hayden described such built projects as the work of "dissident idealists."[51] In the 1930s, however, Schapiro and his fellow writers did not seek to be dissidents; they sought to orient modern architecture in the United States around the central concerns of the left. Social and political concerns were no longer marginal or peripheral—they became one with the process of aesthetic creation. Furthermore, where in the past the joining of architecture and social change dictated departure and isolation from the surrounding society (as in the case of those "dissident idealists"), modern architecture, as envisioned in the pages of the *New Masses*, offered the possibility of reorganizing society as a whole.

By uniting political possibilities with aesthetic ones, Schapiro stakes out a critical position that is important for the way it counters two trends in architectural history. The first is the tendency to judge the political content or impact of architecture by analyzing, nearly exclusively, the politics of architects and patrons; "political architecture" results from the union of politically committed architects and patrons. Given this precondition and taking into account the degree to which historians agree that "in its transition to the United States the modern movement lost its social project," a "lament" about modernism in the American context developed that "suggests that the formalization of modernism as the 'International Style' eliminated any avant-garde tendencies (political and aesthetic) evident in the original European context."[52] This view, while accurately charting a dominant historical and critical line of thought, nonetheless denies the possibility of an avant-garde *reception* (either political or aesthetic) of modern architecture. It specifies that political and aesthetic meaning are formed during the process of creation, and therefore ignores the creative possibilities of different communities of reception.

Inevitably, then, critics have described architectural modernism as apolitical because its leading proponents in the United States (like Mies van der Rohe and Walter Gropius) were, in their assessment, apolitical (as were, presumably, the curricula they instituted at the Illinois Institute of Technology and Harvard University's Graduate School of Design).[53] Even if the individuals themselves were not apolitical, their architecture remained so because, in the words of Joan Ockman, architects like "Gropius and Mies van der Rohe . . . believed that aesthetic culture had the option to remain 'apolitical,' that it could exist untainted by political ideology."[54] The review in *New Masses* asserts an alternate position, noting that buildings can communicate meanings and messages outside or beyond the intent of their designers. The revolutionary possibilities of modern architecture extended beyond the process of creation, and therefore architecture could be revolutionary even when, in Schapiro's words, "the architects themselves are conservative or ignorant of basic facts."[55]

This is not to say that the issues of meaning and representation were treated cavalierly, for the second important element of Schapiro's position is that architecture is neither the embodiment of the political economy, nor a form of culture free from its bounds. Rather, it functions in between these two extremes, capable of mediating boundaries or, conversely, reinforcing them. And so Schapiro praised the "new architecture" on display as "international, classless and practical," but reminded his readers that the "technical, esthetic form is not enough to ensure the social value of this architecture." While Exhibition 15 "provided the indispensable technique and esthetic of a Socialist community," it was, like any technique, capable of serving as the means to a number of ends. "Without the will to apply it for a common end," Schapiro warned, "this style, which has grown out of industrial society, will remain a means of exploitation, or the newest fad of the richest class, the symbol of a profitable, spectacular efficiency."[56] He noted that while the style of architecture on display at MoMA was doubtless shaped by industrialization, commercialization, and the influence of "bourgeois culture . . . these forces do not themselves explain the emergence of the new style."

How then were architecture and social revolution related? What role did those on the American left imagine architecture might take in the "social revolution" of which Schapiro wrote? Many historians pondering the relationship between social change and modern architecture in its early years in the United States have noted that "measures of economy, efficiency, and technical innovation" were the means by which "architecture could serve as an agent of social redemption."[57] The failure of technology to achieve a measure of "social redemption" is well documented. But looking through the pages of the *New Masses* raises the question whether this narrative of naïve technological idealism is accurate. In an article titled "Architecture Under Capitalism," Schapiro wrote: "As a perfected technique architecture points to the greatest social possibilities; but these possibilities cannot be realized in their fullness in a capitalist society where technical advances are inseparable from exploitation and misery."[58]

The engineering feats that raised buildings ever faster and to ever greater heights were viewed with suspicion as innovations that, in Schapiro's words, "do not in the least change the relation of boss and worker."[59] Modern architecture, in order to play a role in the social revolution its designs implied, had to provide more than technical advances and cheaper means of production, for these alone would simply make architects "highly paid employees of builders and realtors." In "Architecture Under Capitalism" Schapiro went so far as to attack Buckminster Fuller, the Structural Studies Associates (SSA), and their journal *Shelter* for, in his words, proposing "that change from capitalism to a better system of communal service will come about automatically from the social attitudes resulting from improved technology."[60] Schapiro insisted that architecture, technology, and the political economy were intertwined social elements; advances in one but not the others solved little. Seventy years of theorizing about the role of architecture in society have passed since then, but Schapiro's point is as valid today as then.

Faced with what Dolores Hayden calls the "Corbusian blackmail" of "Architecture or Revolution" that has so often preoccupied historians tracing the politics of modern architecture, Schapiro would no doubt respond "Architecture *and* Revolution."[61] The rarely quoted second half of Le Corbusier's famous phrase, "Revolution can be avoided," seems, in the context of Schapiro's comments about the mutability of modern architecture, to reflect anything but the revolutionary spirit commentators often afford it.

For Schapiro, the style of the show was a response to changing social conditions and needs, not a statement of artistic petulance. Surely Schapiro would have found the *New York Times* out of step and archaic in its anti-modernism. In fact, the streamlined, "monolithic" forms decried by the *Times* would soon become, as the *New Masses* had predicted, the "dominant manner of building," which is to say, modernism as presented at MoMA achieved supremacy in architecture, even if it did not make similar inroads with the vast majority of building that occurs without the services of an architect.[62] What the *New Masses* did not predict, and perhaps could not have, was the fashion in which International Style modern architecture would achieve this dominance.

PART II

The Seagram Building:
The Ascension of
the International Style
and a Somber Monument
to Corporate Authority

5

Architecture Culture into the 1950s

Looking at the 1950s, and the Seagram Building, it is worthwhile to survey briefly the broader architecture culture of the era. As it had in the 1930s, modern architecture served as a medium that could convey a variety of messages. At the same time, political, economic, and cultural shifts around the world profoundly altered the architectural landscape of the United States. In the year of the MoMA exhibit, Soviet modern architecture was featured in the American magazine *Soviet Russia Today* as a demonstration that "Socialism is no longer a dream, but a living reality."[1] Yet such a definition of modern architecture, as James Sloan Allen points out, stood in stark contrast to the growing alliance in the postwar United States between "twentieth century art and commerce . . . that drew them inevitably together."[2] Indeed, by the mid-1940s, modern architecture was used in a variety of advertising, for both building products (which is to be expected), as well as (unexpectedly) consumer goods such as whiskey. At the same time, novelists and filmmakers employed modern architecture as a symbol of progress, aligning it with a host of political and economic virtues.

The influence in popular culture of modern architecture as an idea versus a built reality was aided by various other factors as well. By the time the Modern Architecture: International Exhibition closed in 1932, commercial and domestic construction in New York and many other major cities had slowed to a near standstill. In New York this decline was especially notable because the pace of construction had been so furious. The construction boom of the late 1920s alone saw the construction of such notable edifices as the Chrysler, McGraw-Hill, and Daily News Buildings, as well as the drawing up of plans for both the Empire State Building and Rockefeller Center. With the exception of Rockefeller Center—which took nearly a decade to complete—the years between MoMA's famous exhibit and the start of World War II were ones of declining architectural production. And while the massive manufacturing boom spurred by the war jump-started the economy, wartime restrictions on materials and construction meant that most architects in the United States were designing buildings that could be built only at some unknown point in the future.

During these lean years, political events in Europe sent modernist architects packing, and many of them arrived in the United States. In the fall of 1933, amid a crushing depression that had left most architects unemployed, the Nazis finally closed the Bauhaus for good, claiming it was a "foreign virus" that needed to be "purged."[3] The now famous Bauhaus building was called "un-German," a "somber glass palace of oriental taste," and an "aquarium." Its professors and students were accused of engaging in artistic and architectural practices that were decadent, rootless, "Jewish-Marxist," unclean, and ugly.[4] The Nazis could tolerate glass and steel structures for factories, but the Third Reich would be represented by the austere neoclassicism of Albert Speer's designs, buildings that would make "beautiful ruins" a thousand years from now.[5]

In the Soviet Union, a few months after Exhibition 15 ended, the Central Committee of the Party decreed that all private, autonomous artist and architects' groups were now dissolved. They were replaced by official unions, given orders to create art, literature, and architecture in the style of Socialist Realism. Socialist Realism, as Richard Weston notes, required that architecture be "monumental in character and draw upon appropriate historical styles. . . . Avant-garde art became a crime against the state."[6] The Soviet and Nazi states, William Curtis points out, regarded modern architecture (except in the case of strictly utilitarian programs and designs) "with suspicion," and directed architecture to return to "pre-revolutionary frames of reference."[7]

And so, while in the late 1920s many avant-garde German architects had moved to the Soviet Union to experience the freedoms afforded them there, by the late 1930s major Bauhaus architects like Walter Gropius, Marcel Breuer, and Ludwig Mies van der Rohe had emigrated to the United States. Prior to their arrival, as Curtis notes, the "Beaux-Arts system of education remained virtually unchallenged" in architecture schools in the United States.[8] Gropius and Mies changed that when they took leading positions at the Harvard School of Design and the Illinois Institute of Technology respectively, and established curricula that diverged dramatically from the Beaux-Arts model. Their arrival at these two schools established the foundation not only of postwar architectural education, but of the ascension of modern architecture in the United States.[9]

The rising legitimacy of modernism in the United States was also boosted by events during World War II, when the American press began popularizing modernism, as Serge Guilbaut notes, by writing articles that "gave currency to the erroneous notion that Fascism was destroying all culture. In reality Fascism was getting rid of a certain kind of culture: modernism. . . . As a result, what the mass media were defending without knowing it was the concept of modernism."[10] In tune with this defense of modernism was a particular American historical legacy in which, as Dell Upton writes, "mechanistic imagery was regularly equated with modernity."[11] The mobilization the nation underwent during the war effort meant that such mechanistic imagery, whether of tanks, planes, boats, bridges, or the vast production lines and factories required to construct them, was very much in the forefront of American popular culture.

Ayn Rand, Howard Roark, and Architectural Genius

Novelists and film-makers were sensitive to the changing meanings of modern architecture and the political uses to which they could be put. In the 1930s, Le Corbusier was well known among architectural circles, and even quoted in the *New York Times*, for making such claims as "we have sacrificed conscience for wealth, and wealth is the one brutal aim pursued by everyone."[12] In 1943, however, Ayn Rand's novel *The Fountainhead*[13] depicted the visionary modernist architect as the ideal heroic man for a postwar capitalist America. While advertisers touted the visionary qualities of modern architecture, Rand went much farther as, according to the logic of her narrative, the genius implicit in modern architecture is recognized only by those who understand the true nature of human progress. For Rand, as critic Nancy Levinson notes, that progress rests on the recognition of the "supreme importance of the individual ego."[14] The hero of her novel is Howard Roark, an architect whose "integrity is as unyielding as granite," a man who refuses to compromise for anyone or any reason. Alfred Barr, Jr., thought exhibitions and competitions had been the primary influence on American architecture in the last forty years; Rand's novel treats such events with the same exaggerated seriousness: the dramatic denouement of her story depends on the result of an architectural competition.

Rand began writing the novel in 1935. It was rejected by twelve publishers before Bobbs-Merrill Company agreed to publish it. Critics took only slight notice of it on publication. It was reviewed in both *The Nation* and the *New York Times*, but did not make any major literary waves, although the fiftieth anniversary edition assures us that, "through word of mouth," it became a "best-seller" two years after publication.[15] The *New York Times* offered backhand praise, concluding that *The Fountainhead* was "the only novel of ideas written by an American woman that I can recall."[16] On reading the opening lines of the book ("Howard Roark laughed. He stood naked at the edge of a cliff"), however, one is inclined to heed Diana Trilling's caveat in *The Nation* that readers buying Rand's novel in search of entertainment or enjoyment would be wasting paper.[17] The novel remains popular today, particularly on college campuses, and has been the topic of at least one architectural symposium and numerous articles in various architecture journals.[18]

In fact, the most interesting elements of the novel seem to exist in spite of Rand's flat, didactic prose and painfully stereotyped characters: Howard Roark, the architect *Übermensch* (who bears more than a passing resemblance to Frank Lloyd Wright); Dominique Francon, a wealthy heiress unsatisfied by the weak men around her and Roark's sexual foil; Gail Wynand, the Hearst-like publishing magnate; and Ellsworth Toohey, a critic and public intellectual rumored to be patterned after Lewis Mumford. The predictable behavior of Rand's characters and her obvious determination to choreograph them gives the story its polemical quality. One of the key elements of this polemic is the disdain Rand feels for "the masses" and their refusal to bow down before their social superiors. In her notes for the novel, Rand describes her anger at "the rising power of the masses—The open arrogance of the inferior who no longer try to imitate their superiors, but boldly flaunt their inferiority, their averageness, their popular appeal."[19]

This distaste for people who "flaunt their inferiority" finds expression in the novel in a variety of ways, most obviously in the long lines of dialogue. At one point media mogul Gail Wynand asks Roark: "Did you want to scream, when you were a child, seeing nothing but fat ineptitude around you, knowing how many things could be done and done so well, but having no power over them? Having to take orders—and that's bad enough—but to take orders from your inferiors! Have you felt that?" Roark, who earlier has noted that he "doesn't build in order to have clients," of course answers "Yes."[20] In 1949 the novel was translated for the silver screen, with Rand writing the script in order to guarantee the fluid translation of her themes from paper to celluloid. As one critic put it, "the central point of *The Fountainhead*, of course, is the supreme importance of the individual ego; both book and movie are paeans to the 'I' against the 'We.'"[21]

Both book and film exerted influence on the public perception of the profession for years. If in the translation to film much from the book inevitably was lost, the core elements of Rand's narrative remain. Roark's greatness is expressed via "the exaltation of the architect as a privileged visionary."[22] In Roark, the architect is a figure of decisive individualism who champions the values of capitalist democracy. As Lary May has shown, this association, far from unusual, was a staple element of postwar film when the movie industry was responding to the pressures of the Cold War. Hollywood films during the late 1940s and 1950s sought to craft "a new Americanism rooted in big business, class consensus, and consumer democracy," in the process transforming "the content of film-making [and] creating the basis for a new Cold War culture and ideology."[23]

In many respects this characterization of the figure of the architect remains the most influential aspect of both the novel and film. While in reality Frank Lloyd Wright had been, as May notes, concerned with "architecture as a vehicle for modernizing a producer's democracy at odd with monopoly capitalism," *The Fountainhead* transforms

Wright, via his cinematic simulacrum Roark, into a partisan of the "ethos of the lone genius and entrepreneur" who discovers that "social reformers and the people are corrupt."[24] Rand depicts Roark as a glass and steel uber-modernist who believes that the problems architecture should address are ones of design, not social welfare. The unregulated marketplace and individual effort should combine to solve problems of poverty and housing, for instance. According to Roark, architects and the government joining together to build public housing only makes matters worse. Conversely, the novel is filled with parlor-room socialists and thinly veiled New Dealers whose affiliation with what Rand terms "collectivist" political causes is outweighed only by their commitment to architectural forms steeped in historical styles. Readers of the novel could justifiably come away from it thinking it was individualistic young titans of capitalism who championed modernism in the 1930s, and not leftist radical intellectuals associated with the *New Masses*. Certainly they would be surprised to find out that a glass and steel modernist like Mies van der Rohe had in 1926 designed a monument to the Communist martyrs Rosa Luxemburg and Karl Liebknecht. Or that in his memoirs modern architect and influential writer and editor Peter Blake might write:

> We realized that mankind was faced by all sorts of predictable disasters—population explosion, hence wars, disease, poverty, and so on. We believed, quite sincerely, that modern architecture could do something about all these things—especially housing the poor, and about creating viable, healthy, democratic (and, incidentally, beautiful) communities. We believed that we could slay the automobile, defeat fascism and abolish disease. We were starry-eyed, and beautifully naïve.[25]

Today, decades after *The Fountainhead*, most architects practice in firms where design work is done in teams and often parceled out according to narrow subspecialties, just the sort of arrangement Rand condemned in her novel. Nonetheless, many in the general public continue to think about the profession in Roarkian terms. Many of the best-known architects at the turn of this century marshal their fame by cultivating a persona of individual creative genius that has more in common with Howard Roark than with the relative anonymity of a career in the middle echelons of a large corporate firm. And, like Roark, many of these architects bluntly suggest that architecture cannot and should not try to solve problems that aren't aesthetic or tectonic at their core. At the same time, formal education and training in most schools of architecture in the United States continue to emphasize the role of the single creative figure. Students take on projects alone, managing them from beginning to end, from the smallest detail to the largest element. Teamwork is present, but studio work, the awards system, and admissions process all favor the individual over the team. Rand would be pleased to see how very Roarkian architecture culture remains today.

Advertising the "City of the Future"

Novelists and film-makers were not the only ones to use the architect and architecture as a vehicle for their ideas. Architecture, and in particular the tall office building, was already an standard feature of American advertising in the 1940s. As Katherine Solomonson has observed, "Tall office buildings had provided publicity for the corporations that constructed them since the inception of the skyscraper as a building type . . . companies cultivated the advertising value of the distinctive buildings they erected while reaping financial rewards from leased retail and office space."[26] These corporate headquarters, if their design was distinctive enough, could even take on the role of company trademark or logo, as in the case of the Metropolitan Life Building, which appeared in print ads for the company.[27] This "alliance of the consumer economy and modernism" inevitably altered the political, social, and economic milieu of modern architecture.[28] Here distinctive architecture (in the form of a company's headquarters) crafted an identity for a particular corporation or business.

A series of advertisements in the 1940s, however, used generic modern architecture not to identify a corporate identity but to represent a particular way of life, economic condition, and technological innovation. The advertisements sought to link products or services with a modern lifestyle, so they promoted not only the selling points of a particular good or service, but a whole way of living.

During the years of rationing in World War II, advertisers in mainstream magazines like *Newsweek* assured the public that shortages would be replaced by bounty when the war ended. Ads for Bell Telephone, for instance, told readers that as soon as the war ended and production restrictions were eased, new phone lines would be put up. The copy for an ad, superimposed over the figure of an Air Force bomber-gunner carrying ammunition for a fifty-caliber machine gun, read "In peace, a lot of that copper would have gone into new telephone lines. Now it's needed for shooting and winning the war. That's why we can't build new lines right now."[29]

Architecture-centric advertising similarly blended references to wartime restrictions on the consumer economy with representations of postwar life where prosperity was defined by modernity. These advertisements present a vision of America where modern architecture is allied with the values of a new consumer society in which abundance assures social and political stability. Years of deferred gratification, these ads assured, would be repaid in full with an era of prosperity. An advertisement for Revere Copper and Brass—featuring a couple gazing over a newly minted cityscape complete with flat-roofed modernist buildings—put it: "After total war can come total living."[30] While it is natural to expect such advertising in architecture or building journals, its prominence in popular newsweeklies and magazines suggests increasing public interest in modern architecture and the benefits it presumably could provide the nation. Corporations attempted to capitalize on that sense of potential with depictions of a new and improved future replete with magnificent architectural designs.

The Bohn Aluminum and Brass Corporation, for example, used a series of images depicting the improvements Bohn products would make in the life of Americans after the war. These featured a range of modernist architecture, from apartment buildings, individual single-family homes, to entire cityscapes. The architecture was distinctive enough to attract the eye of the reader, but the ads were not the work of architects, nor did they depict well-known buildings or designs. Rather, they were amalgamations, a sort of cliché that advertisers thought readers would easily recognize as "modern" architecture. The claims that went along with this modernist imagery ranged from the seemingly modest, "Girders, pillars, and innumerable alloys produced by Bohn, will mean new designs for more attractive living," to the sensational, "The City of the Future will be born—startling new architectural designs will be an everyday occurrence!"[31] Rather than touting the quality of Bohn products, these ads projected a vision of the future and the life Americans would enjoy in that future. Associating their products with modern architecture allowed Bohn to sell a way of living, not just building materials.

Of course, the Bohn ads were also an attempt to sell the public a positive image of the corporation by mixing the realities of wartime production and scarcity (ads for the companies repeatedly made the point that they were "exclusively" engaged in production for the war effort at this time, and hence had nothing to offer the consumer market) with a vision of the future where their products would be used by architects to create a world of beauty, economic opportunity, and even leisure. Modern architecture would address social problems—the scarcity of housing, the instability of the economy, the demand for more functional, hygienic design in housing and workplaces—with Bohn products of course, through the mechanisms of the capitalist marketplace, not through any reform of it.

In a series of ads titled "Men Who Plan Beyond Tomorrow Like . . . Seagram's V.O.," Seagram (the corporation that would later build the most significant modern skyscraper of the postwar era) also attempted to link its products with imagined postwar social innovation through the vehicle of modern architecture. One ad featured a modernist white villa (the design a mix of Le Corbusier and Walter Gropius's Bauhaus) with its own swimming pool and airplane runway and a four-vehicle garage. The copy described this "house of the future, turning automatically to face the sun all day long—

so healthful rays may stream through special ultra-violet windows into spacious rooms." It came with an "amphibious car, for land or water . . . and the family plane—a flying wing." The sun-worshiping, "healthful ray"-filled house reminded readers of the ad's caption, that "Men Who Plan Beyond Tomorrow like the *Lightness* of Seagram's V.O."[32] Modern architecture would not only offer new forms of housing and transportation, it would offer Americans a new way of life, one where the physical and societal restrictions of the past were erased by flying wings, amphibious cars, and the easy availability of once-prohibited whiskey.

Another ad in the series featured a rendering of the city of the future, one bearing an uncanny resemblance to Le Corbusier's proposal for a city of towers.[33] The caption beneath the illustration read: "High-speed, amphibious motors will whisk along highways or skim across waterways with equal ease. . . . Sky-scrapers will rise from spacious lawns . . . when Health Authorities abolish over-crowding of buildings. . . . Fantastic? Not at all! These things are being developed today by Men Who Plan Beyond Tomorrow!" The advertisement made sure to remind readers that "Seagram, too, plans beyond Tomorrow—*always*."[34] By participating in the consumer economy, the ad suggests, one joins the ranks of builders of skyscrapers, one becomes an example of "men who plan beyond tomorrow." Seagram employed modern architecture as a proxy for a better future.

Published almost a decade before the earliest stages of planning for the future Seagram Building, these advertisements used modern architecture a symbol of progress and faith in the future, and linked progress to the abundant consumer culture predicted to emerge at the war's end. Abundance would provide gleaming new cities to replace the decline that the years of Depression had wrought, as well as new and innovative solutions to the shortages that had ravaged the U.S. economy and continued to wear on daily life. While in the 1930s modern architecture had been linked by many critics with the cause of reforming the social chaos that resulted from the excesses of capitalism, now architecture served as a vehicle to valorize the benefits that same system would produce for (in the logic of the advertisements) all Americans. While the practice of distilling spirits is thousands of years old, these advertisements generally eschew history. Instead the text and imagery link the consumption of alcohol to a particular vision of modernity largely defined by architecture. In the 1950s, Seagram once again turned to modern architecture to enlarge and refine the company's reputation.

6

Clients and Architect

In the years following the "conspicuously American" Empire State Building, modern architecture in the United States underwent a period of transformation with the introduction of the European-influenced international style. The international style, in turn, was defined by its promoters at institutions like MoMA as a reaction against skyscrapers like the Empire State Building, which they condemned as a reflection of the "architectural taste of real estate speculators, renting agents, and mortgage brokers."[1] Looking today at the Empire State Building and the Seagram Building, we move from a building that celebrated the republican convergence of business and the higher aspirations of civic duty to one that celebrates a growing consumer culture and liberation from older, constrictive social values. Yet both skyscrapers were built by clients who sought to gain legitimacy through architecture, and who sought to build in a style free of particular symbols from the exclusionary culture of the past. That similar quests could result in such different buildings highlights the extent of the changes between the two eras of their construction. These shifts in architectural form and style were not just reflections of changes in the discipline and practice of architecture. Developments in architecture culture occurred at the same time as (and were influenced by) significant changes in the economy, the public sphere, and global politics, in particular the Cold War.

Completed in 1958, the Seagram Building cost a small fortune to build.[2] Indeed, *Architectural Forum* claimed that, at $45 per square foot, it was the most expensive office tower ever built "in Manhattan or anywhere else."[3] In addition, the building occupies only about half its site, sacrificing valuable (and obviously rentable) square footage. Mies van der Rohe had already secured a reputation as a modern architect who embraced sumptuous materials, and the Seagram Building proved beyond doubt that Miesian minimalism could take an extremely luxurious form. The building embodies luxury in a number of forms: of materials, beauty, uniqueness, indulgence, technology, and power.

Figure 19. Seagram Building, 1958. Reprinted by permission from Ezra Stoller © Esto.

It is worth noting at the outset that the building was not mortgaged, but paid for in cash from the company coffers. With bronze I-beams and spandrels, marble-clad shear walls and elevator cores, furnished with pieces designed by Hans Wegner, Charles and Ray Eames, Florence Knoll, and Eero Saarinen (among others), appointed with works of modern art in numbers great enough to fill a small museum, and with its dramatic setback and plaza located on very expensive Manhattan real estate, the Seagram Building redefined corporate luxury in the late 1950s. What program was this luxury designed to serve? What motives fueled this expenditure?

An examination of corporate records and the cavalcade of voices that greeted the building when it opened reveal the wide variety of ends to which the Seagram Building's luxury was seen as a means. While the classical geometry of Mies's design is often called timeless, contemporary responses to the building without doubt highlight the social, political, and cultural tensions prevalent in the United States in the 1950s. For some the luxury of the Seagram Building was an index of the rising prosperity of the nation and the strength of American capitalist democracy. Others mixed their awe of the building's opulence with the atomic anxieties of the era, leading one magazine to comment that the building can "boast of more superlatives than the H-bomb." Indeed, such anx-

Figure 20. Seagram offices, 1958. Reprinted by permission from Ezra Stoller © Esto.

ieties are evident in the plans (later abandoned) to construct an atomic blast shelter in the basement, a move some executives thought would advertise Seagram's good corporate citizenship. Finally, many regarded the building's luxury as an advertisement for the whiskey (and other liquors) the Seagram Company sold and took to calling it the "big, bronze, booze building" and the "world's tallest high-ball." Here I explore the motivations behind the Seagram Company's construction of their corporate headquarters as well as the popular and critical responses to it in order to better understand the changing significance of postwar modern corporate architecture.[4]

Located in the city that epitomizes the restless activity of the American marketplace, it seems inevitable that the Seagram Building should express the particular mode of capitalist organization of its time, and do so in a laudatory fashion. The Seagram Building, built in an era when, as Lary May notes, "politicians and businessmen spoke with one voice in praise of the modern corporation," explicitly identified itself with just such a large modern corporation.[5] In addition, while earlier skyscrapers such as the Empire State Building were symbols rooted in the values of an older producer economy and its attendant definitions of Americanism, the Seagram Building emerged from an expanding consumer culture amid the tensions of the Cold War. This particular economic and geopolitical context (aligned with the increasing importance of marketing and public relations in corporate America) meant that the Seagram Building was engaged in the construction of both a business entity and a particular way of life. In the popular press and architecture journals of the time the skyscraper symbolized not just material power but national identity. Exploring these different manifestations offers us the chance to understand what modern architecture meant both for building and for society.

When the Seagram Building first opened, critics focused on the abstract, timeless, and classical elegance of the building. Roger Montgomery, writing about "The Goal of Architecture," approvingly cited the Seagram Building as a building that "transcends the meaningless idea of taste and the equally meaningless fetishism of technique for its own sake."[6] *Progressive Architecture* praised "its arrangement of space" and was "tremendously moved by the suave beauty of the shaft."[7] The *New York Herald Tribune* editorial page stated that the Seagram Building was one of the few new buildings to "breathe whole new shapes into our lives . . . [it] creates around itself a feeling of space and light that is rare in Manhattan."[8] The *Wall Street Journal*, mingling aesthetic and economic assessments, found the "bronze-sheathed tower with a plaza" made "extravagant use of land."[9] Lewis Mumford, in his lengthy appraisal of the building, wrote: "this seems to me the best skyscraper New York has seen since Hood's Daily News Building; in classic execution it towers above the doubled height of the Empire State Building, while its nearest later rival, Lever House, more package than Pyramid, looks curiously transitory

Figure 21. Lobby, Seagram Building, 1958. Reprinted by permission from Ezra Stoller © Esto.

and ephemeral when one turns from one to the other." He concluded that "Somber, unsmiling, yet not grim, 375 is a muted masterpiece—but a masterpiece."[10]

Much of the writing about the building over the years retained this formal focus, generally describing the building as sober, elegant, and pure in its geometry. William J. R. Curtis's words, "[the building is a] hieratic, stable geometry . . . with an underlying classical echo," are fairly characteristic.[11] Leland Roth, echoing Curtis's reference to things "hieratic," notes that the building, with its "frigid hauteur" and "elegantly uniform fenestration . . . manifests a highly focused artistic energy that previously had been employed for buildings of the church."[12] Kenneth Frampton, impressed by the "Semperian interweaving of fenestration with structure," calls the building Mies's "monument in Manhattan."[13]

The building is a fine example of modern architecture, and one of the most sensitively proportioned structures in New York. Surrounded by the constant activity of Manhattan, the Seagram Building demands more than a momentary glance. The double-height glazed lobby is uncluttered and composed almost entirely of fenestration and the elevator and service cores. Spare and elegant, it offers no hint as to what sort of business takes place in the building.[14] The defining visual elements of the building on its Park Avenue façade, set back some ninety feet from the street, include the extruded bronze I-beams that divide the trabeated tower into thirty vertical ribbons balancing the horizontal emphasis of the bronze spandrels. Six massive bronze-wrapped columns support the building, and the four marble rectangles that contain the elevator and service cores extend outside the building, blurring the distinction between interior and exterior space. In spite of the presence of so much glass and metal, the building is neither translucent nor shiny; during the day it is deep, rich, and dark. Only when it is illuminated from the interior at night does the building take on the quality of a luminous glass box. Along the Fifty-Third and Fifty-Fourth Street sides, the marble shear walls are visible, along with the rectangular "bustle" at the rear of the building. These volumes, solutions to the need for space that cannot be accommodated by the tower alone, are often excluded from photographs of the building through careful composition.

The commentary in the popular and non-architectural press surrounding the Seagram Building at the time of its completion was imbued with the near absolute faith in technology that characterized American society after World War II. The building was lauded as a marvel of technology, of the technological advances that could and would revolutionize American society and solve the problems of scarcity, economic instability, and social inequality (with its attendant class conflict) that had constrained life in the past. At the same time, fears about the Cold War, and the dark side of technology contained in them, also became a feature of the discourse about and life of the Seagram Building. In the early 1960s, for instance, a full-scale model of the Polaris missile was put on display in Mies's famous plaza. The classical geometry of Mies's design may be timeless, but the voices that greeted the construction of the Seagram Building reveal the social, political, and cultural tensions of the time.

In addition to its formal composition and characteristics, another widely discussed aspect of the Seagram Building is the influence it had on urban design around the world. Imitations of the building began cropping up in cities all over the United States, Europe, and elsewhere. By the late 1960s the glass-box office tower, often in iterations far shinier and slicker than the Seagram Building, was ubiquitous. With ubiquity came the expected decline into cliché and banality: most of Mies's imitators, with little of his ability to make the abstract and repetitious seem sublime, created buildings that reproduced many of Seagram's "limitations and few of [its] qualities."[15] Glass and metal towers rose from plazas all over the city. This wave of imitations did much to damage Mies's reputation even though few of these imitations were truly Miesian in proportion, detailing, or richness of materials. But while Mies's reputation—fairly or not—has endured cycles of ascension and decline in the decades since, the Seagram Building remains one of the most important buildings of the twentieth century.

But what more is there to this building? What can we glean from it that moves beyond analyzing the elements responsible for its form, or categorizing the building as the first in a long line of glass boxes? What, in the end, does the form of the Seagram Building tell us? What meanings are there to find or decode?

Clearly we can only hope to find the answers to such questions through treating the building's history as part of its totality. And perhaps the first step in that process is to ask why the building was commissioned in the first place. The Seagram Building became the model for a great many other office towers; however, the corporation behind it was atypical of those generally associated with the gleaming towers of Park Avenue. The nature of the Seagram Corporation, and the family who controlled it, had a tremendous impact on the eventual form of the Seagram Building, and this influence has received far too little attention.

The Bronfman Family: Smuggling Roots

The Seagram Building, like the Empire State Building, dramatizes the gulf between intention and reception. For most of the twentieth century and the twenty-first, the public and even many historians agreed that New York's skyscrapers were the architectural offspring of ideas and designs hatched by powerful, well-established corporations headed by scions of elite society. And, in many cases this is so. With the Seagram Building, however, this view requires revision. First, the family that built the Seagram empire was Jewish and came from outside the United States (from Bessarabia via Canada). Second, Seagram was a distiller and distributor of liquor—one of the largest in the world. The liquor business in the 1950s still carried the whiff of Prohibition and the criminal activity associated with it. Consumption of hard liquor was still not entirely acceptable in polite society. The expressed desire of corporations to use their headquarters as a form of public promotion took on an extra dimension with the Seagram Building. It was a key aspect in a struggle for cultural legitimacy as well as one of many tools used to burnish the reputation of a family with an ambiguous public reputation.

If the liquor industry in general was suspect in the 1950s, many thought the Bronfmans particularly so, for several reasons. The Bronfman family made its initial fortune as suppliers for bootleggers smuggling liquor into the United States during Prohibition. In all his years as head of one of the wealthiest families in the world, Samuel Bronfman felt that he never lived down his past as a bootlegger. He was, according to his son Edgar, obsessed with achieving respectability and entering the upper echelons of society. This required a careful editing of family history.

Furthermore, just as plans to build a new corporate headquarters got underway, Senator Estes Kefauver from Tennessee launched a well-publicized investigation of the role of organized crime in big business. Top Seagram executives were called to testify amid allegations that the company's distribution network was made up of gangsters and hoodlums. Old rumors about bootlegging resurfaced, as well as testimony before the Senate committee to the effect that the Bronfmans had also run brothels in their early days as liquor distributors. It was not the sort of publicity that a family and company deeply concerned with respectability welcomed. Other significant corporate architecture of the early postwar era—the Equitable Building in Portland (Pietro Belluschi, 1948), Lever House (Gordon Bunshaft of Skidmore, Owings and Merrill, 1952)—was for clients whose public reputation was generally positive and well established. Certainly cleaning products and insurance were not popularly associated with crime and controversy as was the liquor industry. Under such conditions it seems fair to say that there was a greater desire to use architecture as a form of public relations with the Seagram Building than with many of its contemporaries.

Carol Willis reiterates a widely agreed upon point about tall office buildings in the postwar era when she notes that they were built to "project an image of affluence and prestige."[16] When the Seagram Building opened, the *Wall Street Journal* was quick to point out that its luxurious appointments and use of land meant that it cost "about double what it would take to erect a building of comparable size."[17] A few years later, *Time* magazine, reviewing recent developments in New York City, noted that "the rich, understated dignity of Mies van der Rohe's bronze Seagram Building set the style for a lavish squandering of space for plazas and fountains."[18] Clearly a corporation that built in such a manner was affluent and willing to pay for prestige. Other architectural historians have commented about postwar corporate office towers, describing them as conjurers of "efficiency, cleanliness, organization and standardization."[19] No doubt this is true. An article *Engineering News-Record* titled "A Skyscraper Crammed with Innovations" remarked that the "newest addition to New York City's changing midtown skyline . . . has many advanced concepts in architecture and engineering," designed "to provide future tenants a maximum of amenities both in rented spaces and public areas."[20]

In the case of the Seagram Building, the office tower was expected to communicate other virtues as well, namely, respectability and power. Two members of the Bronfman family, Samuel Bronfman and his daughter Phyllis Bronfman Lambert, were the key figures in the construction. Mr. Sam, as he was often referred to in Seagram documents, was the patriarch of the family's business empire. His father, Ekiel Bronfman, a Bessarabian Jew, brought his wife and children to Canada in 1891, when Samuel was two years old.[21] They lived in Saskatchewan and later in Brandon, Manitoba. They had eight children, and, like many first generation immigrants, were quite poor. This experience of childhood poverty drove Samuel Bronfman throughout his life to continue to expand his business long after his family had become among the wealthiest in Canada and the United States. Even in the waning years of his life, more than half a century removed from poverty, his daughter Phyllis noted that her father's "horror of being poor was just so tremendous."[22] His son Edgar wrote that his father, "grew up to detest poverty . . . [and] was determined to be someone."[23]

The path to becoming someone took Samuel Bronfman into the world of hotel management in Winnipeg. Hotels in the region at that time were spare and often mean affairs, little more than bars with rooms above. In 1916 the family branched out into the liquor industry. Taking advantage of regulatory loopholes in Canadian law, they quickly became prominent distributors of beverage alcohol.[24] In 1924, two years after he married Saidye Rosner, Samuel and several of his brothers expanded into the production end of the market and invested in their first distillery, which they built in Ville LaSalle, on the outskirts of Montreal and close to the St. Lawrence River. Montreal became the headquarters of the Bronfman commercial activity and of the Bronfman family. Until his death, Samuel Bronfman would divide his time between New York and Montreal (often for the express purpose of eluding tax laws in both Canada and the United States). Four years later, in 1928, the Bronfmans bought a distillery from the Seagram family of Waterloo, and the modern day Seagram Company was born.[25]

From their earliest forays into the liquor trade the Bronfmans had lived on the edge of legal business practice; with their move into full-scale production it was not much of a leap to the shadier markets along the U.S. border, supplying bootleggers with liquor to smuggle into the United States during Prohibition.[26] Samuel Bronfman always insisted that his company never did anything illegal, but his own son acknowledges that "from the beginning of their experience in the beverage-alcohol business until the end of American Prohibition, the Bronfmans dealt with bootleggers . . . they had storage facilities on the French-owned islands of St. Pierre and Miquelon in the Gulf of St. Lawrence, where goods were kept ready to be transshipped across the American border."[27] This was not a small operation, and the profits that accumulated during this time weren't small either. According to some estimates, nearly half the liquor that made its way into the United States during Prohibition had its origins with the Bronfmans.[28]

Paradoxically, the trade that fulfilled one of Sam Bronfman's greatest desires, to be rich, was also responsible for denying him the other thing he wanted most in life, respectability. The association with bootlegging was one Sam Bronfman and the Seagram Company struggled for decades to shrug off. After the end of Prohibition the U.S. government took several Canadian distillers to court on charges of tax evasion, Seagram among them. The notoriety that accompanied the charges was deeply upsetting to Sam Bronfman, who in his later years, in the rare moments he let his true feelings slip, would ask: "How long do you think it'll be before they stop calling me a goddamn bootlegger?"[29] The association with bootlegging and organized crime came to the forefront in the early 1950s in the course of a congressional inquiry into the influence of organized crime on American big business.[30] This investigation took place just as the company was in the midst of deciding to centralize operations in the United States and considering what type of headquarters to build for its offices in New York City. The sting of these associations was slow to fade. Five decades after the Seagram Building opened, one biographer of the Bronfmans wrote about "the continuing atmosphere of threat and mystery that still surrounds the family."[31]

Another hurdle in Sam Bronfman's quest for respectability was his status as a Jew in a time when Jews composed a miniscule part of the Canadian elite, and even in the 1950s were rare presences in American corporate boardrooms.[32] In the early 1920s and 1930s, the Bronfmans' association with bootlegging was often connected to their status as Jews in the eyes of their critics. One Canadian temperance crusader, archdeacon G. E. Lloyd, noted that "of the forty-six liquor export houses in Saskatchewan, sixteen are owned and run by Jews." "When the Jews form one-half of one per cent of the population," he continued, "it is time that they be given to understand that since they have been received in this country, and have been given the rights enjoyed by other white men, they must not defile the country by engaging in disreputable pursuits."[33] Attacks on the evils of liquor and bootlegging by government officials and private groups could easily turn into attacks on Jews in general, and often they did.[34] Similarly, since Prohibition-era attacks on the vice of drinking in the United States often took shape as narratives of the social threat of alcohol, the predominance of Jews in the bootlegging business meant that whatever ills temperance reformers associated with liquor were by extension often associated with Jews. When the Anti-Saloon League of New York attacked alcohol as the precursor of violent revolution in their official bulletin announcing "Bolshevism lives on Booze," it was only a small leap to assume that most Jews (well represented in the liquor business) were sympathetic to Bolshevism.[35]

Phyllis Bronfman Lambert, "the Chairman of Planning"

Although it was Samuel Bronfman who wanted to build an office tower as a symbol of corporate success, it was his daughter, Phyllis Bronfman Lambert, who guided the final choice of architect and even a great deal of the design. Phyllis Bronfman was born in 1927 when the family was already quite wealthy, and was raised in the family mansion

Figure 22. Phyllis Lambert, 1966. Reprinted by permission from Arthur Schatz, Time & Life Pictures Collection © Getty Images.

in Montreal in a cloistered world of privilege. As a child, she would later recall, "our house was a most forbidding place . . . we [the children] hated it, despised [it]."[36] She was from her earliest years involved with art projects and was regarded by the family as "adorable, very cute, tiny, tiny, tiny." Describing her childhood as the second child and second daughter, Lambert notes, "my father was a patriarch—girls were bearable—and you had girls, but my God you wanted a boy." Later, when Edgar and Charles were born, parental interactions followed strict gender divisions: "My father sat at the head of the table with my brother Edgar on his right side and my brother Charles on his left side . . . the boys were my father's thing and the girls were my mother's thing and it was a very macho boy girl thing."[37]

Phyllis Bronfman attended Cornell University for a year and then transferred to Vassar, where she studied art and literature and completed her B.A. in 1948. In 1949 she married Jean Lambert, by all accounts a suave Frenchman who parlayed his minor role in the French delegation at the Bretton Woods Conference into a career in American banking. Their wedding was lavish, announced in the society pages of the important papers, and decorations included "fifteen thousand lilac blooms, plucked in a nursery at Windsor, Ontario, and flown to Montreal by chartered plane." The marriage, which Lambert describes as "just a way of winning my freedom," was annulled five years later.[38]

In 1954 Lambert was living in France and, according to her mother, received a copy of an article in a U.S. paper announcing the construction of the new Seagram Building.[39] The article was illustrated with a model of the proposed $15 million office building, designed by the firm of Pereira & Luckman, to commemorate, in the words of a company press release, the "100th anniversary of the House of Seagram."[40] It was a squat thirty-story tower with twenty-six-story-square tourelles set on a four-story base, the whole thing sheathed in marble, glass, and bronze. In retrospect it is hard to imagine the building arousing any response other than indifference. Pereira & Luckman presumably were hired based on the earlier success of the now-famous Lever Brothers headquarters, which may at first seem confusing, as they did not design that building. But Charles Luckman was trained as an architect before he went to work for Lever as a salesman during the Great Depression. He was president of Lever Brothers when the company built Lever House, and shortly afterward returned to full-time practice as an architect.[41] An architect with experience as a corporate executive probably appealed to Samuel Bronfman, certainly more than the architecture of Lever House did. Lambert was horrified by the Pereira & Luckman design and wrote her father a sixteen-page letter outlining her problems with the plans and her ideas for what the new headquarters should symbolize and the appropriate mode in which to build.[42]

Years later Lambert described the letter as an attempt "to discover what was the most significant statement the building could make. The responsibility for superior planning and painstaking detail required to make a building's spatial intangibles pleasing to the eye and spirit falls on the architect. But,the moment business organizations decide to build they take a moral position; and it's upon the choice of architect that the quality of their statement depends."[43] According to Samuel Bronfman's wife Saidye, that letter convinced him that he needed guidance on building the company headquarters. He was, in Mrs. Bronfman's words, "very Victorian . . . he didn't intend to have a modern building."[44] She noted that "We [lived] at the St. Regis Hotel, our office was at the Chrysler Building and he'd walk or take a taxi and then he'd come home, that's as much as he saw of buildings."[45] She told her husband to ask their daughter to return to the States to "see what she'd suggest . . . she always had wonderful taste."[46] Phyllis Lambert returned, and after some arguments with her father about what kind of building he was going to pay for, found herself, according to her mother, appointed "chairman of planning" for the new Seagram Building.[47] The post carried a salary of $20,000 a year.[48] In an unpublished interview twenty-six years later Lambert claimed: "He never gave me the job of being director of planning—I took it."[49]

Lambert called on a Vassar schoolmate who worked at the Museum of Modern Art for an introduction to Alfred Barr, Jr. Barr suggested that she meet with Philip Johnson, who was then in charge of the museum's Department of Architecture and Design. The two discussed the possibilities for a building that Lambert declared would be "a structure of major architectural significance."[50] Johnson advised her to study the work of the "leading Modernist figures of the day, including Walter Gropius, Marcel Breuer, George Howe, William Lescaze, Eero Saarinen, Louis Kahn, Minoru Yamasaki, I. M. Pei, Frank Lloyd Wright, Le Corbusier, and Mies van der Rohe."[51] According to Meredith Clausen, Lambert also consulted the noted modern architect Pietro Belluschi for advice.[52] After finishing her survey, Lambert and Johnson divided the architects into three groups. First, in her words, were "those who should but couldn't—Paul Rudolph, Eero Saarinen, Marcel Breuer, Louis Kahn—all good but with insufficient experience." Next came those "who could, but shouldn't: the big firms, including Skidmore, all competent enough but indebted in every case to someone more original." Finally there remained "those who could and should. On that list were Wright, Le Corbusier, and Mies."[53]

While unlikely to hire them, Johnson and Lambert nevertheless interviewed Pei, Saarinen, and Breuer; George Howe was also interviewed, "more as a consultant than a candidate." Of the three who both "could and should," Wright was rejected because Lambert thought "his is not the statement needed now," and because of his "comparably unmanageable temperament."[54] In fact as early as 1952, before she and Johnson had included Wright as a potential choice, one Seagram executive composed a memo outlining the dangers of hiring the famous architect:

> Frank Lloyd Wright will undoubtedly design the most unique building in New York and it will surely be good architecture—it will have advertising value.
>
> But he cannot get beyond the sketch stage. It is impossible for him to get up proper working drawings. Much of the engineering and the drawings will have to be worked out as the building goes up.
>
> You will have your own Engineering Department—and probably hire your own architect—otherwise the building will never be finished. The roof will probably leak; the heating system and the lights probably won't work; he will make it extremely difficult to house your employees because he will place them where he wants them, not where they are practically located.

When you get through (if you ever finish it) it will cost twice as much as any other building.

He will want a full 10% for himself and other architects will have to be hired at extra cost.

Because of his egotism it is doubtful whether he would work as a design consultant with other architects.[55]

Lambert told her father that she had narrowed down the list of potential architects to two, and that a final decision would be made within two weeks. At the end of that time, she told him "I think it should be Mies van der Rohe." Mies flew out from Chicago, showed some models of his ideas to Samuel Bronfman, and was hired.[56]

From the earliest days of planning, it appears that Samuel Bronfman never gave much thought to creating a monumental building for his corporation, while his daughter Phyllis Lambert pushed her father and his company not just to invest in a building, but to take "a moral position" and make a commitment to greatness, not mediocrity. While corporate office towers are often treated as visual representations of "big business," it would be more appropriate to regard the Seagram Building as the product of divergent passions in two wildly different people. Public announcements trumpeted the building as a commemoration of the "100th anniversary of the House of Seagram," but Samuel Bronfman offered an alternate purpose when he told Mies van der Rohe to "make this building the crowning achievement of your life and mine."[57] For the man who grew up one of eight children in a poor family, who had been excluded from elite society because of his religion and his bootlegging past, the Seagram Building would serve as a monument to him, not to some faceless corporation (that was, after all, named after someone else).

His shrewd business sense kept Samuel Bronfman from naming it the Bronfman Building, but for the rest of his life he kept vigilant watch over the Seagram Building, never missing an opportunity to promote it and by extension himself. Just as he built his company through careful managing of the smallest detail, Sam controlled the public image of the Seagram Building. In this regard he resembled John J. Raskob, who came to great wealth from poverty but who had been excluded from the upper echelons of New York society because of his Irish Catholic background. For Bronfman, as for Raskob, a great building offered the chance to grasp previously denied social and cultural prominence. For both men, modern architecture (in two distinct forms) was a tool used to secure legitimacy in the eyes of wider society.

For Lambert, the Seagram Building was the launching pad for a lifelong career in architecture. She studied at Yale, and later with Mies at the Illinois Institute of Technology, before starting her own design firm. Some years later she founded the Centre

Canadien d'Architecture, through which she maintains an active and influential presence in the world of architecture.

The Figure of Mies

Choosing Mies to design the Seagram Building had a considerable impact on the publicity the project garnered. Contemporary accounts in the business, architectural, and general interest press hailed the choice of Mies. As the *New York Times* put it, "A distinguished architectural career that began in Berlin fifty-two years ago is reaching its greatest heights here on Park Avenue."[58] *Fortune* called Mies "The architect who has achieved perhaps the most effective synthesis of aesthetics and technology," a synthesis the magazine applauded as a valuable public relations tool.[59] *Architectural Forum*, assessing the

Figure 23. Mies van der Rohe, 1958. Courtesy of the Library of Congress.

importance of the Seagram Building, concluded, "In Mies' career, Seagram is something of a milestone: it is his first building in New York; it is the largest structure he has ever built anywhere; and it is finally, the climax of Mies' 40-year search for a new kind of skyscraper . . . [it] is a monument that will be recorded as one of the great events in twentieth century architecture."[60]

The Seagram Building cemented the public image of Mies as an architectural genius, and assertions of his genius appeared in unexpected places. An editorial in *Playboy*, featuring a photograph of a brooding Mies addressing the reader, said: "his [Mies's] genius might never have acknowledged outside the circle of *Architectural Forum* readers if the Seagram people hadn't been seeking fresh talent for the New York scene. . . . Now that Mies, like his building, enjoys a place in the sun, the paeans to his artistry are filling the air."[61] Whether one was reading *Architectural Forum* or *Playboy* (or perhaps both, in spite of what the editors of the latter clearly thought), Mies's reputation was represented in Roarkian proportions. His identity and his architecture were fused, creating a public persona ripe for publicity.

This presentation of Mies was carefully orchestrated by the Seagram Company in its internal documents and promotional materials. A press release written in the form of a "confidential memo" distributed to Seagram executives in 1954 laid the groundwork

slenderella in the sky

ONE OF THE LATEST giants to thrust its head into New York's skyline is a stern but startling 38-story edifice sheathed in stunning bronze. Austerely geometrical and devoid of any ornamentation, the House of Seagram is referred to sneeringly as "that whiskey building" by Frank Lloyd Wright. But to the rapidly multiplying admirers of its 72-year-old architect, Mies van der Rohe, the building is the crowning manifestation of a lifelong principle: maximum effect with minimum means. Mies (as he prefers to be called) is a man of ample proportion and great personal warmth; his architecture is spare and rigid ("skin and bones," he calls it). Mies' career began officially in 1919 in his native Germany, where he designed a truly revolutionary skyscraper, sheathed wholly in glass and stripped almost to the structural skeleton. After 20 years of advancing his avant-garde theories in Europe, he came to this country. At the Illinois Institute of Technology, he headed up the Department of Architecture (a job he still holds). With relish he proceeded to re-do the entire I.I.T. campus, making bold use of immense glass areas and blanketing the 100-acre project with his architectural X-ray look. Then in 1948 the

unique Mies touch appeared on Chicago's Lake Shore Drive in two towering apartment houses with floor-to-ceiling windows, standing on stilts of steel. Though somewhat resembling up-ended ice-cube trays and thus termed "icy cold" by critics, this Slenderella approach to architecture elicited huzzahs from many of Mies' confreres in the field. But his genius might never have been acknowledged outside the circle of *Architectural Forum* readers if the Seagram people hadn't been seeking fresh talent for the New York scene. With the assistance of architect Philip Johnson, Mies gave them the world's first bronze skyscraper, with huge, tinted, glare-resistant windows, overlooking a paved, fountain-dotted plaza (Park Avenue's first "park"). Now that Mies, like his building, enjoys a place in the sun, the paeans to his artistry are filling the air. They are summed up in the words of one of his fellow architects:

"Mies' very perfectionist attitude toward detail, his insistence on order, his uncompromising truth to material, his precise adjustments of scale and proportion have all been brought together to achieve an architecture for the 'whole man' of the 20th Century."

Figure 24. "Slenderella in the Sky," from "Playboy on the Scene: Mies van der Rohe," *Playboy* (August 1958). © 1958 Playboy.

for a promotional campaign based on Mies's reputation. In it he is described as "one of the all-time great pioneers of architecture," an architect whose "work has influenced the new generation of architects to a degree perhaps more than any other modern architect." "His visionary concepts of the type of tall, office structure contemplated for Seagram's executive headquarters which have been a decade ahead of the entire field, and his mastership as a builder, attracted our attention to him." The elevation of the figure of Mies in turn elevated the purposes behind the construction of the building: "It is our conviction that the new Seagram Building will make a lasting contribution to the further cultural development of New York City by setting standards of excellence for a modern office building in public and civic usefulness, in visual beauty, and will stand as a symbol for the qualities which have made our family of companies great."[62]

The press eagerly adopted a similar tone. *Time* magazine called the building "the definitive statement of what a skyscraper can be by the architect whom most purists hail as the master of glass-and-steel design."[63] It is somewhat ironic that the public persona surrounding Mies, whose earlier work on the Luxemburg and Liebknecht memorial was the antithesis of what Ayn Rand would champion, would by the late 1950s be supremely Roarkian. The traits Rand gave Roark—his insistence on "honest building," his "cold, intellectual approach"—as symbols of his genius are strikingly similar to descriptions of Mies's attitude.[64] *Time* pointed out that Mies's aim "is to express the skyscraper's essential steel cage as dramatically as possible and with a maximum of economy."[65] Roark is a "supreme egotist"; Mies likewise gained a reputation (not entirely justified) as an architect who refused to alter his work or his life to suit the needs of others. In *The Fountainhead*, one of Roark's clients complains that his design for their summer home fails to provide sufficient closet space; Roark cannot be bothered to comply with such petty demands. In real life, when Edith Farnsworth told Mies the weekend home he was designing for her needed more closet space for her dresses, he is said to have replied "It's a weekend house. You only need one dress. Hang it on the hook on the back of the bathroom door."[66] One of Mies's early, and now very famous, projects was his entry for a competition to design a skyscraper along the Friedrichstrasse. It was rejected by the jury for failing to meet the basic criteria set forth by the competition.[67] Seagram understood the potential publicity a new building could provide them, but they also grasped that their choice of architect could also play a role in their public relations campaigns.

In order to cast Mies as a visionary architect, a genius of modern design, both Seagram and the popular press chose language that echoed the language of *The Fountainhead*. Rand's definition of architectural genius depended on a number of elements. First was her vision of the lone creative spirit, of the man (and indeed her misogyny is clear on this point) who will not, cannot, work in a team. Rand's animosity toward all forms of "collectivism" meant that she cast the process of planning, designing, and constructing a building as a solitary effort marshaled by a single, dominant individual, even though at the time architects were increasingly working in teams with engineers, planners, associate architects, and real estate experts.[68] The publicity surrounding the Seagram Building likewise emphasized Mies's creative authority—his genius—while minimizing the extent to which engineers, associate architects, and others assisted in the process of designing and constructing his buildings. The title of Lewis Mumford's review of the building in the *New Yorker* is telling: "The Lesson of the Master."[69]

This impression was reflected and reinforced by the many photographs of Mies in any number of buildings standing or sitting alone (often with a cigar), assuming a pensive air. While his office employed nearly thirty architects, few if any of the famous and widely reproduced photos of Mies show him in their company. Unlike contemporaries such as Walter Gropius, who was often photographed with other members of the Architects' Collaborative, or earlier architects like Bernard Maybeck, who posed among his various assistants in publicity photographs, Mies is most commonly (and powerfully) posed alone.

Mies's presumed indifference to opinions of others, needs of clients, and restrictions of budgets and his solitary creative power all became elements of his fame. To some degree they help explain the continuing public interest in Mies. Mies fits the romantic notion of the creative and psychologically complex artistic figure far better than any team of designers could. In some ways he is the architectural counterpart of Jackson Pollock, even down to the heavy drinking and difficult personality. Both men, after all, found a range of expressive gestures at a critical juncture of their careers that were then refined over time into a host of iconic images.[70]

The name recognition today of Mies van der Rohe is far greater than that of the firm of Shreve, Lamb & Harmon, even though more people know the Empire State Building than the Seagram Building by sight. But of course Shreve, Lamb & Harmon were decidedly non-Roarkian architects. Their reputation rested on producing designs on time, under budget, for buildings that suited the demands of clients, not of fame.[71] Today, even among architectural historians, the Empire State Building conjures up King Kong rather more easily than the names of Shreve, Lamb & Harmon.[72]

7

Gangland's Grip on Business

How did corporate and business concerns shape the creation of the Seagram Building? A revealing set of company memos and plans created in 1951, three years before the unveiling of the Pereira & Luckman design, under the aegis of "Project Skytop" help answer that question. Skytop was the internal nickname for a committee convened to develop the "Program for Development of Building to House the Seagram Companies."[1] Documents produced by the committee included lists of potential architects, studies of "various [building] schemes showing building size and comparable financial set up," and a memo assessing Frank Lloyd Wright's difficult disposition and unreasonable salary demands.[2] These, along with various correspondences between company executives, promotional materials dedicated to the new building, press releases, and even a script written for the tour guides in the finished building, all flesh out the Seagram company's interest in building an icon of modern architecture in the United States.

Project Skytop

The earliest document relating to the Seagram Building is a memorandum from July 1951 that details company concerns about a possible new building and establishes a timeline for its consideration and construction. The unsigned memo was in all likelihood created under the aegis of Project Skytop, and probably the work of Ellis D. Slater, an executive with Seagram Company and a member of Project Skytop. It raises a number of issues; as was the case with the Empire State Building during the planning stage, most of them are concerned with finances rather than design:

1. Will a building occupied by our companies alone be practical—
   economic—distinctive—arouse public interest—give the proper
   impression to shareholders, trade, public—will it have advertising value?
2. Should such a building occupy full ground area or only the Park Avenue
   front—leaving back lot for leasing? Air rights can be maintained.
3. Considering the size of the lot and its cost would a building of maximum
   floor space, providing rentable areas, result in lower cost for company
   used space? Can the building be made to produce profits? Would such a
   larger building be more impressive among other neighboring properties?
4. Should the building be modern or traditional?
   If traditional, will it soon be outmoded—just another office building.
   Do modern concepts of building fit in with our ideas of background,
   age, stability?
   What type of building will best compete with Lever Brothers [sic],
   the Ambassador, other buildings eventually to be erected on neighboring
   sites?
5. What unusual features are to be embodied in this new structure?
   Auditorium—restaurants—florists—garage—distillery exhibit—living
   quarters—terraces—set backs—towers. Stone or metal facings. Seagram
   building alone, or Calvert, Frankfort [other Seagram Company brands
   of liquor] as well.[3]

A similar set of concerns was raised by the Seagram Company "Advisory Committee" nearly a year later. Formed in 1952, the Advisory Committee met twice a month to discuss a wide range of company issues, and was actively involved in the planning of the Seagram Building from 1952 through 1955,when plans for the final design were submitted to the New York City Building Department. The committee included a number of Seagram executives, for example, Ellis Slater and the president of Seagram-Distillers, Victor A. Fischel. When they met for the first time on May 27, 1952, in the Seagram offices at the Chrysler Building, they raised five questions and came to three conclusions:

1. Should we build a new building?
2. Should we invest our own money?
3. Should we arrange for investment through an insurance company?
4. Should a building be built in Westchester or out of metropolitan
   New York?
5. Whether or not this is the peak period of building costs?

Conclusion—

1. Mr. Friel to talk to Cross & Brown [a real estate agency] to see if they can enable us to be released from our present lease.
2. We are to build a building.
3. Plans for building and size of building to depend on investigation of possible tenants, etc.[4]

The question of building in suburban Westchester or out of metropolitan New York altogether was not raised again, suggesting that the idea was quickly dismissed. Samuel Bronfman probably thought (correctly) that a suburban campus headquarters carried far less prestige than a tall office building on Park Avenue. In 1952 the Skytop committee hired a builder, the George A. Fuller Company, and requested a report on the estimated costs of operation and income for a new building from the real estate firm of Cross & Brown. Cross & Brown's report cataloged a number of mid-town lots between Avenue of the Americas and Lexington Avenue where office building construction was expected in the near future, and noted that the real estate market was going to absorb 2.1 million square feet of "comparable" office space by 1955. In light of these conditions, the firm concluded, "We believe a bulk building would be a sounder building to build because the space is developed at the least cost of construction and the least cost of operation." The report further cautioned, "We do not believe in a tower building because of the present construction costs . . . and the higher rentals that must be obtained to make it a paying proposition." Cross & Brown noted, however, that these conclusions were drawn only "from an economic point of view." "If your clients wish a building for their own use solely and bring in special promotional ideas, then they might desire to do something like the Lever Bros. Building."[5]

Similar concerns about the relationship between cost and return on any new building were evident in a more extensive design study produced for Project Skytop by the George A. Fuller Company, the firm of Kahn and Jacobs, and the property management company Cushman and Wakefield (who had managed the Empire State Building). The study produced eleven different designs to illustrate "various schemes showing allowable building size and comparable financial set up."[6] The eleven proposed designs ranged from a squat seven story building occupying the entire lot to a fifty-story tower set back some 100 feet from Park Avenue.[7] Costs varied with size and the complexity of design from $14 million on the low end (for a building "without towers or embellishments") to over $34 million. Rentable square footage ranged from roughly 330,000 square feet (for a "building figured as a 'distinctive' type") to just over a million.[8] Two designs made concessions on profitability in the interests of visual distinction: one a near replica of Lever House and the other a tower set back from the street to create "advertising space."[9] The neo-Lever House design, along with the mention of that building in an earlier 1951 memo, is a testament to its immediate impact in the world of New York corporate architecture. By the time it opened in 1952, Lever House's success at yoking architecture to the service of corporate publicity established it as the benchmark any new office building in New York would "compete" against.[10] In the same vein, it is apparent as early as 1952, long before Mies van der Rohe was hired, that Seagram was considering employing a grand setback in order to take advantage of the "advertising" effect it offered.

While these early setback designs were fussier than Mies's—often with elaborate landscaping and monumental decorative elements—they are nevertheless clear progenitors of his final design. Similarly, one of the setback tower schemes designed to "dominate Park Avenue" foreshadows the "bustle" solution Mies arrived at years later. As with Mies's design, a tower rises straight from the ground level, with additional construction wrapping around the sides and rear for the first several stories. Given that Kahn and Jacobs were later hired as associate architects for Mies on the Seagram Building, it is reasonable to assume that he was exposed to the ideas raised in these early proposed schemes. While none of the proposals in Project Skytop exactly resembled the final solutions Mies arrived at, some of the elements of his design—the setback, the "bustle," and the sheer tower façade along Park Avenue—began to take shape by late 1952.

As 1952 drew to a close, Seagram executives remained undecided about what type of building should house the company. It was clear, however, that whatever was built would have to "compete" with Lever House in the marketplace of the skyline. Similarly, building size was raised as an issue in relation to both cost and appearance: would a "larger building be more impressive among other neighboring properties?" Additional early design concerns raised the question of whether modern architecture was consistent with Seagram's corporate and public identity. Would modern architecture communicate the impression of age and stability Samuel Bronfman pursued throughout his life for the "House of Seagram?" How would Seagram's different business constituencies—"shareholders, trade, public"—view the building; would it leave them with "the proper impression"?

"Gangland's Grip on Business"

This seemingly innocuous phrase, "the proper impression," needs to be understood as something other than a standard business generality; in the context of the time its obliqueness speaks volumes. As mentioned earlier, a 1950-1951 Senate investigation into the presence of organized crime in corporate America had generated a great deal of negative publicity for the liquor trade. Much of that negative publicity accrued to Seagram's, and in addition resurrected stories of the company's origin as a supplier for bootleggers. Even worse now, though, were accusations raised by the investigation that Seagram's and other distillers served as fronts for the mob. An article in *Business Week* about the hearings titled "Gangland's Grip on Business" leveled the following accusation: "The top-notch companies, such as Schenley and Seagram, grant exclusive area franchises to the country's top-notch hoodlums."[11] Many of the hearings were televised by local channel WPIX, with 25 to 30 percent of TV sets in the New York area tuning in.[12] Movie theaters even showed the hearings at free screenings. This was decidedly not the sort of publicity Samuel Bronfman wanted.

Figure 25. Kefauver Hearings shown at local movie houses. Reprinted by permission from Michael Rougier, Time & Life Pictures Collection © Getty Images.

Figure 26. Estes Kefauver (far right) presiding over the hearings on organized crime, 1951. Reprinted by permission from Hank Walker, Time & Life Pictures Collection © Getty Images.

The investigations were headed by Estes Kefauver, a Democratic senator from Tennessee who had set his sights on a spot in the upcoming presidential elections. According to one biographer, Kefauver thought the investigations could put "him in a position where lightning just might strike in 1952." It was unlikely, however, that Kefauver "foresaw the impact of the crime investigation on the public."[13] Initial committee hearings were held behind closed doors. However, the committee then made three critical decisions: to hold public hearings, to turn the hearings into a "road show" traveling from city to city to investigate corruption, and to allow television cameras into the hearings.[14] In the fifteen months of its existence, the committee held hearings in Washington, D.C., New York, Miami, Tampa, St. Louis, Kansas City, Chicago, Las Vegas, Los Angeles, New Orleans, San Francisco, Cleveland, Philadelphia, and Detroit. Kefauver's new-found fame landed him on the cover of Time, alongside a masked and criminal octopus.

The hearings were carefully planned. Research on those who testified was conducted in advance by chief counsel for the committee, Rudolph Halley, and his staff. In city after city public officials and reputed mobsters testified about organized crime

TIME

THE WEEKLY NEWSMAGAZINE

CRIME HUNTER KEFAUVER
Gamblers + Politicians = Corruption.

Figure 27. Kefauver on the cover of *Time*, 1951. Reprinted by permission from Time Life Pictures, Time & Life Pictures Collection © Getty Images.

in American business and its relationship to municipal corruption. Evidence emerged not only of the presence of gangsters in "legitimate" business, but of "political ties between gangsters and politicians of both parties."[15] Figures such as Paul (the Waiter) Ricca and Jacob (Greasy Thumb) Guzik pleaded the Fifth Amendment, while Meyer Lansky and Frank Costello were questioned about the criminal organization Murder Incorporated. Testifying along with this rogues' gallery was Victor Fischel, president of Seagram Distiller Corporation, who was asked, as the press put it, about "how extensively gangsters may have muscled into liquor distribution."[16] Testimony by others dealt with Samuel's and his brothers' origins as bootleggers and allegations that the family hotels in Canada were actually brothels, or as one witness put it, places where "people sleep very fast, they rent them [rooms] quite a few times during the night."

The publicity clearly was a problem for the company, and the Seagram's public relations department, headed by Harry Bulow, scrambled to put the best possible gloss

Figure 28. Frank Costello testifying before the Kefauver Committee, 1951. Courtesy of the Library of Congress.

Figure 29. Frank Costello's hands during the Kefauver hearing. Reprinted by permission from Alfred Eisenstaedt, Time & Life Pictures Collection © Getty Images.

on the revelations coming out of the hearings. In response to allegations in *Business Week* about relations between the company and gangsters, Harry Bulow wrote the editor of the magazine a letter explaining:

> In "Business Week" for May 12, on page 22 in your article dealing with gang-land's grip on business, you note that Seagram's has granted exclusive area franchises to this country's top-notch hoodlums. You based this apparently on the Kefauver Report early in May.
>
>   This is in error. Seagram's has never granted any exclusive area franchises to any top-notch hoodlum.[17]

In addition to these straightforward public relations efforts, a document in the archives of the Seagram Corporation hints at other labors undertaken to secure the company's reputation in the face of distasteful allegations. Tucked away in the files of the public relations department from 1951 is a two-page document, single-spaced, unsigned and undated, printed on plain paper free of letterhead and labeled simply "CONFIDENTIAL." Its first line reads:

> Dear Sir:
>   In response to your inquiry concerning RUDOLPH HALLEY, whose address was given as 1411 Pennsylvania Avenue, N.W., Washington, D.C., Chief Legal Counsel, Senator Kefauver Investigating Committee, we report that the subject of your inquiry was born in this country on June 19, 1913.

The report covers, in some detail, Halley's family life, including his ex-wife ("described as a high type woman"), his divorce ("our consultants advise that the circumstances leading up to the divorce referred to do not in any way reflect upon either Mr. or Mrs. Halley"), and his child support ("R. Halley provides amply for his two children"). It details Halley's educational and work background, including salary history and estimated net worth, and includes two paragraphs that discuss Halley's personality ("married to his job"), drinking habits ("takes a social drink but is not given to excess in any way whatever"), and social acquaintances (moves "in the best of circles"). The report closes by noting "Nothing adverse is found to be recorded against him, and it appears that he has developed a name for himself in Washington, D.C. as a highly competent attorney with excellent connections and undoubtedly profiting therefrom."[18]

It is unclear who conducted this research for the Seagram Corporation, or what the company hoped to find by investigating Halley's personal affairs (perhaps a few skeletons in the closet that might serve to discredit his investigative work for the Kefauver committee). Perhaps Seagram executives came into possession of investigative work done on the behalf of unnamed others.[19] Nevertheless, the document suggests one response to the heightened scrutiny the corporation felt it was facing at a time when it was engaged in the planning process for new headquarters.

It was in this context that Seagram faced the question of what type of headquarters to build. If a traditional design at first seemed more appropriate for a business still in pursuit of legitimacy, would such a design, as an early memo asked, "soon be outmoded?" In its Canadian headquarters in Montreal, Seagram's had pursued such legitimacy by hiring David Spence to design a replica of a sixteenth-century Scottish castle on a site chosen by Samuel Bronfman. Bronfman regarded the building—which locals called the "Peele Street Castle"—as a tribute to the Scottish origins of the Seagram Company, and the company's name was proudly and prominently appended to the façade. In the United States, however, and in light of the allegations of criminal activity in the liquor business, the company chose a design without corporate signage and that made no reference at all to the history (either storied or not) of the businesses it housed. The popular associations of modern architecture with efficiency, cleanliness, and advanced technology all made sense for businesses in fields where such attributes were part of already extant corporate identities (e.g., cleanliness and soap, as is the case with Lever House). It is less obvious why a distiller would pursue those associations. Distilling is after all not a new process, but a craft handed down over time and one where quality and reputation are not generally associated with technological innovation. The associations of modern architecture with bureaucratic "organization and standardization," or "modular techniques of factory production" that might have appealed to Seagram executives could certainly be accommodated by the original Pereira & Luckman design, or by any other number of architects and firms less expensive than Mies.[20] We are left with the conclusion that it was the opportunity to use a design that elided the past and could simultaneously serve to garner cultural capital and respectability that appealed to Sam Bronfman.

The choice of design was fortuitous in other ways. As William Jordy points out, it is in its deviation from the norm in materials and color that the building takes on a character appropriate to the business it houses. The bronze and warm-toned glass Seagram Building is "the first major metal-and-glass skyscraper consciously designed to age as masonry buildings age—an architectural property as appropriate for Seagram's whisky as sheen for Lever's soap."[21] A letter from a member of the general public to Seagram in 1958 proposed one way to extend the benefit of the "architectural property" to which Jordy referred. The author opened by congratulating Seagram for "the fine architec-

Figure 30. Seagram Headquarters building in Montreal. Reprinted by permission from Pierre Roussel, Getty Images News Collection © Getty Images.

tural gem you have recently erected on Park Avenue, New York City," and noted that upon spending time contemplating the building:

> Suddenly a sinner's idea hit me over the head . . .
>
> If only, God forbid, every Saturday night, no, say every once a year, on New Year's Eve, those two rows of silvery fountains were give some of the Seagram Spirit, or a little of the V.O. Bouquet and charged, say with only a little bit of the 86 Proof you are so well famous for. . . . What a sales promotion and "Public Relations" idea that would make.[22]

The public clearly made the same connection Jordy did, referring to the building (to the great distress of the Seagram Company) as a "a whiskey colored edifice" and "the world's tallest high-ball."[23] Executives at Seagram's were so concerned about how the building was referred to on television and radio that for years they hired a manuscript service to monitor the airwaves and provide them with daily reports of all known references to the building on New York TV and radio broadcasts. In those broadcasts some called the Seagram Building the "booze building," and one local radio host went the extra mile and called it "the B.B.B.B . . . the big brass [sic] brown booze building."[24] When the fountains were turned on in spring, some commented that "Over at the new Seagram's [sic] Building they've got the chasers out in front now."[25] When the trees along the street side of the building were replaced, the same wags suggested, "How about some Spanish stuffed olive trees on one side and maraschino cherries on the other, huh?"[26] Perhaps the best play off the association with the building and the liquor business it housed came when a radio host, referring to the practice of keeping the building's lights on until midnight, said: "It gives me the chance to say that over at Seagram's even the building is lit up."[27] Others saw the bronze as something besides a metaphor for whiskey, calling the building "dirty brown."[28] All these comments were carefully recorded for Seagram and filed in the corporation's public relations department. Seagram was so distressed by the antics of one repeat offender, Jack Sterling on CBS, that a letter was drafted to William Paley, then president of CBS that read in part:

> I hate to introduce a jarring note during this season of goodwill. But I must as the result of a recent broadcast by Jack Sterling.
>
> Of course, I do not question Mr. Sterling's right to his personal views, and to his individual expression. But his flippancy does suggest unawareness of the social problems surrounding liquor which the entire liquor industry has been laboring to overcome for years. *References to whiskey as booze and to the Seagram Building as a booze building are certainly derogatory and harmful.*[29]

Such seemingly innocuous humor was taken very seriously by the company, and throughout the 1950s and 1960s great pains were taken to control the public image of the building. Seagram's corporate headquarters garnered significant media attention, and the company zealously attempted to manipulate the public uses of the Seagram Building to its advantage. When their new headquarters was completed, the advertising and public relations arms of the Seagram Company were centralized in one building, with an annual advertising budget reported as "well in excess of $14,000,000."[30] A great deal of energy was subsequently put into promoting the new building and countering any perceived negative publicity, such as references to the building as "dirty" or the "booze building." A barrage of press releases accompanied the unveiling of the new building and the awards it received, carefully scripted tour guide materials were produced, numerous well-publicized events were held at the building, and a promotional booklet was given to Seagram employees enumerating the benefits their new workplace offered and the accolades the building had garnered. These promotional materials make clear what aspects of the new building the House of Seagram wanted to emphasize to consumers, investors, and fellow businesses, as well as how the Seagram Building was used to burnish the company's corporate identity.

8

Modern Architecture and Corporate America in the 1950s

Of course, from the Pyramids of Egypt to the monuments of Rome to today's shopping centers, "clients" have seen architecture as a means by which institutions could manifest and solidify their presence in society.

—Bernard Tschumi

New York during the 1950s underwent a variety of profound transformations, not the least of them a dramatic boom in construction. The Great Depression and later the economic restrictions imposed by World War II meant that building activity was nearly non-existent in the city for almost two decades. The construction slowdown, Carol Krinsky writes, "brought an end to many conservative, long-established firms, leaving the field open to younger ones."[1] Architecture firms were not only fewer and younger, they were ready to embrace modern architecture to a far greater degree than their conservative predecessors. Transatlantic émigrés took teaching positions at architecture schools across the country, bringing with them an appreciation for modern architecture that differed greatly from the Beaux Arts traditions that had held sway in American architecture throughout the nineteenth and early twentieth centuries. Mies van der Rohe and Gropius took charge of the Illinois Institute of Technology and Harvard schools of architecture, transforming their curricula into one grounded in the appreciation of modern architecture. Other schools across the nation followed suit. When building commissions began to pour in, younger firms staffed with architects trained in Bauhaus-inspired curricula responded with designs indebted to the lessons expounded on by Philip Johnson and Henry-Russell Hitchcock in the 1932 Modern Architecture: International exhibition.

Lever House opened in New York in 1952. Taking great advantage of Mies's formal innovations, Gordon Bunshaft's design "received universal praise from architects, critics, and laymen, all of whom acclaimed the new architectural image it created for New York City business."[2] Just as politicians and business executives praised the modern corporation for its positive impact on American economic, social, and political life, so too did critics consider modern corporate architecture by standards beyond the bottom line. This was in many respects the fulfillment of a trend that started in the 1920s, when, Katherine Solomonson notes, "the distinctions between commerce, culture, and civic life narrowed."[3] Reflecting this critical tendency to evaluate the corporate office tower as a socially and culturally significant architectural intervention into the urban landscape, Paul Goldberger called Lever House "a stunning act of corporate philanthropy."[4]

This form of architectural expression was embraced as readily by business executives as by architects. Bunshaft recalls, "We never had to sell modernism to anybody . . . these big corporations needed new facilities and they all wanted something new-looking. I'm sure these corporate presidents all lived in colonial houses in Connecticut, but for their offices they wouldn't consider anything but modern. They all wanted buildings they could be proud of."[5] Speculating why modern buildings were now the ones corporate executives "could be proud of," Krinsky notes that by mid-century modern architecture "had become associated with the Establishment, to be fostered in America and then reexported."[6]

Architecture was part of the increasing dominance of American big business at home and abroad. That John F. Kennedy invited Mies van der Rohe to his inauguration only hints at the symbolic political value of modern architecture.[7] Corporations ostensibly chose modern designs for a variety of reasons ranging from its association with functionalism to a desire to appear aesthetically or even socially progressive. The proliferation in New York and elsewhere of corporate office towers built in the same modernist vein as Lever House has led some to conclude that, as Bunshaft said, corporations refused to "consider anything but modern." According to others, however, the ubiquity of the glass box is to be laid at the feet of architects: "ironically, as technology freed tall buildings to take any form, the orthodoxy of high modernism tended to standardize them."[8]

The answer surely lies somewhere in between. However, rather than trying to pinpoint the driving force (or blame) behind the proliferation of modern architecture in cities like New York, I would like to return to the point raised by Bernard Tschumi. Clearly both architects and corporate clients embraced modern architecture: The question then really is "Why?" Why did corporations in the 1950s adopt modern architecture as the mode through which they would manifest their presence? How did it establish connections with social and cultural values to which corporations responded

Figure 31. Seagram bar, Chrysler Building, designed by Morris Lapidus (ca. 1939). Courtesy of the Library of Congress.

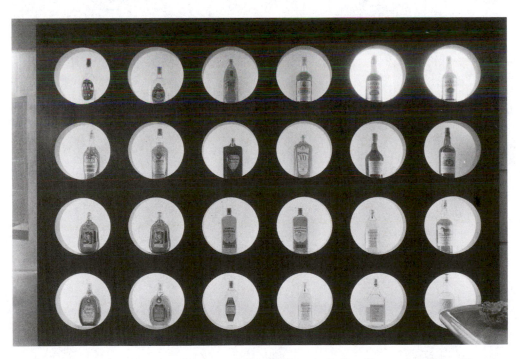

Figure 32. Morris Lapidus-designed bottle display at Seagram offices, Chrysler Building. Courtesy of the Library of Congress.

favorably? The orthodoxy of architects alone cannot explain this. Does it speak to an alteration in the nature of architecture, corporate America, society, or all three?

In spite of Bunshaft's comments about executives demanding to build modern, we have already seen that Samuel Bronfman had to be convinced to do so.[9] There is a great deal of variation in the scope of "modern"designs; a commitment to modern design does not mean a commitment to hiring Mies van der Rohe. While the original Pereira & Luckman proposal was not historical, as Seagram's Canadian headquarters was, it was nonetheless little more than a workable, inexpensive, relatively anonymous, but clearly modern design. Franz Schulze describes Samuel Bronfman's choice of Pereira & Luckman as "well advised" given the "standards most familiar to him." After all, the firm "had ample experience with large commercial structures that were normally neither very expensive to build nor troublesome to maintain. Bronfman was a businessman, no esthete."[10] Prior to the Seagram Building, the firm's New York headquarters was located in the Chrysler Building, where their offices were designed by Morris Lapidus in an exuberant, bright and shiny deco-moderne style that was quite the anti-

Figure 33. Bottle display with modern art and furniture designed by Mies, Seagram Building, 1958. Reprinted with permission from Ezra Stoller © Esto.

Figure 34. Four Seasons restaurant, Seagram Building, 1958. Jeff Goldbert © Esto.

thesis of Miesian restraint. The question of how and why the company ended up with a building that was in many ways the antithesis of the Lapidus and Pereira & Luckman designs—expensive to build (in fact the most expensive of its day), expensive to maintain, a work of architecture individualized in and out—cannot be satisfactorily answered with the generalization that all corporations embraced modernism.

Publicity, Architecture, and Reception

Publicity and the chance to burnish a reputation are part of the answer to the above question. Seagram and the Bronfmans (Samuel and Phyllis) were not content to rely on the general or popular attributes of modern architecture alone, but used publicity to describe it in terms favorable to both company and family. They likewise made every effort to define Seagram's embrace of modern architecture as a form of civic duty. Their success was due in part to the fact that no other building of its time was the subject of so much publicity. Articles about the Seagram Building, detailing its cost, its use of bronze, its setback and plaza, the fame of its severe German architect, and much more appeared in newspapers in every state of the nation.[11] While much of this publicity was the result of curiosity aroused by the cost of the building, the fame of the architect designing it, and the uniqueness of the design, much of it was also generated through a carefully choreographed campaign by Seagram to maximize press coverage. A wide range of details were marshaled to promote the building. It was supposed to open in 1957 to celebrate 100 years of the House of Seagram, but the dedication ceremony had to be moved to spring 1959 because the scope of the event was simply too large. As one memo from a public relations firm hired by Seagram put it: "it is Phyllis' feeling that a proper dedication ceremony cannot be done as early as September and, following conversations with Mr. Sam, that it should be planned for next spring so as to coincide with the opening of the new restaurant." The memo went on to outline some of the preparations, making it clear why the delay was now necessary.

> To bring you up to date:
>
> Paris reports that the first known Rembrandt will be available, provided our dates are okay with the French museum.
>
>   Israel is trying to get permission for us to borrow some copper or bronze scrolls dug up from the Dead Sea which are over 6,000 years old.
>
>   Italy is trying to get one of Michelangelo's famous sculptures, if possible.
>
>   Greece is running into difficulty because of government restrictions there, but I am awaiting further replies.
>
>   Germany is working on original scores of Beethoven, Bach, etc.
>
>   London—still awaiting report of what is available.
>
>   We are awaiting results on the above before going on to other parts of the world.[12]

The Seagram Building was treated as a work of art, not merely a work space, and the memo establishes the company's intent to situate the building within the context of international high culture. This clearly would not be a modest dedication ceremony.

    Events leading up to it were nearly as elaborate. By 1956 stories about the construction of the Seagram Building had appeared in newspapers in all 48 states and the District of Columbia, and had been carefully clipped and filed by A. A. Schechter and Associates, a public relations firm hired by Seagram.[13] A number of activities at the construction site helped generate interest and provided a stream of subjects for newspapers

Figure 35. Seagram Building under construction, viewed from the courtyard of Lever House. Reprinted by permission from Frank Scherschel, Time & Life Pictures Collection © Getty Images.

across the country. One of the most popular moves Seagram made was to encourage so-called "sidewalk superintendents," private citizens who spent time around the construction site observing the activity within. Such "superintendents" generally had to peer through gaps in the fences around construction sites and were sometimes considered nuisances by builders or contractors. Seagram instead encouraged them by installing

Plexiglas portholes at various heights and intervals in the fences. In addition, informa-
tional broadcasts about the progress of construction in English, French, and Spanish
were carried on speaker systems mounted along the fences. Broadcasts in English were
recorded by well-known personalities including Steve Allen and Will Rogers, Jr.[14]

Other ground-level promotional efforts included a 10,500-piece scale model of the
finished building placed at the construction site "so that the public may judge daily
progress." The model took five months to build and weighed half a ton. Stories about
the model, spurred no doubt by the barrage of press releases Seagram sent out about
every aspect of the building and its construction, were printed in newspapers from New
York to Peoria to El Paso.[15] Seagram hired scenic artists to paint murals that changed
with the season on the construction fencing, and bronze-encased bulletin boards with
information about construction materials and other items were placed at the site.[16] All
these developments were the topics of Seagram press releases and were dutifully reported in papers across the nation.

Elements about the building and its appointments that today seem mundane or
even outdated were widely reported in the late 1950s. The building was the first in New
York, a Seagram press release noted, to be equipped with a machine that "will usher in
a new era in customer automation," one that "changes dollar bills into coins automatically." The release touted the "Bill Changer" as the "first machine of its kind" and noted
that while currently set to dispense "two quarters, three dimes and four nickels" as
change for a dollar, the machine "can be adapted to give different amounts of change,
from two half-dollars to 100 pennies."[17] Other technological innovations reported included a lobby lighting system in which "by use of an astronomical clock . . . lights will
automatically get brighter as the sun shines and dimmer as the day wanes."[18] Syndicated
columnist Mel Heimer in his column "My New York" applauded the fact that the elevator system would not require operators, as "the average lift jockey may not be quite the
equivalent of bus drivers in sheer neglect and unawareness of his passengers, but he runs
a close second."[19] Another symbol of change that had a debut of sorts at the Seagram
Building was the "Forty-Niner," a 49-star American flag. Flying from a 50-foot bronze
pole (of course) and measuring 12 by 18 feet, the Forty-Niner, according to several reports, was "believed to be the first to fly at a major office building in New York."[20]

In addition to these largely non-architectural details, the relationship of the building to its site captivated the public's interest. News stories throughout the nation referred to it as "the first Park on Park Avenue," and embraced the idea of a skyscraper
with a "front yard" as an unexpected bonus for pedestrians.[21] The plaza quickly became
a popular location for fashion shoots; a 1958 fact sheet distributed by A. A. Schechter
claimed that "102 photographers representing most of the leading general, women's,
fashion, farm, business, etc., publications and newspapers have taken photos at the

building."[22] What a farm publication would photograph at the Seagram Building remains, sadly, unknown.

Within five years the plaza was an established spot for New Yorkers to spend a free moment or more during the day. As the *New Yorker* Talk of the Town column put it in 1963, "Since the start of spring, we have taken to spending an occasional lunch hour in front of the Seagram Building. . . . After considerable experimentation we have found what seems to us to be the ideal spot on the wall. It is on the Fifty-third street corner." The Talk of the Town thought this spot was the best because you could dangle your feet over the wall, listen to the fountains, and "observe pretty girls daydreaming."[23] Years later, in 1971, urban sociologist William H. Whyte conducted a survey of plazas in New York and likewise found that the Seagram Plaza—the inspiration for the "plaza bonus" change in the city code—"had not been designed as a people's plaza, but that is what it became."[24] Time lapse cameras mounted on top of the Racquet Club across the street recorded activity in the plaza from dawn to dusk. At lunch time on a day with good weather, the plaza routinely had 150 people in it. Visitors were plentiful and regular; a hot dog vendor at the corner, there for over fifteen years, reported to Whyte that he had put a son through college and grad school with the earnings.[25] While most plazas built after the Seagram Building remained empty, the Seagram plaza had, in Whyte's words, a sense of "genial permissiveness." There was always activity in the plaza, which Whyte described as the "hallmark of a great urban space."[26]

In the late 1950s this plaza, with its innovations that melted snow off the granite and kept the fountains from freezing, with its 180foot Vertgard marble benches weighing half a million pounds, provided a setting for the Seagram Building that reinforced perceptions about the relationship between its architecture and the values of its client (both company and family). Many of the accolades drew links between the aesthetics and materials of the Seagram Building and the larger economy and society. The Republic of Chile, for instance, awarded the Seagram Building a citation of honor in 1956. Delivered to Samuel Bronfman by the Chilean Consul General in New York, the citation praised the Seagram Building as "an outstanding and original contribution to world architecture embodying copper, one of Chile's primary natural resources." "The erection of the House of Seagram," which would eventually use some three million pounds of bronze, "bespeaks initiative and enterprise of the highest order."[27] This initiative and enterprise led to accolades not only for Seagram but also for Samuel Bronfman. His use of architecture to achieve status and respectability paid off grandly. As one newspaper put it, "Samuel Bronfman, Canadian philanthropist and community leader, head of Seagram's, is the inspiration for the world's first bronze skyscraper now being erected at 375 Park Avenue." The paper went on to treat the building as an index of the economic future, a symbol of hope: "Designed by Mies van der Rohe and Philip Johnson, it reflects

Figure 36. Samuel and Edgar Bronfman in front of the Seagram Building, 1966. Reprinted by permission from Arthur Schatz, Time & Life Pictures Collection © Getty Images.

Mr. Bronfman's desire that the building serve as a symbol of confidence in the strength of the industrial and business future of America."[28]

A Building That Can "boast more superlatives than the H-bomb"

Such reassurances were welcome in the face of concerns about the future of the country during the years of rising anxiety in the late 1950s. Connections between a symbol of confidence like the Seagram Building and the Cold War were materialized in a variety of forms, often in unexpected fashions. The *Centralizer*, published by the Central Mutual Insurance Company, put the Seagram Building on the cover of its August 1958 issue. The magazine generally dealt with issues relevant to the insurance industry, so the building's appearance at first seems surprising, but a blurb on the inside cover explained: "This outstanding example of Tomorrow-Minded architecture can boast more superlatives than the H-bomb."[29] The phrase "Tomorrow-Minded architecture" even echoed the language of Seagram's World War II advertising campaign, "Men who plan beyond tomorrow." The Seagram Building was celebrated as an example of great architecture and evidence of the strength of the postwar American social project. The *Centralizer* declared it a "bold step into the future."[30]

In the face of the threat of nuclear war, the Seagram Building was welcome evidence of the prowess and ingenuity of American engineering and design. The wealth, imagination, and advanced technology necessary to construct it were cast as the very forces that would serve the United States on the geopolitical stage and preserve the vitality of American business, culture, and society. The distinctions between civilian life and the machinations of the militarized state had narrowed, and a building could be lauded by comparing it with a strategic nuclear weapon.

This intersection between the bomb and the Seagram Building was made even more apparent during Armed Forces Week 1962, when a full-scale model of a Polaris missile was placed in the plaza. Accompanied by five "Miss Armed Forces" (beauty queens chosen from each branch of the military) the submarine-launched nuclear missile was on view for the first time in New York City.[31] That it went on display on the plaza of the Seagram Building, and not in some seemingly more appropriate military setting, is critical in assessing the relationship between corporate America and the expanding military-industrial complex during the Cold War. Just as the Polaris missile epitomized the technological power of the military, the Seagram Building epitomized the innovative technological and imaginative forces driving American capitalism. It was a surreal mix of sex and power in the form of beauty queens and bombs set on the stage of a skyscraper with its own peculiar phallic metaphor.

This was not the only time in the early years of the building that its strong right angle architecture was linked with sex. A short 1958 piece in *Playboy* entitled "Slenderella in the Sky" featured a photograph of a typically stern Mies (see Figure 24). If calling the building Slenderella implied a feminine association, however, the copy that accompanied the image reads: "One of the latest giants to thrust its head into New York's skyline is a stern but startling 38-story edifice sheathed in stunning bronze."[32] Other advertisements cast the tower as female, calling it "shapely" and adorning it with women's sunglasses, but—whether Slenderella or a thrusting giant, host to Miss Armed Forces or a missile—sex, the bomb, and modern architecture offered an apparently irresistible mix.[33]

In a 1951 memo Seagram executives had pondered making additions to the standard program of the office tower in order to assist in promoting their future headquarters: "What unusual features are to be embodied in this new structure? Auditorium—restaurants—florists—garage—distillery exhibit—living quarters—terraces—set backs—towers."[34] The "unusual feature" they came up with a few years later surpassed all of these. The promotional interests that motivated parading a missile in front of the Seagram Building spurred an effort to build a bomb shelter within it. A 1955 series of documents record discussions about whether the Seagram Building would have a shelter capable of withstanding an atomic blast. The apparent incongruity of such an idea disappears when one considers that at the time it was understood that a vibrant and expanding capitalist economy, dependent on corporations for continued growth, would form a bulwark of our defense against the threat and appeal of Marxism. After all, the Polaris missile was designed and built not by the military but by a corporation—Lockheed. It followed that the corporations whose economic and technological power would protect us from the Soviet Union would construct buildings that would save us from the bomb. The more abstract security provided by the economic power of corporations was conjoined with the more concrete security of the corporate bomb shelter.

Indeed, the very profit motive that animated corporate behavior in general was assumed to be the one that would motivate their public service on this matter in particular. As one official in the City of New York's Office of Civil Defense, commenting on the possibility of Seagram constructing a bomb shelter in their new building, put it,

> Should favorable consideration be given this project, I would like to mention that the House of Seagrams [sic] would have the distinction of being pioneers in this area of public service, since it would be the first building in the City of New York to provide such a facility and, perhaps in major respects, in the Nation. The well-established and well-known prestige of Seagrams [sic], I am sure, would be measurably enhanced.[35]

Presumably the "measurably enhanced" prestige of Seagram would lead to measurably enhanced sales of Seagram's various products.

Seagram executives agreed that a bomb shelter would garner good publicity for the company. In a 1955 office memo, one executive noted that "considerable favorable publicity could be given the building," as its provision of a civil defense shelter would make it unique among buildings in New York.[36] By February 1956, the engineering firm of Severud, Elstad and Krueger (consulting engineers for the Seagram Building) had produced a report on "how Civil Defence considerations would affect the structure and its inhabitants," which it sent to Mies and Philip Johnson.

In that report Fred Severud laid out the various effects an atomic blast would have on the building. His assessments are particularly interesting because he had recently written a book on atomic blast survival techniques.[37] He noted that the impact of an atomic blast was akin to a massive wave slamming into one side of the building and then "hugging" the whole building as the impact wrapped around it. The Seagram Building was better equipped than most to handle such forces because "special means have been taken (due to other considerations), both to stiffen the building and to give it mass." In fact, Severud continued, "Experience during the Nagasaki and Hiroshima attacks has shown that the human body has a really remarkable resistance against hugging forces of short duration." This meant that if "a tenant is sitting at his desk when the blast hits, he may survive the hugging action of the blast at a surprisingly small distance from ground zero." The bad news was that "he will most certainly not survive the machine-gun fire of flying glass" produced by the shattering of windows that would accompany any "atomic hug."[38]

Protection for inhabitants of the building could be provided on each floor, Severud noted, but added that it "would be very costly and space consuming." He proposed using the sub-basement as a refuge in case of an atomic attack, and closed his report with the following: "we have not carried out our various suggestions. . . . When you decide how to proceed in this matter we could rather quickly develop the necessary details."[39] It appears that in the end few if any changes were made in the design to accommodate civil defense concerns. A 1956 letter from the office of Philip Johnson to Fred Kramer states that after consultation with "Mrs. Lambert, Mr. Severud, and myself" and "due to the fact that building the floor baffles, as discussed by Mr. Severud, would restrict the planning and utilization of the tower floor areas," the decision was made that "shielding wall could be built when an emergency arises." Furthermore, the parties involved thought "a successful attack would not initially be launched in the vicinity of the New York area, or, more particularly, to strike close enough to damage the Seagram Building." In the event of an attack, "the materials and labor . . . would be on hand when required" to construct the necessary sheltering additions to the building.[40]

The faith in technology suggested by these comments was not limited to a prospective bomb shelter. Articles in the architectural and popular press linked technology and aesthetics, and events organized by Seagram to celebrate the opening of the building reinforced these connections. A 1956 article in *Fortune* magazine cast the headquarters of corporate America as the "architecture that most vividly reveals the life of its time." The examples offered—"the brilliantly organized General Motors Technical Center in Detroit, the Alcoa Building in Pittsburgh, or, in New York, at Lever House, the magnificent crystal cage of the Manufacturers Trust, or the new Seagram Tower"— were cited as evidence that "within the last decade a whole society has been captivated by fresh forms, fresh materials, and fresh building techniques." The not yet completed Seagram Building affirmed Mies's status as "the architect who has achieved perhaps the most effective synthesis of aesthetics and technology."[41] *Engineering News-Record* likewise trumpeted the building for its "many advanced concepts in architecture and engineering."[42]

These architectural, technological, and engineering advances were, as in the case of the proposal for a bomb shelter, freighted with Cold War anxiety. One of the events Seagram held to celebrate the formal opening of the building was a symposium titled "The Future of Man," held at the Waldorf-Astoria and "attended by 1,500 leaders in industry, science, education and government."[43] Speakers, advertised as "Six of the World's Great Thinkers," included poet Robert Frost, philosopher Bertrand Russell, the Nobel-prize winning zoologist Hermann J. Muller, and the anthropologist Ashley Montagu. The chair of the symposium, Dr. Milton Eisenhower (president of The Johns Hopkins University), warned that unless the expansion of human knowledge served the purpose of expanding peace and justice, society was condemned "to live in fear—the fear that terrible forces will, by design or miscalculation, break loose and destroy mankind."[44]

> New Yorkers owe Seagram a debt of gratitude not only for commissioning a building of beauty, style, and enduring elegance, but for now trying to find a way to safeguard those qualities. The Seagram Building is for a buyer who wants the best.[45]

In retrospect it is not surprising that Mies, Lambert, and Johnson were not eager to alter the design of the Seagram Building in the manner that addressing the concerns of the Office for Civil Defense required. Mies rarely accommodated much input from outsiders, especially non-architects, on his designs, and at this stage in his career and with his affection for Mies, Johnson wasn't likely to have a different opinion. For her part, Lambert was actively involved in any number of issues concerning the building's design, decoration, and public image. It was, as she has said many times, a labor of love: "from the framing of the windows to the total building, love has gone into it, love for every detail." With her predilection for describing the building as "austere strength . . . ugly beauty, terribly severe [with] all the more beauty in it," it doesn't seem likely she would embrace the symbolic opportunity the creation of a bomb shelter offered if it came at the expense of the design she fought for the company to accept.[46]

Phyllis Lambert's characterization of the building as a carefully and thoughtfully designed work of architectural significance and beauty was reiterated in two booklets produced by the Seagram Company: a guide to the building written for company employees and a script composed for the employees who led guided tours of the building for the general public. The employee guide described various innovations in the building related to elevators, air-conditioning, office layout, lighting, and so forth, noting that "in our new home are a number of architectural 'firsts.' Worldwide architectural authorities have praised the concept and design of this structure and its plaza as heralding a new golden age of architecture." The guide unambiguously laid the success of the building and its intervention into the urban landscape at the feet of Samuel Bronfman: "Those who view our building and those who visit it will find it a worthy addition to the world's mightiest skyline. The vision responsible for the creation of the first headquarters building for a major distilling firm in the United States was that of Samuel Bronfman." As in its public promotional materials, the employee guide defined the skyscraper as a form of civic generosity: "He and his associates who have made possible this crowning achievement for all of us and for New York City itself, deserve the accolade of present and future generations."[47]

The narrative for tour guides, in 36 brief, numbered paragraphs, reiterated some of these points and also offered elaborate descriptions of the artwork and furniture in Seagram's offices. The first paragraph welcomed guests to the building; the second informed them, "First occupied in January 1958, the Seagram Building already has received wide acclaim for its architectural perfection. For example, *Architectural Forum* described it as New York's most beautiful building." Details large and small were pointed out in the text: "All lettering and numbers in the building, such as the office numbers and the lettering you see in the lobby, were especially designed for Seagram. The typeface is known as square serif." In the reception area of the Seagram offices "The modern leather-and-steel chairs and the glass-and-steel coffee table were designed by Mies van der Rohe, the architect for the building. He designed them for the German exhibit at the Barcelona fair in 1930, and they are known as Barcelona chairs." The name of the artist and the title of the work were given for the myriad works of art hanging on the wall.

To ensure uniform pronunciation, the guide provided phonetic spelling for each artist whose name might cause confusion: "Leger (Leh-jay)," "Lurçat's 'Le Jardin' (Lure-sah's Le Jhar-dan)," and "the lithograph on the wall is 'Jeux de Pages' (Zhe de pazhes) (Game of Pages) by Pablo Picasso (Pah-blow Pih-cass-o." Furniture designers were given equal treatment, so Hans Wegner was "Vague-ner," Eero Saarinen "Sarah-nen," and Jens Risom "Ree-som." Evidently the company wanted its investment in these works of art and furnishings to bespeak a degree of class and refinement. The stage-managing of the tour guide booklet suggests that the tactics in traditional advertising campaigns were applied to promoting the building both within the company and to the general public.

The integration of modern marketing and brand management concepts, along with the construction of the headquarters, offered the opportunity to create a new,

Figure 37. Washroom, Seagram Building, 1958. Reprinted with permission from Ezra Stoller © Esto.

polished corporate identity. In his memoirs, Edgar Bronfman, who took over the company from his father, writes that the belief that the Seagram Building was a "brilliant distillation" of the values and identity the corporation wished to advertise for itself was the reason "company stationery, calling cards, even interoffice memos bore its image."[48] Just as Seagram advertisements in the postwar years insisted that their whiskey was for "Men who plan beyond tomorrow," consumers of distinction and taste presumably, so too would their headquarters attract a buyer "who was interested in the best."

PART III

The World Trade Center:
Urban Renewal,
Global Capitalism,
and Regeneration
Through Violence

9

Regeneration Through Violence

Trade in all its vicissitudes is a defining force in the history of Manhattan. Representatives of the Dutch West India Company arrived in 1625 with the goal of establishing a trade outpost. In the twentieth century trade helped generate the profits that found material expression in skyscrapers and ordered the labor of the men and women who filled those tall buildings. The Empire State Building provided office space for small-scale enterprises engaged in trade at both the domestic and international scale. The Seagram Building housed a growing multinational corporation that grew into a colossus by purchasing companies around the globe and developing new markets at home and abroad. The World Trade Center established the link between global trade, Manhattan, and the skyscraper in bold and uncompromising terms. Larger than either of the others, the twin towers adopted trade as the defining element of their program and nomenclature. Not one but two flags were planted in lower Manhattan in the name of trade.

International trade and the global flow of capital are therefore at the heart of the history of the World Trade Center. Lower Manhattan's role in the city's rise as a center of global finance and trade made it, in Michael Sorkin and Sharon Zukin's words, the "historic cradle of New York."[1] But this sense of place and connection to the world was not without cost. Edwin Burrows, exploring how the conflicts in Manhattan's past shaped the sensibility of those who lived on the island, notes that a "sense of exposure, of precariousness, of vulnerability was central to their historical experience." The attacks on the World Trade Center of September 11 were, he writes, "an unwelcome reminder that Lower Manhattan has abundant experience with the violence spawned by international trade."[2]

Constructed in a process that eradicated the built record of the site's past, the twin towers of the WTC nevertheless can be fully understood only in the context of the long and rich history of Lower Manhattan. After 9/11 Lower Manhattan's role as the birthplace of New York was invoked by writers and politicians. As Pete Hamill put it, the WTC was located in "the birth canal" of the city.[3] Ann Buttenwieser wrote that "New York City was born of its harbor and its port," crediting Lower Manhattan as the source of the city's wealth and economic prosperity.[4] Planners referred to Lower Manhattan as the "cradle of the city."[5] Others argued that Lower Manhattan was the birthplace not just of the city, but of the United States.[6] In their urge to connect Lower Manhattan in 2001 with its seventeenth-century form, these writers unconsciously linked the twin towers and their site to the violence and displacement woven into the island's history. Elements of the collective historical memory were selectively deployed in a narrative of loss, violence, and grief, and these could not help referring to the role of capital and violence in shaping the landscape of Lower Manhattan in general and the World Trade Center in particular.

A complication of unraveling the story of the WTC and Lower Manhattan is that since 9/11 both building and site have been transformed in a process of mythmaking. Out of the absence of the twin towers emerged a set of powerful narratives connecting them retrospectively to social, political, and economic agendas at domestic and global scales. Political leaders of certain stripes quickly and determinedly appropriated the attack on the World Trade Center as the opening salvo in a "war on terror," a war cast as a totalizing conflict between civilization and savagery. In the process, twin buildings erected to serve a specialized sector of the globalizing economy were transformed into stand-ins for a set of values far more vast and complex than their original program.

During the 1960s Minoru Yamasaki, architect of the WTC, in the face of hostile public and critical reactions to his designs, insisted the buildings were material instruments of a path to global peace via world trade. In the towers' absence, political figures have made equally generous and broad claims about the towers representing "freedom," or "democracy," or "our way of life." Simultaneously, the particular socioeconomic order housed by the twin towers is cast in the role of "civilization" under attack in a savage war. The broad range of possibilities imaginable under the title of democracy, much less civilization, are reduced to the interactions of global finance and trade—practices that at their core demand neither freedom nor democracy. The history and meaning of the buildings, manipulated via their deployment in mythic language, casts them into new roles as political justifications for martial action.

At the heart of the transformation of the twin towers from object to myth is the need, as Richard Slotkin points out, to preserve historical experience in the "form of narrative." Through a process of retelling, the narratives of the twin towers and 9/11 become formalized and abstracted into myth and the buildings are "reduced to a set of powerfully evocative and resonant icons . . . in which history becomes a cliché."[7] At the same time, mythmaking is "an intellectual or artistic construct that bridges the gap between the world of the mind and the world of affairs, between dream and reality, between impulse or desire and action." Thus the myth serves not just to define the contours of the past, but also to direct action in the future: "Myth describes a process, credible to its audience, by which knowledge is transformed into power: it provides a scenario or prescription for action, defining and limiting the possibilities for human response to the universe."[8]

The discourse of myth in the wake of that day in September inexorably stripped away the contentious history of the construction of the World Trade Center. In that process a vast, sixteen acre, multi-building development was compressed (reduced, distilled) into the iconic image of the "Twin Towers." The largely negative reactions of critics and the public to the buildings and their original narrow, commercial purpose were treated as peripheral or irrelevant to the towers' newly minted identity. This transformation via erasure of collective memory was both figurative and literal: the Port Authority archives documenting the creation of the WTC, housed in the North Tower, were destroyed when the tower collapsed. In public discussions, real estate was transformed into sacred ground. In practice, these sixteen acres remained real estate, although politicians, architects, and developers together spoke in language that sought to elide this reality.

A common lament since the attack on the WTC is that after 9/11 "everything changed." This lament, echoed variously in the halls of legislatures, the security checkpoints of airports, or the press, argues that the events of 9/11 heralded the fracturing of a formerly comprehensible world. A new "clash of civilizations" demanded shedding the codes of conduct of the past, whether those were concerned with civil liberties, the need to debate expanding presidential power in a time of war, the conduct of soldiers in distant battlefields, or even the utility of defining the temporal limits of the war itself. The lament that "everything changed" after 9/11 sets the stage for demands that architecture and the urban landscape be transformed into secured outposts in the war for civilization. This broad appropriation of the attack on the WTC insists that the United States was entering a period of history unlike any in its past. As Burrows describes it, the attack was interpreted as "the end of a long period of untroubled isolation from global events and the warning of new, almost certainly dangerous engagements ahead."[9]

Burrows reminds us, however, that New York City "has always been deeply implicated in the world and that this is not the first time its people have paid a heavy price as well."[10] Sorkin and Zukin agree, noting "the destruction of the Twin Towers has reformulated the terms of conflict for the foreseeable present, it does not change this history."[11] Indeed, even the rhetorical use of the violence of 9/11 and the violence in response to it are tied to historical traditions in American history and thought. Richard Slotkin notes that "The first colonists saw in America an opportunity to regenerate their fortunes," but "the means to that regeneration ultimately became the means of violence, and the myth of regeneration through violence became the structuring metaphor of the American experience."[12] "What is distinctively 'American' is not necessarily the amount or kind of violence that characterizes our history, but the mythic significance we have assigned to the kinds of violence we have actually experienced, the forms of symbolic violence we imagine or invent, and the political uses to which we put that symbolism."[13]

In order to deconstruct the myths that have arisen around the World Trade Center, and to come to terms with the buildings themselves, it is necessary to understand the legacy of violence at the buildings' site and the ends that violence served. The early settlers sent by the Dutch West India Company to secure the company's claim to lower Manhattan—missionaries seeking to expand the reach of capitalism rather than any church—were Walloons, "an oft-persecuted Belgian minority."[14] Their 1625 arrival initiated two distinct waves of exploitation, displacement, and violent conflict. The first was with the Manhasset and Munsee Lenape.[15] The second came a year later when the Company imported eleven African slaves to the colony. From the outset, European settlement of lower Manhattan and the desire for global trade at the heart of that settlement depended on displacement and enslaved labor. Leslie Harris points out:

> African slaves became the most stable element of the New Netherland working class and population. The Dutch West India Company's importation and employment of most of the colony's slave labor enabled the settlement and survival of the Europeans at New Amsterdam as well as the limited economic success the colony experienced. . . . The company, not individuals, owned these slaves, who provided labor for the building and upkeep of the colony's infrastructure. In addition to aiding in the construction of Fort Amsterdam, completed in 1635, slaves also built roads, cut timber and firewood, cleared land, and burned limestone and oyster shells to make the lime used in outhouses and in burying the dead.[16]

Although the arrival of slaves in the colony signaled the efforts of the Dutch West India Company to control the trans-Atlantic slave trade, throughout the 1630s and 1640s the Company imported slaves largely on an irregular basis. Nonetheless, by the 1650s in New Amsterdam slave labor fed the settlers; other Dutch colonies and even the Netherlands received grain harvested and livestock tended by slave labor. Members of the merchant class, businessmen, and even artisans bought slaves to work in their industries. Secondary markets for the purchase and sale of slaves developed, and by 1660, Harris notes, "New Amsterdam was the most important slave port in North America."[17]

By the mid-seventeenth century the Dutch dominion was perceived as a threat to British economic interests. In 1664, encouraged by the presence of four British warships and hundreds of soldiers, the Dutch ceded authority over Lower Manhattan. Both the island and New Amsterdam were renamed New York. The shift in authority brought an elaboration and entrenchment of the role of slavery in the colony as the British sought to increase their own involvement in the African slave trade generally and the market in New York in particular. To that end the British eliminated the "property tax on slaves and imposed tariffs on imported slaves that favored African imports" over those from elsewhere in North America and the Caribbean.[18]

These taxation and tariff policies suggest that slaves were understood less as human beings than as commodities to be traded. The inhumane conditions of the Middle Passage responded to and reinforced "the British belief that Africans were lesser humans, subject to enslavement."[19] The global slave trade surely depended on the depravity of those who traded in human bondage. But it also depended on systems of storage, transport, and capitalist innovation: the warehousing of slaves on the coast of Africa, the murderous efficiency of ships in manipulating the maximum amount of human cargo in their holds, and the marketplace in New York to distribute the enslaved at a profit.[20] These systems later facilitated trade in the goods produced in the New World through slave labor: sugar, cotton, rice, tobacco, and so forth. World trade in New York had its roots in systems of bondage and the goods produced under bondage.[21]

The slave trade in the late seventeenth and early eighteenth centuries boomed as demand increased in New York. Indeed, in the first half-decade of the 1700s the slave population grew at a faster pace than the white population. The increased supply of slaves—at points in the eighteenth century "New Amsterdam and then New York City housed the largest slave population in mainland North America, with more slaves than any other city on the continent"—was nevertheless outstripped by demand.[22] The price for a "healthy, male slave" in 1700 was forty pounds; by 1760 it was one hundred pounds.[23] As the value of slaves as individual commodities and as the key sector of the colony's labor market increased, so did legal controls over slaves' daily lives and interaction with whites. Slaveholding households were common, and the trade in supplies to support the expanding market for slavery fueled the area's wealth.

At the close of the eighteenth and into the nineteenth century, New York slowly began the process of abolishing slavery. The Revolutionary War was a major force in the transformation of the slave empire built by the British, but emancipation came gradually and slowly. New York legislators made a commitment to ending slavery in 1799, and a final end was declared in 1827, but hundreds were left in apprenticeship until the 1840s.[24]

These changes did not mean that the political economy of New York, and trade in particular, was no longer dependent on slavery. Indeed, quite the opposite was the case. At the close of the War of 1812, New York merchants and bankers found a world of wealth in exporting cotton to textile manufacturers in Europe. Ships arrived at Manhattan's ports laden with European goods to satisfy consumer demand in the United States. New York merchants had in the past struggled to profit on the return voyages of these vessels because of British embargos on various American agricultural products combined with low European demand for American finished goods. By the second decade of the nineteenth century, however, the growing British textile manufacturing industry created a voracious demand for raw cotton. Slave labor, along with the development of the cotton gin, spurred the dramatic growth of cotton production in the South. New York was the critical site where supply and demand were accommodated. Historian David Quigley notes: "By the 1820s, New York investors and their firms secured leading roles in regularizing the movement of capital and supplies between the plantations of the black belt and the mill towns of Britain. In the process, New York's merchant houses created a network of Northern agents who spread across the South, developing lasting business and personal connections."[25]

Trade in slave-produced cotton necessitated both institutional investments and personal relationships between New Yorkers and their plantation counterparts in the South. Just as trade produced great wealth for Southern plantation owners and their New York counterparts, so too did it establish New York as "the center of American banking and finance by the middle of the nineteenth century."[26] By 1822 over half of New York's exports were produced in the South; slave cotton alone accounted for 40 percent of city exports and in dollar terms dwarfed second-place flour.[27] The very mechanism of its export, the cotton bale, uniform in size and weight, designed to be stacked with ease and stability in transport ships, presaged the containers and freight vessels that carried an increasing percentage of goods around the globe in the late twentieth century when the World Trade Center was under construction.

Some 20,000 enslaved and freed African Americans were buried just blocks east of where the WTC would rise centuries later. The burial site was largely ignored by the city until 1991, when builders stumbled on it while excavating a construction site. Both the public sphere and the built environment responded to and accommodated the role of slavery in New York's economy and daily life.[28] The proponents of the WTC sought to preserve Lower Manhattan's dominant position in world trade. The origins of this dominance—little spoken of at the time—were in the trade in slaves in the seventeenth and eighteenth and in slave cotton in the nineteenth century.

The construction of the urban built environment that sustained New York's rapacious economic development was neither peaceful nor orderly. Major slave rebellions took place in 1712 and 1741. Fires swept through the city in 1776 (likely caused by arson), 1835, and 1845, destroying nearly a third of the city's buildings each time. Violence tore at the fabric of the island's social life as well, as through the eighteenth and into the nineteenth century riots were a common tool for the expression of political power. Prior to 9/11, the most violent terrorist act in the city's history was the 1920 bombing of Wall Street, an attack that like 9/11 was used to justify political actions taken at a variety of scales unrelated to the site of violence itself.[29]

The violence and destruction in real life were mirrored and even exaggerated in popular literature and film, where Manhattan was destroyed multiple times over. In spite (or perhaps because) of the history of violence against Indians and the enslaved in Manhattan, the American "disaster novel," Mike Davis notes, was "fixated on the specter of subversive immigrants and non-whites." The fictional narratives of dystopian futures revealed the anxieties at the heart of "nativist fears" that were layered onto Manhattan. In *The Last American* (1889), by John Ames Mitchell, "the alien hordes actually turn green and destroy New York after massacring its Protestant bourgeoisie."[30] In *Caesar's Column* (1890), Ignatius Donnelly depicted the efforts of "slum hordes" to destroy modern civilization in a battle where the victors, after defeating the hordes, "monopolize the scorched earth of a ruinous war of extermination."[31] H. G. Wells's *The War in the Air* (1908) imagined Manhattan reduced to fiery rubble; a city of death and the twisted remnants of its once great skyscrapers. Films too numerous to mention condemned New York as a reservoir of depravity, licentiousness, crime, and violence; others, such as *Independence Day* (1996), *Godzilla* (1998), *The Day After Tomorrow* (2004), and *Cloverfield* (2008), and many more, sought dramatic frisson via its destruction.[32]

The wealth and power centered in Lower Manhattan was the source of great enmity long before 9/11. Lower Manhattan was built on a foundation of cycles of eviction, destruction, and redevelopment that made and remade the urban landscape time and time again. The World Trade Center rose on a site cleared by a mighty wave of demolition justified by the imperative to develop land to its most profitable use. While little remembered today, coverage of the planning and construction of the WTC was replete with references to regeneration, death, ghosts, and destruction. The predilection for destruction to precede creation led architecture critic Ada Louise Huxtable to comment that at the World Trade Center site "the death of the past [was] framed by the birth of the future." Amid the violence of destruction, birth and death commingled in the "regeneration" of the city. "New York rises not from ashes but from rubble." Haunted by the past, "everything that economics, expediency and unfeeling blindness can do to exorcise these ghosts has been done, but they will not go."[33] Although averring that the WTC was "on balance . . . not the city-destroyer" it was "popularly represented to be," Huxtable nonetheless rued that "megalomania" meant that the city's "skyline would be broken again . . . [a] dramatic testament of the city's brutally competitive grandeur and vitality."[34] The brutality of the marketplace and the megalomania it served ruptured the prized skyline of the city by inserting in it twin towers alien in both scale and aesthetics.

Figure 38. World Trade Center, 1974. Reprinted by permission from Peter Keegan, Hulton Archive © Getty Images.

The skyline, of course, was not the only part of the city fractured by the construction of the WTC. Clearing the sixteen-acre site on which the buildings rose meant destroying what the *New York Times* called "one of the city's oldest and most colorful commercial centers."[35] Huxtable, in less impassioned tones, lamented the use of eminent domain in the "destruction of a small but irreplaceable business community."[36] In the years of legal battles to halt the project, the *Times* was peppered with stories about the impending demise of the neighborhood. Small business owners criticized the construction of the WTC as a death knell for a whole community and way of life: "Some of us have been in business for 35, 45 years," said one. "They're dealing in human lives here."[37] Shop owners paraded a coffin draped in black up and down the streets of Lower Manhattan with a sign reading "Here Lies Mr. Small Businessman."[38] The remorseless exercise of eminent domain forcibly removed hundreds of small business owners, many of them less than moved by the rhetoric of urban renewal in which the demolition of their livelihoods was couched. "In the end," one former resident said, "we were pushed out by the goons."[39] Her view colored by the context of their creation, Huxtable gloomily warned in 1966 that the towers "could be the start of a new skyscraper age or the biggest tombstones in the world."[40]

Today the twin towers and Ground Zero are characters in an unfolding drama about the ability of architecture to memorialize violence and loss, about the relationship between form and meaning, and about the appropriate way to build on ground claimed by a broad spectrum of interests often in conflict with one another. Debates about rebuilding the site raise questions again and again about national security, the blowback of American cultural, political, and economic power across the globe, and the presumptive capacity and need for architecture to embody the virtues of capitalist democracy and the nation-state. These debates layer the World Trade Center site with associations and meanings that diverge dramatically from those it carried prior to 9/11. Huxtable wrote nearly four years after the attack: "the World Trade Center site was turned into a giant memorial and bizarre pairing of art and patriotism, a place for political grandstanding while security fought architecture to a draw."[41]

Commenting in 2003 on the rebuilding of Ground Zero, Governor George Pataki described Daniel Libeskind's designs as "plans born out of tragedy but forged in democracy."[42] "Centuries from now," Pataki said in public comments about the rebuilding process, "history will record September 11th, 2001, as a turning point for humanity—a date when those who believe in fear were overcome by those who believe in freedom." Out of the violence of 9/11 emerged a political consensus that insisted that the rebuilding effort must deny an act of terrorism the power to define Ground Zero, and that through rebuilding architecture would materialize the greatness of American society. Architecture, Pataki said, would allow the United States to "defiantly reclaim our skyline with a new beacon symbolizing all that makes our nation great."

Destroyed, the Twin Towers and Ground Zero in general assumed new symbolic dimensions and overtones. In the late 1970s architecture critic Paul Goldberger, mingling critical judgment with a coastal disdain for the land mass between the two coasts, dismissed the Twin Towers as "boring, so utterly banal as to be unworthy of the headquarters of a bank in Omaha."[43] Shortly after 9/11, however, no less a figure than Robert A. M. Stern, dean of Yale School of Architecture, said of the loss of the buildings, "the World Trade Center was a powerful symbol of our city. . . . When a landmark is torn down, we lose witness to our humanity. Buildings are at once silent witnesses and yet they speak."[44] What one critic in 1966 called a "fearful instrument of urbicide" was transformed into a landmark, a witness to our humanity.[45] Through the violence of their destruction, the meaning of the Twin Towers was transformed, progressing from tools of "urbicide" to a powerful symbol of "our city." In years since 2001, a cacophony of voices have echoed Stern's assessment, these interlocutors seemingly able to hear the buildings speak to any number of agendas. But this was not always the case. Prior to 9/11 the "inarticulate two," as one architect called them, did not speak in the fashion Stern described.[46] Rather, people looked on these acres of vertical sameness, "monoliths" as one architecture guide put it, and saw in them what they wanted to see, what they believed an architecture of such scale was *supposed* to convey.[47]

Rashomon-like, of course, not everyone saw the same thing in the Twin Towers. Architectural critics (as we have seen) saw one thing when gazing at the towers. Builders, real estate developers, and others less sensitive to aesthetics but deeply concerned with the exercise of eminent domain probably saw something else entirely. The popular press and the endless waves of tourists from far and wide seemed to read in them something not too different from a barbaric yawp. How could the towers inspire this range of reactions when they stood? How do they now—as symbols rather than objects—continue to serve a range of agendas often at odds with one another?

In the years since 9/11, a parade of architectural visions for a new Lower Manhattan have been displayed in museum exhibits, magazines, newspapers, and journals. Politicians have devoted endless words and press conferences to prove their commitment to rebuilding the site, in its manifest variations. Design competitions have been held, scuttled, held again. Winners have been announced, their designs heralded, and then attenuated beyond recognition by the inexorable and undemocratic forces of commerce. Whatever else the World Trade Center was, and whatever the site may become, it was and remains a plot of valuable real estate and, as architecture critic Philip Nobel observes, "New York only knows how to do one thing with a hole in the ground."[48]

10

The Rhetoric and Reality of Urban Renewal

. . . the critics, detractors, adepts at sneer and innuendo, apostles of backwoods Americanism and pristine Aryanism, suffer less from fancied superiority than from high-minded envy.
—Robert Moses

To get to the heart of how and why the World Trade Center came to bear so many interpretations, it helps to know something about the things themselves, rather than the symbols they are now. The initial discussions that led to the project began in 1955. Construction stretched into the early 1970s, and the WTC did not turn a profit until 1981. At completion, the twin towers replaced the Empire State Building as the tallest skyscrapers in New York City and the world. Their total cost, more than $1 billion, dwarfed that of the Seagram Building, until then the most expensive office tower ever built. At more than 10 million square feet of office space, it was an astoundingly large project: two towers of 110 stories, each floor an acre in size.

The Empire State Building was a speculative venture undertaken by a small group of wealthy and politically well-connected individuals who sought to use architecture to gain access to the ranks of society's elite. The Seagram Building was built by a corporation that hoped to use architecture to elevate the reputation of the business and the family that owned it. While both buildings were cast by their clients as structures whose size, beauty, and aesthetics improved the quality of life in Manhattan, they were privately funded developments. The World Trade Center from the moment of its inception likewise assumed the cloak of civic improvement and urban renewal. But while the rhetoric used to justify the project was familiar enough, the financing, planning, and construction were quite distinct. The clients for the earlier skyscrapers, although politically well con-nected, were not themselves active members of the political bureaucracy. The WTC went from idea to built reality under the direction of banker David Rockefeller, grandson of John D. Rockefeller; his brother Nelson, four-time governor of New York, one-time vice president of the United States, and repeat candidate for president (shades of Al Smith); and the Port Authority of New York and New Jersey, a government corporation entirely removed from public oversight.

Figure 39. David Rockefeller, 1954. Courtesy of the Library of Congress.

Figure 40. Vice-President Nelson Rockefeller with President Gerald Ford, First Lady Betty Ford, and Bob Dole, Republican National Convention, 1976. Courtesy of the Library of Congress.

No single figure involved in the creation of the WTC—David or Nelson Rockefeller or the Port Authority—could on its own have engineered a development of this scale. Every agent in the project used the rhetoric of civic benefit and urban improvement to gain public approval and funding, but they all had their own agendas for the WTC, agendas rarely stated in public. All figures in this process quickly learned to employ the rhetoric of architectural discourse and civic benefit to disguise concrete demands of their own.

John Raskob and Samuel Bronfman were self-made men; born poor, they built empires of great wealth but were often regarded as outsiders because of their background or faith. David Rockefeller's story was quite different, as was his relationship with architecture. He was born in 1915 at 10 West Fifty-Fourth Street in a nine-story home, the largest private residence in New York City. As a teenager in the 1930s he saw out his bedroom window the Empire State Building, the building the World Trade Center would eventually replace as the world's tallest.[1] During his teenage years his father began building Rockefeller Center, one of New York's grandest architectural developments. Certainly privileged position in society, great wealth, and experience watching his father spearhead the construction of Rockefeller Center all contributed to David Rockefeller's quest to build his own skyscraper. Like Raskob and Bronfman (and his own father),

David Rockefeller was a central figure behind the construction of one of New York's most famous buildings; unlike Raskob and Bronfman (and his father), he managed to do so without spending a dime of his own money.

In his memoirs, David Rockefeller introduces the story of the World Trade Center by recalling how his interest in the affairs of New York City was shaped by his experiences growing up and attending school in the city. In the late 1920s, he recounts, he went to Harlem to deliver Thanksgiving baskets as part of a school project. The baskets were for poor families living in "old law" tenements. "Accompanied by a liveried chauffeur in full uniform," he writes, "this was a very memorable experience because I was faced for the first time with the reality that many people in the City were living in dire poverty and would not have had a Thanksgiving meal had we not brought it."[2] In his memoirs, Rockefeller presents this brush with poverty, albeit soothed by the presence of the chauffeur, as the first of several events that convinced him that New Deal-style government policies (like "New York City's invidious rent control laws") were flawed and that "the most effective response to urban problems would result from intelligent public-private cooperation."[3] Throughout his life Rockefeller stepped comfortably into leadership roles to marshal what he considered such cooperation.

In the late 1950s Rockefeller concluded that Lower Manhattan, Wall Street in particular, was in serious decline, and that the flight of banks, insurance companies, and other corporations was not likely to stop unless dramatic action was taken. Of course, Rockefeller's interest in the renewal of Lower Manhattan was not purely philanthropic. In 1955, as president of Chase Manhattan, he decided that the bank's new 60-story headquarters would be built in Lower Manhattan. To assemble a lot of sufficient size he met with Robert Moses and asked "the City's permission to 'demap' or close a one-block stretch of Cedar Street, a narrow but heavily traveled thoroughfare." Moses agreed, but warned that "many Wall Street businesses had already moved uptown or were about to leave the City altogether."[4] Although chastened by Moses's warning, Rockefeller pressed on with his plans for a modern skyscraper headquarters. Designed by Gordon Bunshaft of Skidmore, Owings & Merrill (SOM), it was clad in anodized aluminum (cheaper than stainless steel) and glass. The investment in this massive, shiny hulk of a building was in serious jeopardy if real estate values fell as financial institutions fled uptown or (more likely) to the ostensibly tamer, quieter suburbs of New York, Connecticut, and New Jersey.

The situation, Rockefeller felt, called for action. In 1958, at a time when only one-fifth of new commercial construction was being built south of City Hall, he organized the Downtown Lower Manhattan Association (DLMA) with the goal of restoring "downtown's former luster" and stemming the tide of falling property values.[5] One of the ironies of David Rockefeller's desire to resurrect Lower Manhattan as a center of financial activity and construction is that its decline was in part sealed by his father's construction of Rockefeller Center, which cemented Midtown's position as the most important business district in the city.[6]

When Robert Moses helped Rockefeller assemble the lot to build Chase Manhattan's headquarters, he suggested that Rockefeller "put together an organization that could speak on behalf of the downtown financial community." The DLMA would do more than offer a voice to a group not heretofore known as shy and retiring; it would "offer a cohesive plan for the physical redevelopment of Wall Street to persuade the politicians to allocate the necessary resources." In 1958 the DLMA hired Skidmore, Owings & Merrill to create a plan for a "new Lower Manhattan."[7] The SOM proposal, the first to raise the idea of a World Trade Center, called for reorganizing the downtown street grid and razing more than 100 blocks. It suggested, Plan Voisin-like, that renewal required a blank slate as its starting point. The proposal was Joseph Schumpeter's creative destruction acted out on the urban landscape, the regeneration of Lower Manhattan achieved through the violence of wide-scale demolition.[8] It was philosophically in line with the mindset of many of Manhattan's postwar planners, who, as Christine Boyer notes, "considered industrial uses to be obnoxious and signs of blight." Although David Rockefeller envisioned Manhattan as a center of white-collar residences and office space, it was the city's planners who "set about trampling tens of thousands of blue-collar jobs under their urban-renewal bulldozers until they had completely eradicated manufacturing from the urban mix."[9]

The idea of a World Trade Center intrigued David Rockefeller, who asked SOM to work out in more detail what such a development might entail and also forwarded the initial plan to Mayor Robert F. Wagner. In January 1960 SOM returned to the DLMA with a revised proposal: a $250 million complex to be located on the east end of Wall Street on a thirteen-acre site. Rockefeller liked the plan, perhaps in no small part because, as one observer noted, it "had many of the features of other multi-building complexes that the Rockefellers had a hand in developing: the United Nations, Lincoln Center, and above all, midtown's architectural jewel, Rockefeller Center."[10] Rockefeller believed the development would cement Manhattan's position as center of global trade and finance, a move that would serve the interests of his bank and its new downtown headquarters. The project's size, cost, and location required a developer with the power to exercise eminent domain and secure credit. Rockefeller knew that only the Port Authority of New York and New Jersey could do both to the degree required.

The Port Authority is a curious creature, created in 1921 to build and manage ports and transportation infrastructure within a twenty-five-mile radius of the Statue of Liberty in New York and New Jersey.[11] This was a powerful mandate, but precisely how the construction of a World Trade Center complex fit into it is certainly unclear. This potential complication, however, did not trouble David Rockefeller. Nor, apparently, did it trouble the Port Authority. Rockefeller approached the head of the Authority, Austin Tobin, with the SOM plan, and Tobin agreed it was a project the Authority should undertake.[12] Rockefeller saw to it that the DLMA sent copies of the plan to Nelson Rockefeller, his brother and governor of New York, Mayor Wagner, and Robert Meyner, governor of New Jersey.

The Port Authority assembled an advisory panel of architects (including Wallace K. Harrison, Edward Durrell Stone, and Gordon Bunshaft), planners, and engineers to study and revise the initial plan. The plan the advisory panel released in March 1961 called for a $335-million multi-building development dominated by a 72-story tower and providing 11 million square feet of office space. This proposal would have satisfied the ambitions of most developers at the time, but not the Port Authority. When exactly the Port Authority decided to build the largest office development in the world is the subject of some dispute. But according to multiple accounts, by 1960 its marketing department had already concluded that the Authority "should build the world's tallest building" in an effort to attract tenants.[13] Although Rockefeller had reservations about "publicly financed housing schemes," he and the Port Authority were about to engineer public financing of "a massive and fully tax-exempt intervention in the private real estate market through the development of the world's largest office building."[14] Three years earlier, when he organized the DLMA, David Rockefeller spoke about revitalizing downtown Manhattan by building housing in order to promote Wall Street as an "around-the-clock community."[15] By 1961 the banker's grandest plans instead would house yet more offices and white-collar commuters.

Legislative wrangling in New York and New Jersey in 1962 and 1963 slowed but did not stop the passage of bills authorizing the creation of the World Trade Center. To satisfy the demands of politicians in New Jersey, the project was moved from the proposed location along the East River to a site on the West Side occupied by a terminal for a rail line connecting New Jersey and Manhattan. The Port Authority announced it would take over operation of the unprofitable rail connection and upgrade its infrastructure, which at that point was in serious decline. Unfortunately for Rockefeller and the Port Authority, the move that pacified politicians in New Jersey set off its own protest in Manhattan. The area along the West Side that would be razed to make way for the proposed World Trade Center was a commercial district occupied by nearly 1,000 offices and 300 small businesses and known as Radio Row after the electronic goods in which most of the shops dealt. Rockefeller described the area as "commercial slums,"[16] but a 1963 *New York Times* article characterized the neighborhood as "mainly known as the East Coast's electronics center." The merchants of Radio Row, the article went on, were "its economic heart."[17]

Figure 41. Cortlandt Street, Radio Row, ca. 1930. Reprinted by permission from Hulton Archive © Getty Images.

The modest merchants of Radio Row displayed a pronounced skepticism for Rock-efeller's plans to "revitalize" Lower Manhattan by demolishing their livelihoods. An owner of a radio shop summarized the sentiment of many when he said "the Port Authority will tear down my business. . . . If it were for the betterment of the city, that would be one thing. But this is simply big business running over us."[18] A similar condemnation of efforts to evict businesses to make way for the World Trade Center was voiced by Oscar Nadel, president of the Downtown West Businessmen's Association.[19] As the *New York Times* reported, "Mr. Nadel said that the 325 store-level businesses and 1,000 above-street-level businesses employed more than 30,000 persons who would be thrown out of work if the buildings were razed. 'This project is to benefit banks, insurance companies, brokers, people dealing in international trade,' Nadel said. 'Why should the Port Authority put us out of business for something like that?' " Public protests organized by the Downtown West Businessmen's Association reiterated Nadel's populist critique, featuring "a black-draped coffin containing the life-size figure of a man labeled 'Small Business Man,' " and broadcasts of a recorded speech urging passersby to sign a petition to "stave off the forces of injustice to working people in this area."[20]

Justified skepticism and protest on the part of the soon-to-be-displaced, however, is little obstacle for the power of eminent domain. Reports spread of unexplained fires and break-ins in the businesses of holdouts who refused to accept the Port Authority's relocation offers.[21] A restaurant that opened in 1882 and employed three generations of a family would not occupy the energies of a fourth; the Port Authority offered the owners a fraction of what it would cost to move the business.[22] Bad publicity in the form of press articles detailing the efforts of small businesses to fight for their place in Manhattan no doubt irked the Port Authority. But the real concern for David Rockefeller and the Authority were the legal challenges. These were filed by both the merchants of Radio Row and Midtown real estate developers who saw their property values threatened by such a massive development. The legal battles over the use of eminent domain in the World Trade Center traveled through the New York state court system, with the New York Court of Appeals upholding the rights of the Port Authority. In 1963 the Supreme Court refused to review the Appellate decision, ending the legal challenge to the World Trade Center.[23] Faced with defeat, Oscar Nadel was defiant: "Public opinion and the little guy have yet to be heard from. This is far from over."[24]

True to his word, Nadel and the Downtown West Businessmen's Association announced plans to follow Nelson Rockefeller during his travels as a candidate for the Republican presidential nomination. In January 1964 Nadel organized a busload of sixty protesters to follow Rockefeller during a "hand-shaking tour of Concord, NH." The Downtown Businessmen's Association, Nadel warned, "was determined to follow Rockefeller throughout his primary campaign."[25] Just over two weeks later plans and models of the twin towers and the World Trade Center complex were revealed to the public at the New York Hilton Hotel. Also at the event were Nelson Rockefeller and Austin Tobin, executive director of the Port Authority. As Governor Rockefeller spoke about how "construction of the center would take up the slack in the building industry," "fifty men, women, and children representing the Downtown West Businessmen's Association picketed outside." Children carried placards that asked: "Gov. Rockefeller, Do You Want My Dad to Lose His Job?" The same newspaper article that covered the unveiling and protest also noted that, in spite of the claim that the center was designed to serve businesses involved in international trade, "only 4 million of the 10 million square feet will be occupied by private businesses. The balance will be taken up by Federal, regional and state government units."[26]

Later that year Barry Ray, the owner of a delicatessen, began an effort to lobby European governments to refuse offices in the World Trade Center. In a letter to the heads of "eleven Western European governments," in advance of visits to those countries by a delegation from the Port Authority, Ray wrote: "We feel it incumbent upon us to warn you of a scheme which is shortly to be perpetrated on you, your government, and your people under the thinly veiled lie of a 'World Trade Center.'" He warned, "You will very shortly be swarmed upon by an extremely energetic group of salesmen. They will submit beautiful brochures filled with deliberate lies." The World Trade Center "is sponsored by financiers who have no honest interest in world trade, but who believe they have found a way to create the issuance of almost a billion dollars of tax-free bonds which they are in a favorable position to exploit." The letter closed raising the specter of negative publicity for any foreign nation that occupied office space in the World Trade Center: "We respectfully urge you to make no commitment. To do otherwise would be going over the heads of the American people, taking sides against the American businessman on an issue foreign to you. It seems ridiculous to risk your foreign trade in the hands of an independent, irresponsible Port of New York Authority founded years ago to handle bridges and tunnels and now seeking to control the field of free enterprise."[27]

Ray's resistance held out for less than two years; in 1966 he accepted a check for $3,739.77 from the Port Authority and shuttered his business. A still defiant Oscar Nadel, facing the imminent demolition of his shop, refused to give up the fight. Speaking from Oscar's Radio Shop at 63 Cortlandt, he vowed to "fight to the very end." "They've knocked out 32 of us, but we still have nearly 200 left. If they want to evict us, let them try."[28] Four years later, while heavy machinery cleared the ways for the foundations of the twin towers, 160 claims for compensation were still unresolved.[29]

In 1964, in the midst of this rancor about the size of the World Trade Center and its effect (positive or negative) on life in Lower Manhattan, the Port Authority announced that the cost was to rise to $525 million. By now the project was under attack by a range of interests as too large and too risky, and derided by a young Ed Koch as led by "a conspiracy by people who think they know what's best for New York."[30] Real estate magnate Leonard Wien (who, along with Harry Helmsley, owned the Empire State Building), organized the Committee for a Reasonable World Trade Center. In letters to politicians and advertisements in the *New York Times*, Wien claimed that the acres of office space in the WTC would glut the commercial real estate sector, causing chaos in rental rates. Wien called the Port Authority an "unconquerable Frankenstein," and characterized the World Trade Center as a vast, publicly financed real estate development that threatened the profits of private developers throughout the city. When the final design, twin 110-story towers, was revealed to the public Wien suggested the sheer size was a public safety hazard, illustrated in advertisements showing a passenger jet about to crash into one of the towers.

The Committee's advertisements presented the tremendous height of the towers as a threat to public safety. In the years that followed, advertisements featuring the towers directly and indirectly referenced similar anxieties about the safety of tall buildings and the risks associated with habitation within them. One ad, for asbestos fireproofing,

Figure 42. Radio Row, 1966, demolished to make way for the World Trade Center. Reprinted by permission from Hulton Archive © Getty Images.

shows the twin towers from ground level with black letters over them reading: "When The Fire Alarms Went Off, It Took Two Hours to Evacuate New York's World Trade Center." The ad closes by noting that "the taller the building, the more important fire-proofing becomes," and affirming "When life depends on it, you use asbestos."[31] While the technological acumen that allowed for such tall buildings was not explicitly criticized, the ad carries a subtext of fear about the incompatibility with easy evacuation in the face of calamity presented by structures so tall. The marvel of great height was burdened by an often unspoken fear of the cost of living at such heights. The Port Authority advertisements cast an interpretation of the significance of height that in light of history seems forebodingly ambiguous. These were illustrated by an image of the twin towers taken from the sky and carried the text: "The closest some of us will get to heaven."[32]

The battles and the losses that accompanied construction preparations recall Boyer's insight that "War is a contest between two sides, and injuring is its central activity. So might the building of Manhattan be described as a battle over terrain in which one victor remains standing after inflicting considerable injury."[33] In her discussion of Rockefeller Center, Carole Krinsky describes the complex as the product of architects guided by an owner "who was interested in the maximum beauty consistent with profitability."[34] Unlike Rockefeller Center, where the interests of profit and power were dressed in an architectural cloak of beauty and civic obligations, the World Trade Center was largely discussed as an economic intervention, with beauty a distant second (if not third or fourth). The architect for the complex faced the challenge of designing in an environment rife with conflict and where the exigencies of program superseded notions of beauty. What kind of architect would accept a commission so encumbered?

11

Cathedrals of Commerce: Minoru Yamasaki, Skyscraper Design, and the Rise of Postmodernism

Until Minoru Yamasaki was hired as architect, the World Trade Center was a project guided entirely by a coterie of well-connected individuals, firmly ensconced among the power elite of New York City. The architects on the Port Authority's advisory board, known as David Rockefeller's "genius committee," would not unreasonably have imagined they were likely candidates for the job that went instead to Yamasaki.[1] They had, after all, been involved with the planning and design of the World Trade Center up to that point, and they were all architects with established reputations and substantial experience working on large scale projects in Manhattan and elsewhere.

Gordon Bunshaft was a partner in Skidmore, Owings & Merrill, one of the largest architecture firms in the world, and had ample experience designing office buildings, including New York's famous Lever House and David Rockefeller's Chase Manhattan headquarters. Wallace K. Harrison, often regarded as the Rockefeller "family architect," worked on Rockefeller Center, and was one of the principal architects for the United Nations Secretariat, and later for Lincoln Center. In the late 1950s, when David Rockefeller was guiding the construction of Chase Manhattan Bank's new downtown headquarters, he called on "Wally" for advice about whom to hire, and Harrison suggested SOM.[2] Edward Durrell Stone designed the Museum of Modern Art, an institution closely associated with the Rockefellers and the United States Embassy in New Delhi, and by the mid-1960s had an office with nearly a billion dollars in construction underway, including the State University of New York at Albany complex.[3] But instead, in 1962, the Port Authority decided to hire Minoru Yamasaki, a Seattle-born architect with an office in the Midwest (recall Goldberger's disdain for all things Omaha) and without a single building in New York to his name. What the Port Authority asked of Yamasaki was at

Figure 43. Minoru Yamasaki, 1952. Reprinted by permission from Hulton Archive © Getty Images.

once simple and complex: he could design whatever he wanted so long as it housed 10 million square feet of rentable space. This vast, non-negotiable, and largely arbitrary amount of space was what the Port Authority shorthanded as "the Program."

Yamasaki was an unusual choice. In the early 1960s he had completed only one high-rise building, the relatively modest 28-story Michigan Consolidated Gas building in Detroit. Yamasaki topped that structure with a crown of gas-fed flames, a design choice that highlighted his aesthetic and geographic remove from the more reserved New York City corporate architecture of the Seagram Building and other office towers of the late 1950s and 1960s. The Port Authority was not your typical corporation, however, and Austin Tobin was not your typical chief corporate officer. The Port Authority sold neither goods nor services (unlike corporations such as Seagram or Chase Manhattan), had no shareholders, and had no competitors. Austin Tobin thought of the Port Authority as the nation's preeminent planner and engineer of public works, an organization staffed and managed by a group of dedicated, technically savvy professionals. Tobin admired efficiency and skillful engineering over high-art architecture. Prior to hiring Yamasaki, Tobin rejected forty competing proposals from other architects, including Walter Gropius, Philip Johnson, Louis Kahn, and I. M. Pei. While Gropius's reputation was at that point in decline—albeit for his work on the Pan Am Building, a project whose size and scale made it something of a precursor to the Twin Towers—Johnson, Kahn, and Pei's careers were still on the rise. But, as Eric Darton notes, Tobin felt that "high-modernist aesthetics could no more appropriately be applied to the World Trade Center than to the designs of the PA's bridges, bus terminals, or freight facilities." So Tobin chose Yamasaki, "an ambitious climber with the soul of an engineer."[4]

Yamasaki's professional persona and reputation—a careful engineer but also an outsider "driven to assert his presence within the elite ranks of American architecture"—were in large part the product of his background.[5] Minoru Yamasaki was born in 1912 in Seattle, the son of Japanese immigrants; his father worked a number of jobs including clerking at a shoe store and cleaning the floors of a chocolate factory. As a young child Yamasaki and his family lived in a cold water tenement with an outhouse. Recalling his youth as a Nisei in Seattle, he wrote that he was keenly aware of the "strong racial prejudice that existed against Orientals." "It was as bad for the Japanese there as it has been and continues to be for the blacks throughout the country." While some of his peers protested the racist culture of the Northwest and the treatment they received—being forced to sit in the balconies at movie theaters, denied access to public swimming pools—Yamasaki threw himself into his studies.[6] He excelled in math and science and graduated with honors, but had no real interest in a particular career. All that changed when his uncle, who had recently graduated with an architecture degree from the University of California and was on his way to a job in Chicago, stopped in Seattle for a visit. "He unrolled the drawings he had made at the university, and I almost exploded with excitement when I saw them."[7] Yamasaki decided to become an architect.

Yamasaki's architectural education took place far from the elite schools of the East Coast, at the University of Washington, where, in his own words, he exhibited "no drawing skills" or "aptitude for sculpture."[8] While excelling at his coursework in structures, he struggled with design. He considered dropping out of school, but was encouraged by a trusted faculty member who predicted he would become one of the school's best graduates. Paying for university training during the Great Depression was a constant struggle for Yamasaki as his father endured several cuts in pay. To help pay for his education Yamasaki found work in an Alaskan salmon cannery, where he worked with other Nisei and Filipinos in generally deplorable conditions. The experience of the "greed of these unregulated companies and their exploitation of the workers" had a lasting impact on Yamasaki.[9] His time working at the canneries occupies more pages in his autobiography than his years at school. After graduating with a bachelor's degree in architecture he went to New York City in search of a job.

Arriving in New York with letters of recommendation from his faculty at the University of Washington, Yamasaki crisscrossed the city from office to office, finding them closed "or being greeted by architects acting as their own receptionists."[10] With no architectural jobs available, Yamasaki went to work packing Noritake china for a Japanese importer and began attending night school at New York University to pursue his master's degree in architecture. After NYU and a year of design-drafting piecework, he got a job in the firm whose most famous design he would one day surpass: Shreve, Lamb & Harmon. He thus spent the late 1930s and early 1940s in a firm known for efficiency and economy as much as design skills. Employed in the working-drawings department, he received a solid training in the business of architecture and of building, elements he knew little about at the time.

Yamasaki later wrote that he "wasn't too sympathetic with the type of design work" Shreve, Lamb & Harmon was doing at that time, and the firm's influence on him may have been more of ethos than of style. His statement years later that "one can't fit the people who use the building into any fashion the architect desires just to suit the exterior appearance" neatly summarized the spirit of Shreve, Lamb & Harmon.[11] Yamasaki later worked in the firms of Wallace K. Harrison and Raymond Loewy. As World War II drew to a close, he movied to Detroit to take a job with the established firm of Smith, Hinchman, and Grylls. In 1949 he struck out on his own, and by 1962 he was the head of a firm with fifty employees.

In both New York and Detroit Yamasaki had faced the anti-Japanese hysteria spurred by World War II, a powerful reminder of his continuing outsider status. Yamasaki's father was fired from his shoe store job of over twenty-five years two days after the attack on Pearl Harbor, and his parents moved from Seattle to New York to live with Yamasaki to avoid internment on the west coast.[12] Life in a highly militarized society made it difficult to avoid the impact of the war on all aspects of private and public life. Advertisements in architecture journals during the war made every effort to link the profession to battles abroad. An advertisement for LCN Door Closers featured illustrations of tanks, bombers, artillery, and battleships and highlighted the various small parts manufactured for their construction by LCN. The text read: "Now 100% Small Parts Production for Victory"; the V was composed by the arm of a door closer, and seemed to fire off a plethora of small parts.[13] Linton Pencil Company ran ads that assured readers "In Defense Art-Guild Pencils Serve Best," atop an illustration of sharpened pencil points forming a protective enclosure around the Statue of Liberty.[14] Todd Combustion ran advertisements with illustration of an American bombers flying through the wreckage of flaming Nazi aircraft with the caption "Buzzards Get Brushed Off like Flies" emblazoned across it. The text read: "Far above the reach of man's eyes or ears, a flock of deadly eagles hovers over Naziland, laying eggs with uncanny accuracy. They are American-flown, American built long range bombers . . . and even the best of the German fighter planes that rise up to give battle are no match for these tough warbirds. They brush the buzzards off like so many flies . . . send them flaming back to the hell they came from."[15]

But while these ads referenced the shortages of war and carried disparaging language about the Nazis generally, ads with anti-Japanese sentiment were far more vicious. The role of racism in marshaling the American public during World War II was until recently, notes John Dower, "one of the great neglected subjects" of that era.[16] Just as the privations of wartime and the better life presumed to follow its conclusion were fodder for advertising, so too were racist sentiments. An advertisement for Timken Tapered Roller Bearings uses a photo of a ruby-cheeked woman of about thirty working at her station in a factory. Her demeanor and pose—focused on her labors, with modest make-up (lipstick) and dressed in simple, clean, sturdy worker's garb—recalls Rosie the Riveter and its iconic depiction of the American woman in terms simultaneously sexual, maternal, and chaste. The caption, in font second in size only to the name of the advertiser, reads, "Jap-Killing Machine." The text below explains, "Geraldine Maher doesn't look like a very belligerent person and she actually isn't one either, but her husband has just gone into the army and she likes to call the machine she operates at one of the Timken Bearing Plants 'her Jap-killing machine.'" The ad notes "Perhaps that is one reason why her daily production is running 20% above the average."[17]

Such anti-Japanese language was common during the war. Commenting on the combat film (a staple of wartime entertainment), Richard Slotkin notes, "Since Japanese faces figured more prominently than Germans in the first wave of visualizations of the enemy, an element of racial symbolism became an essential part of the combat film's symbolic code." The racist thought that permeated the anti-Japanese elements of popular culture drew its inspiration from "the language of American political culture" that was struggling to respond to Pearl Harbor. That attack on American forces by a non-white enemy "who had been stereotyped as racial and technological inferiors . . . went against the expectations ingrained in Americans by the racist imagery of our preferred mythology." "No comparable reversal of mythic expectations had occurred since Custer's Last Stand, and it was to the myth that the media reverted in their search for an explanatory model." By 1942 reports in *Life* magazine described battles on the Bataan peninsula as "a form of 'savage war'" where the "tactics resemble 'old-time Indian fighting.'" A result of this discourse was that the "imputation of savagery linked the Japanese to the oldest of our mythic race-enemies, the Indian."[18] In such an environment, anti-Japanese sentiment presented more than a barrier to entry into polite society. Yamasaki was coming into his own as an architect in an era of intense race prejudice that defined Japanese identity as savage and incapable of assimilating (peacefully or otherwise) into the cultural melting pot of the United States.

The social capital Yamasaki accumulated as an architect could not neutralize the bigotry of his fellow citizens. The manager of an apartment complex designed by Shreve, Lamb & Harmon refused to let Yamasaki rent an apartment there despite the fact that he had been one of its designers. On the subway in Manhattan one evening a fellow passenger grabbed Yamasaki by the collar, demanding to know whether he was "Chinese or Jap." When Yamasaki moved to Detroit he wanted to live in Grosse Point or Bloomfield Hills, choices well within his generous salary from Smith, Hinchman, and Grylls. As he later recalled, however, his realtor "told me in confidence that it was hopeless to try and buy a house in one of those areas. Though he wanted to sell me one, he said he would be driven out of the real estate association if he did so."[19]

It is not surprising in these circumstances that Yamasaki often couched his discussions of architecture and aesthetics in a rhetoric of beauty, spirituality, and peace—ideals far more appealing than the ugly reality around him. He criticized his own early St. Louis Airport Terminal, as lacking "the sense of order and serenity so necessary in buildings [in a society] too often fragmented and discordant."[20] In his autobiography he wrote that he wished to live life "more beautifully" and with more "gentility."[21] Beauty and gentility, however, are hardly the first words that come to mind when reviewing the bulk of Yamasaki's work from the 1950s through the 1970s. In his buildings of those decades he time and again attempted to enliven the façade of a basic built box with vaguely gothic or roman arches. These might be arrayed directly on the exterior walls, as with the Federal Science Pavilion (1962) in Seattle, or in a colonnade, as with the Woodrow Wilson School of Public Policy (1965) at Princeton, or in some combination, as with the Northwestern National Life Insurance Company (1964) in Minneapolis.

Charitably speaking, Yamasaki's work in this period might best be understood as an effort to develop beautiful and genteel architecture for programs and uses that were often paternalistic or banal iterations of corporate power: the Pruitt-Igoe housing projects (1950–54) in St. Louis, the headquarters of Michigan Consolidated Gas (1963) in Detroit, the IBM Office Building (1964) in Seattle, and the Manufacturers and Traders Trust Building (1967) in Buffalo. At times, Philip Nobel writes, Yamasaki's designs looked like "an attempt to weld a sort of sissy finesse to the broad shoulders of America commerce."[22] Nevertheless, the commissions brought fame enough to Yamasaki, who was featured on the cover of Time magazine in 1963.

No single project in Yamasaki's career was more a product of broad shouldered American commerce than the World Trade Center. The 10 million square feet the program called for was "more office space than existed in all of Houston, more than in Detroit or downtown Los Angeles," enough to fill 261 football fields.[23] From the start,

Figure 44. Yamasaki on the cover of *Time*, 1963. Reprinted by permission from Time Life Pictures, Time & Life Pictures Collection © Getty Images.

however, Yamasaki habitually described the project in abstract and emotional terms rather than the language of large-scale speculative architecture that the project was. Early in the design process he wrote that the World Trade Center should be "respectful" of its surroundings, and that the "great scope" of the project "demands a way to scale it to the human being so that . . . it will be inviting, friendly and humane."[24] The search for that "humane" scale led Yamasaki's office to produce 105 possible configurations, each to be studied and photographed set into a detailed 10-foot chipboard site model of Lower Manhattan from City Hall to the Battery. The struggle any architect would have with such an unwieldy program was amplified in Yamasaki's case because he did not instinctively design large. He wrote in his memoirs that if he were free of social and economic constraints, "I'd solve all my problems with one-story buildings."[25] When reviewing Yamasaki's portfolio, the Port Authority was particularly impressed by his

McGregor Memorial Conference Center at Wayne State University in Detroit, a two-story building.[26] Precisely how they expected him to make the transition from such a modest scale to 10 million square feet remains a mystery. For the Port Authority the form the World Trade Center would take was essentially a technical rather than aesthetic problem. Its public comments were couched in the language of public benefit—"the Trade Center will dramatically revitalize a drab and decaying section of Lower Manhattan"— but as a client the organization repeatedly asked the same question about each of the 105 design schemes: did it accommodate the "Program"?[27]

Of the myriad design schemes, Yamasaki eventually settled on a site plan composed of two towers set in a plaza surrounded by a collection of low buildings. The towers were disposed diagonally to each other, an arrangement Yamasaki liked because it allowed offices on all four sides of each tower to have expansive views. In plan it bore some resemblance to Mies van der Rohe's Lake Shore Drive apartments in Chicago, built between 1948 and 1951. But the Miesian elements of Yamasaki's design really were few. The high-rise towers in Mies's design were rectangles, allowing for variations in the façade between long and short axes. The long axes were perpendicular, with one tower pulled farther back from the street line, a move that heightened the visual tension between the two structures. Yamasaki's towers were squares and the façades of all four sides were identical. As a result, the arrangement was far less dramatic, producing an effect nearer to that of a single tower and its mirror image rather than two distinct towers set in relationship. In terms of scale the differences were overwhelming. The Lake Shore Drive apartments were just 26 stories tall; Yamasaki's early two-tower proposal, rejected by the Port Authority because it was 2 million feet short of the "Program," called for towers between 80 and 90 stories. Pushed by the Port Authority up to 110 stories to meet the voracious "Program," the towers were too tall to be meaningfully understood on the basis of their relationship to one another on the ground. While Mies's buildings could be viewed on the ground and in the sky at the same time, most people saw the twin towers (in photos or with their necks craned upward) surrounded by empty sky, removed from any context that would help make sense of their arrangement vis-à-vis one another.[28]

Each façade was clad in aluminum and divided by fifty-nine columns that, as they approached ground level, merged and formed a series of neo-Gothic arches. It was a fairly fussy arrangement, lampooned in the 1970s as "General Motors Gothic," "Moorish filigree," "outmoded [and] Victorian."[29] But if we examine a building with the idea that it can tell us something about the client who had it built, then these comments miss the point. David Rockefeller made his career as a banker, a person with a well-established faith in financial (not social or democratic) institutions as agents of economic innovation and growth and as tools of political influence. The Port Authority joined in Rockefeller's enthusiasm for remaking the landscape and life of Lower Manhattan by

Figure 45. 860–880 Lake Shore Drive. Yamasaki cited Mies's paired towers as one of his inspirations for the World Trade Center. Reprinted with permission from Ezra Stoller © Esto.

Figure 46. General Motors Gothic. Reprinted by permission of Albert Squillace © Esto.

Figure 47. Windows on the World, the restaurant atop the World Trade Center. Reprinted by permission from Ezra Stoller © Esto.

building a trade center to house the very sorts of institutions to which Rockefeller's Chase Manhattan Bank catered. In the late 1970s Rockefeller spoke of how the spread of capitalism united the globe into "one world, governed by the logical motive for profit." For those who, like Rockefeller, believed in a "universal church of money with its own curia," could there be a better place to worship than in Yamasaki's neo-Gothic twin cathedrals of commerce?[30] What more appropriate sacrament to the closing of a business deal than the toast at Windows on the World, with its view that suggested the rightfulness of wealth's claim over the landscape of Manhattan? Architecture critics who complained that the towers were distasteful were perhaps too quick to blame the architect and exculpate the clients. What could anyone expect from a church of money? After all, the impulses that motivated David Rockefeller and the Port Authority were hardly aesthetic. Yamasaki's design was a more adequate symbol of the banal corporatism (or General Motors-ness) of his clients than even Yamasaki might have cared to admit.

It was left to Yamasaki to offer some explanation of his design to the public in terms beyond development for the sake of development (the defense the Port Authority offered). The choice of two towers was favored because, as one architect on Yamasaki's team put it, it worked best "in terms of elegance . . . in terms of symbolism."[31] But what exactly did these two towers symbolize? In order to answer that question, Yamasaki turned to the now familiar cliché of world trade as a generator of world peace. The World Trade Center has "a bigger purpose than just to provide rooms for tenants," he said. "World trade means world peace . . . the World Trade Center is a living symbol of man's dedication to world peace."[32] If world peace and the gargantuan scale of the project caused some raised eyebrows, Yamasaki was ready to reassure the doubtful. In his memoirs, published a few years after the Twin Towers were completed, he wrote "I am happy I was able to design these very large buildings with the proper scale relationship so necessary to man . . . they are intended to give him a soaring feeling, imparting pride and a sense of nobility in his environment."[33] His tendency to describe the towers in such terms may be evidence of his own discomfort with the aesthetic solution he developed to house the "Program." It was his opinion that architecture in the mid-1960s had entered a period "confusion," and "anarchy" in which an "explosion of architectural ideas . . . indiscriminately gushed forth to fill the streets of our cities."[34]

In the midst of this aesthetic anarchy, Yamasaki developed a design that was not high modernist in the vein of the Seagram Building or Lever House (or even the Chase Manhattan Bank headquarters just down the street). Nor, despite historicist elements in their neo-Gothic detailing at the base or references to Arabic architecture at the crown, could the towers be called postmodern, particularly compared to more forceful (if ironic) deployments of historical forms in buildings like Philip Johnson's AT&T. The towers were built in the uncomfortable ideological and aesthetic borderland between the two movements. The design, rather than being energized by this mix, seems paralyzed, capable of making a few faint gestures to decorate the speculative boxes demanded by the "Program." In retrospect his clients didn't seem troubled by the design or particularly moved by it. For the Port Authority the index of the design's success was whether it accommodated the "Program"; style mattered largely to the extent that it had to be amenable to future tenants. In his memoirs, David Rockefeller has nothing to say about the appearance of the Twin Towers beyond their size. Minoru Yamasaki is not mentioned by name. This stands in contrast to Chase Manhattan Bank, whose appearance Rockefeller describes in some (albeit stiff) detail as "contemporary," before quoting positive reviews in a handful of magazines and newspapers. But then, Chase Manhattan had a large public relations effort to marshal, something the Port Authority did not.

The mismatch between the rhetoric and reality around the trade center was probably inevitable given that never before had a project of that size been forced onto the Manhattan grid. There was no precedent for altering the underlying geometry of the urban landscape to this degree. The mismatch between the language of developers, or architects, or politicians, and the reality of what is taking place on the ground continues at the site today. It is as difficult to imagine a way to reconcile that gulf between rhetoric and material reality at Ground Zero at present, as it was when the Twin Towers were built.

CONCLUSION
Into the Future

In the first days and weeks after the destruction of the twin towers, public sentiment about the buildings was far from fixed. Where the force of myth today has refined and narrowed the range of sentiments deemed acceptable to express about the building and site, such was far from the case at the end of 2001. The ambiguity of public sentiment that was part of the (now forgotten) history of the WTC found voice in comments that ranged far from the general tone of discourse surrounding Ground Zero today. Philippe de Montebello, director of the Metropolitan Museum of Art, called the ruin of the towers "in its own way, a masterpiece."[1] What so many elite critics had condemned as banal when it stood could by virtue of its destruction be called a masterpiece. De Montebello's critical assessment found a curious counterpart in the comments of those who lamented the loss of life, but not the loss of the buildings themselves. "If you could have lost the World Trade Center without the loss of life," said Jaquelin T. Robertson, former dean of the School of Architecture at the University of Virginia, "it would have been an incredible victory."[2] Others responded to the destruction more directly: "Thank goodness. At least it's not the Chrysler Building or the Empire State Building."[3]

Coursing through these judgments is an air of critical distinction, a tradition where acumen is displayed via condemnation more readily than by celebration. This discursive trend soon disappeared from discussions about the WTC. Instead, architects, critics, politicians, and a host of other figures of varying aesthetic authority rose to champion the buildings as objects of affection and symbols of broad American civic values. Vincent Scully, the eminent architectural historian at Yale, spoke of this seismic shift when he said: "As you know, very few of us really liked the World Trade Towers. . . . When they got hit all associations changed. All of the sudden, instead of looking inordinately tall, they looked heartbreaking. Now I love them."[4] Architect Daniel Libeskind, speaking about the ruins at Ground Zero, went much farther: "The foundations withstood the unimaginable trauma of the destruction, and stand as eloquent as the Constitution itself, asserting the durability of democracy and the value of individual

Figure 48. World Trade Center, 1999. Reprinted by permission of David Sundberg © Esto.

life."[5] Viewed in the light of today, an image of King Kong (from the 1976 remake) lying at the base of the Twin Towers is one of surprising sorrow and lamentation. The gulf between the emotional resonance of this image now and the cliché it seemed at the time of its release suggests the depth of our retroactive reinterpretation of the buildings and their site.

The destruction of the twin towers curiously wrenched them from the grip of history. The end of their physical presence on earth could be seen as a call for reflection and examination of their history and impact on the urban landscape. It would have been an appropriate moment to try to understand the buildings' historical origins and the complexities inherent in their existence—as figures in the landscape with their own charms and failures rather than isolated objects of reverence stripped of their past. Instead, as the process of mythmaking took hold, something quite different happened. Rather than looking carefully at the towers in an effort to consider why they were such an inviting target for terrorists, politicians, critics, and the general public comforted themselves by defining the WTC in terms that appealed to emotions. Such efforts com-

Figure 49. King Kong felled at the base of the Twin Towers. Reprinted by permission from Paramount Pictures, Hulton Archive © Getty Images.

ported with a portrayal of the world that replaced complexity and contradiction with tales of heroics and glory, mythologizing the WTC in the process.

As we have already seen, the collapse of the twin towers motivated a fresh outpouring of affection for older figures in the Manhattan skyline. Sharon Zukin, reflecting on 9/11, wrote of New Yorkers, "We find comfort in the old-fashioned . . . the Empire State Building."[6] Her views were echoed in the popular press. One piece in the *New York Times* put it: "city residents, traumatized by the collapse of the trade center and the horrific loss of life, seem increasingly attached to the Empire State."[7] In a similar vein, a poster produced after 9/11 showed the Empire State Building weeping at the site of the Twin Towers. This skyscraper, with all its own curious history, once again carried the frisson of awe, danger, and sorrow. The tallest building in New York City once again, its significance resonated as forcefully as it had in the 1930s, but this time for very different reasons. The architecture of the building once again proved itself amenable to a complex range of sentiments. Both the ease with which the World Trade Center's history was elided in the wake of its destruction and the resurrection of attachment to the Empire State Building merit consideration by historians. The "moment of upheaval" of 9/11, Max Page reminds us, should force us to reexamine how the city's "history has been written."[8]

Figure 50. The Empire State Building weeping over the ruins of the World Trade Center. Courtesy of the artist, Peter Kruper, and the Library of Congress.

Richard Slotkin notes, "A people unaware of its myths is likely to continue living by them, though the world around that people may change and demand changes in their psychology, their world view, their ethics, and their institutions."[9] Surely we need to be aware as well of the history and meaning of the buildings around us, for they too shape our daily lives and our conception of self, city, and nation. We certainly have not seen the last transformation of opinion about these buildings. They are, after all, bookends to an era of extraordinary change in American culture, politics, and society. Their continued popularity (as both objects and memories) suggests they resonate with critics and popular audiences alike. Seventy years separate the opening of the Empire State Building and the collapse of the twin towers. In that space and time modern architecture in the United States underwent a dramatic transformation. In order to appreciate fully the history that precedes us and the potential of the future that lies ahead, we must understand how the spheres of politics and culture in the form of architecture are intertwined. This study hopefully has been a part of such an inquiry.

EPILOGUE

The skyscraper's capacity to attract suitors seems impervious to time. The Empire State Building, now nearly eighty years old, remains one of the city's most popular destinations. In the years since Raskob and Pierre du Pont ceded their stake in the building it has been the object of intense bidding wars among a number of real estate barons. Harry Helmsley (today probably best remembered as the husband of Leona Helmsley, who was convicted of tax evasion and on her death bequeathed $12 million to her pet Maltese, Trouble), Lawrence Wien, Donald Trump, and even a reputed boss of the Japanese underworld all claimed full or partial ownership of the building at one time or another. Seagram sold its eponymous headquarters in 1979 to the massive TIAA-CREF pension fund. In 2000 the building was purchased by RFR Holdings (now RFR Realty, LLC), a German real estate investment firm that also presently owns Lever House. Lease rates for the Seagram Building are generally higher than for neighboring Class A office space, as the building remains prized in the New York market. Philip Johnson's iconic Brasserie was recently given a glossy and somewhat ill-considered updating by Diller + Scofidio, but nevertheless it is still a well-trafficked destination, as is the Four Seasons. Successive generations of architects, critics, and real estate mavens in the making have responded to the lure of these buildings, seeing their own ambitions materialized in them.

Of course the ambitions behind the construction of a skyscraper and the desire for its possession are generally as outsized as the building itself. Rebuilding the World Trade Center site, now in its seventh year, rather than scaling down the ambitions of the twin towers (and the rhetoric that accompanied them) is a project of nearly inconceivable proportions. Once completed, this chunk of Lower Manhattan will have perhaps half a dozen skyscrapers with nearly as much office space among them as downtown Atlanta.[1]

But it is not exactly the proportions and scale of construction that are so challenging to comprehend. Making sense of this massive expenditure of labor, time, and capital is, a challenge because size alone does not provide symbolic heft. The Empire State Building carried the title tallest building in the world for more than four decades; for much of the first two decades, as it sat largely empty and hemorrhaging cash, its height was its only superlative. In the past twenty years, however, the title of world's tallest has ping-ponged around the globe. The public eye is jaded to the shock of vastness alone.

Figure 51. World Trade Center Tribute in Light, 2002. Reprinted by permission of David Sundberg © Esto.

Likewise, the sixteen acres of the WTC now seem a less dramatic undertaking than in the 1960s, and it takes more than a grand scale to give an urban project meaning. The recently completed 138-acre redevelopment of a steel mill at Atlantic Station in Atlanta is one of the largest urban redevelopment projects in the nation. Yet even with 6 million square feet of Class A office space, 2 million feet of retail space, 5,000 residential units, 1,000 hotel rooms, 11 acres of parks, and a parking structure underneath it all holding 15,000 cars, Atlantic Station is as mute as any corporate office block or suburban cul-de-sac. Grand as its ambitions may be, those are perhaps most visible in the ledger books, not in its architecture and urban design. In an effort to assign significance,

identity, meaning, something, to the project, a concrete simulacrum of a triumphal arch was erected at Atlantic Station. Overlooking a water retention pond, the arch is a marker of the absence of architectural significance, not its presence.

We should keep in mind that rebuilding the WTC site is but one of many significant construction projects across the city of New York. In 2008, prior to the spectacular meltdown of the financial markets and the recession that followed, $30 billion of investment capital was poised to wash across the city with creative destruction in its wake.[2] The building and buying booms of the first decade of the twenty-first century recall the incessant hum of speculative activity that in the 1920s remade whole portions of the city.

In the past decade residential towers went up at such a clip that architects who formerly designed mostly at the modest domestic scale were charged with multi-million-dollar condominium towers. Just as the design possibilities for the corporate office tower in the 1960s slowly narrowed to variations on a type, the condo towers of the early years of the twenty-first century adopted the once maligned glass box as "the undisputed architectural aesthetic of the moment."[3] The glass curtain wall skyscraper, once indisputably the façade of business and commerce, is now a symbol of a particular kind of urban domesticity.

The wave of construction is also a wave of reconstruction, renovation, and expansion. Existing institutions—Lincoln Center, the Museum of Modern Art—are expanding up and out. Even the venerable Gray Lady, the New York Times, had its headquarters modernized and a sleek, new façade put in place. Edward Durrell Stone's lollipop tower on Columbus Circle is undergoing a transformation, albeit after a heated dispute over the preservation of Stone's original and once little-loved façade. If the ferocious pace of construction was a reminder of the 1920s, so too were many of the disputes that shaped the public's response to the rebuilding of their city. As the Empire State Building rose with unprecedented speed, many wondered whether the safety of labor and the general public was subsumed by the hunger for profit. Eighty years later there are over 4,200 buildings under construction in New York City, most a great deal smaller than the Empire State Building, but a still occasion for pause.[4]

In a particularly gruesome three-month period in 2008, nine people were killed and a dozen injured in two separate tower crane collapses on the East Side of Manhattan. In that time slot, the city's chief crane inspector was arrested on charges of accepting bribes, and a second inspector was charged with filing false inspection reports.[5] These were followed by the arrest of an engineer for filing fraudulent plans with the Department of Buildings and the indictment of the owner of the site for manslaughter following the death of a construction worker.[6] In the first half of 2008 fifteen people died in construction accidents, three more than in all of 2007. Construction in the second half of 2008 slowed substantially, and likely will take years to rebound. The contraction in the building market cannot obscure, however, the failures of regulation during the boom years. Leading up to 2008, construction in the city grew steadily by nearly 20 per year. In spite of this, the number of building inspectors on the city payroll was about half what it was a decade ago.[7] At the World Trade Center site in 2007, where 343 firefighters died on September 11, two firefighters were killed when the Deutsche Bank Building caught fire during preparations for its demolition. The emergency fire safety systems in the building, in spite of daily inspections by various municipal and state agencies, were rendered inoperable through a combination of error and incompetence.[8] It is all another reminder of the often lopsided balance between the broader public good and the need for speed, driven by the inexorable calculus of profit and loss, in construction.

The rebuilding of the WTC site began with the stated goals of producing architecture worthy of "sacred ground." Reality set in during the design selection process as the imaginative and thoughtful was jettisoned in favor of the ordinary and the banal. In spite of this, a chorus of voices insisted that the new World Trade Center would be a symbol of something more than mere building. This is, of course, nothing new. Political agendas and social aspirations raised the height of the Empire State Building, and the WTC was built on a foundation of political power. The reconstruction of the site was quickly, loudly, and visibly adopted as a cause by politicians across the land including two mayors of New York City, two governors of New York, and the president of the United States. In speeches about the future of the site, these politicians defined rebuilding as a symbolic act—a way of distinguishing between winners and losers in the fight against terrorism. Rhetoric aside, the reconstruction of the site continued to be an end in itself as well as the means to other distinct and often vaguely articulated ends. It remains to be seen whether any of these politicians successfully yoked their reputations and aspirations to rebuilding. One wonders, at the very least, what Al Smith and John Raskob would say to those who cast their political lot in with the life (and death) of a skyscraper.

Of course, the skyscraper is a potent (if often misguided) tool for political symbolism because we project so many of our collective anxieties, fears, dreams, and desires on it. The periodic lamentations that accompany the sale of a landmark skyscraper to foreign investors is one index of these passions. A slew of high profile purchases by Japanese firms in the 1980s, most notably the sale of Rockefeller Center to Mitsubishi Estates, set off a protectionist outcry. The sale of the General Motors Building for $2.8 billion in June 2008 to a consortium financed by investors from Dubai, Kuwait, and Qatar, along with the purchase of a 90 percent stake in the Chrysler Building by an investment arm of the government of Abu Dhabi, have raised similar sentiments. These multi-billion-dollar investments are no outliers; they come on the heels of $4.4 billion spent by Middle Eastern investors on New York City real estate in 2007. German and Middle Eastern funds "accounted for $22 billion of the $30.2 billion invested by foreign entities over the past seven years."[9] The wave of capital flowing through the city in search of investment and growth is most visible in the cranes and construction sites. Nevertheless, we should also see the art deco flourishes of the Chrysler Building and the taut, moderne lines of the GM Building not as icons of the past, but standing for the global capital flows that define the present. As wealth is reorganized around the globe, the skyscraper, even one more than seventy years old, remains its preferred urban expression.

Critics accused Yamasaki's twin towers of being "mute," of failing to communicate their purpose for being or place in the world. The disputes and disappointments surrounding the design of the Freedom Tower suggest that too much ideological freight loaded onto a tall building may produce a design that pleases few and disappoints many. The shift in nomenclature alone is illustrative. Yamasaki continually insisted that his twin towers were symbols of world peace, but no one ever suggested that their name baldly made that claim. The title Freedom Tower burdens the structure with a purpose and identity so vast and complex that hardly any three-dimensional form can satisfy expectations. Of the hundreds of proposals for rebuilding the WTC site, we end up years later with a bland corporate tower whose major concession to a sense of place is that it is reinforced like a bunker or outpost on the frontier. Whatever one might imagine the Freedom Tower offering, it probably is not expensive office space and cube farms.

It may be that the reason more people have not balked at the title of the Freedom Tower is that the skyscraper has over the past half century been linked so successfully in the public mind with any number of grand and abstract values beyond the provision of mundane office space. Of course, the ideological freighting of the tall building is also a retrospective act. Looking back at the history of skyscrapers, especially the three examined here, one is struck time and time again by their adoption in popular culture via advertising, movies, and news reports. In the course of researching this book, I found the WTC in advertisements for items as varied as asbestos insulation, cigarettes, and air travel. These were all published in mainstream magazines and can easily be found in the collection of any library. Nevertheless, most of the companies that ran the advertisements were less than enthusiastic about giving permission to reprint the material in question. One company, Pakistani Airlines (PIA), was especially adamant, going so far as to claim that reprinting its 1979 ad featuring the twin towers would "cause severe harm to PIA and our country's good name."[10]

The skyscraper continues to serve as a global barometer of urbanization and the accumulation of wealth and power. A number of ideologically freighted skyscraper projects (Burj Dubai by SOM, Taipei 101 by C. Y. Lee & Partners, Foster's Swiss Re, CCTV Headquarters by OMA, RMJM's Gazprom Tower) located in centers of global capitalism push these associations, as well as formal and tectonic boundaries, even farther. The patterns of financing and patronage that support such projects, however, are often less clearly articulated, and there is attendant ambiguity about the specific social, cultural, and economic agendas for their construction. So too are the labor conditions under which they are built and the larger political aims for their cities and societies. These increasingly varied projects (and the increasingly varied locales in which they rise) serve to underline the importance of investigating the skyscraper not only as an aesthetic object but also as a material expression of the ways wealth and power reorganize the urban landscape. The questions that cry out to be answered when examining these projects are not how they look, but to what ends they were built.

Indeed the explosion of building projects in Asia, the Middle East, and many of the decidedly less democratic nations of the former Soviet Union designed by high-profile architects raises issues of ethics and responsibility many thought buried by the purported postmodernist rejection of modernism's social aspirations. The question resonates more at present than in the past several decades in part because clients around the globe with ambiguous political scruples now prefer their monumental designs modern. The autocratic tendency toward "pachyderm neoclassicism"—as one critic calls it—has been supplanted by the taste for hybrid, grand, and vaguely corporate modernism.[11] Architects whose early careers were defined by theory-laden projects that rarely left the page are hot commodities in locales that twenty years ago would have been considered architectural backwaters.

One such designer, Daniel Libeskind, recently announced that he would not accept commissions for projects in China, stating "I won't work for totalitarian regimes."[12] How precisely he would draw the line between acceptably authoritarian (such as Russia, where he submitted a design proposal for the Gazprom Tower) and totalitarian he left vague. Nevertheless, Libeskind's comments sparked a lively debate harking back to questions raised about Minoru Yamasaki's work at the World Trade Center, Mies's largely mute response to the rise of the Nazis in Germany while he was head of the Bauhaus, and even Shreve, Lamb & Harmon's work on a speculative skyscraper project controlled by two of the wealthiest men in the nation in the midst of the Great Depression. What is architecture's proper relationship to power? Under what conditions are architects responsible for the social, political, environmental, or economic impact of their work? To whom are architects ultimately responsible? In the 1960s Yamasaki publicly suggested that world trade paved the way for world peace—an argument used to justify not only the twin towers but the general political and economic demands of globalization in the postwar era. The cost and benefits to the public of the WTC are open to debate, but certainly such considerations are as critical now as ever in light of the many monumental projects—skyscraper and otherwise—undertaken in the past few years. Foster & Partners' work on a 500-foot "entertainment center" in Kazakhstan, Zaha Hadid's Heydar Aliyev Cultural Centre in Azerbaijan, and OMA's Waterfront City in Dubai are just a few of many projects for client governments that have, at best, a highly flexible definition of democracy and individual freedom. The Port Authority is hardly a paragon of openness and transparency, but it is not Azerbaijan.

Of course, the wealth behind these projects in distant locales is also the wealth buying up skyscrapers in New York. The nascent global corporate economy reflected in the

Chrysler Building has matured. Capital circumnavigates the globe, unfettered by the national boundaries and border crossing regulations that encumber persons as they move from place to place, but it returns time and time again to roost in the tall buildings so closely associated with wealth and power. Indeed, wherever the shifts in wealth, corporate structure, architectural taste, technological innovation, and developments in urbanization take us, they take us to the skyscraper.

NOTES

Introduction: Narratives of the Built Environment: Architecture, Ideology, and Skyscrapers

Epigraphs: Karl Marx, *The Eighteenth Brumaire of Louis Bonaparte* (New York: International Publishers, 1994), 15; Andrei Codrescu, *The Hole in the Flag: A Romanian Exile's Story of Return and Revolution* (New York: Avon, 1991), 15–16.

1. John D. Bell, *The Bulgarian Communist Party from Blagoev to Zhivkov* (Stanford, Calif.: Hoover Press, 1986), x.

2. Atanas Slavov, *The "Thaw" in Bulgarian Literature* (New York: Columbia University Press, 1981), 124.

3. Georgi Markov, *Zodochni Reportazhi za Bulgariia* (Zurich: Fond Georgi Markov, 1980), vol. 1, 312.

4. Generally speaking, specific kinds of movies and programming from the West were shown with some regularity in Bulgaria. Like *The Flintstones*, however, these were expected to depict the negative consequences of life under a capitalist regime.

5. Vladimir Topechnarov, ed., *Sofia* (Sofia: Sofia Press, 1979), 220–21. This was published on the "Occasion of Sofia's 100th Anniversary as the Nation's Capital and the 1300th Anniversary of the Bulgarian State."

6. Yordan S. Tangurov, ed., *The Architecture of Modern Bulgaria* (Sofia: Technika State Publishing House, 1972), 10.

7. Dinu C. Giurescu, *The Razing of Romania's Past: International Preservation Report* (Washington, D.C.: U.S. Committee, International Council on Monuments and Sites, 1989), ii.

8. Codrescu, *The Hole in the Flag*, 20.

9. Giurescu, *The Razing of Romania's Past*, 48.

10. Codrescu, *The Hole in the Flag*, 21.

11. Dana Harhoiu, quoted in Luminita Machedon and Ernie Scoffham, *Romanian Modernism: The Architecture of Bucharest, 1920–1940* (Cambridge, Mass.: MIT Press, 1999), 320.

12. Augustin Ioan, quoted in Scott Heller, "East Meets West in Art History," *Chronicle of Higher Education* 45, 49 (August 13, 1999): A18–A19.

13. Hilde Heynen, *Architecture and Modernity* (Cambridge, Mass.: MIT Press, 1999), 7.

14. Alan Balfour, *Berlin: The Politics of Order* (New York: Rizzoli, 1990), 244.

15. Walter Benjamin, "Surrealism," reprinted in Walter Benjamin, *Reflections: Essays, Aphorisms, Autobiographical Writings* (New York: Schocken, 1986), 183.

16. Gwendolyn Wright, *Building the Dream: A Social History of Housing in America* (New York: Pantheon, 1981), xvi; Max Page, *The Creative Destruction of Manhattan, 1900–1940* (Chicago: University of Chicago Press, 1999), 8; Carol Willis, *Form Follows Finance: Skyscrapers and Skylines in New York and Chicago* (New York: Princeton Architectural Press, 1995), 7.

17. Joseph Siry, *The Chicago Auditorium Building: Adler and Sullivan's Architecture and the City* (Chicago: University of Chicago Press, 2002), 2.

18. William Faulkner, *Requiem for a Nun*, Act I, Scene III, Gavin Stevens to Temple Drake Stevens.

19. Neil Harris, *Building Lives: Constructing Rites and Passages* (New Haven, Conn.: Yale University Press, 1999), 161–66.

20. Dorothy Habel, *The Urban Development of Rome in the Age of Alexander VII* (Cambridge: Cambridge University Press, 2002), 1.

21. Sandy Isenstadt, "Richard Neutra and the Psychology of Architectural Consumption," in *Anxious Modernisms: Experimentation in Postwar Architectural Culture*, ed. Sarah Williams Goldhagen and Réjean Legault (Montreal: Canadian Centre for Architecture and Massachusetts Institute of Technology, 2000), 100.

22. Harris, *Building Lives*, 164.

23. Eric Foner, *Free Soil, Free Labor, Free Men: The Ideology of the Republican Party Before the Civil War* (Oxford and New York: Oxford University Press, 1995), 4.

24. Hilde Heynen, *Architecture and Modernity* (Cambridge, Mass.: MIT Press, 1999), 5–6.

25. Sharon Zukin, *Landscapes of Power: From Detroit to Disney World* (Berkeley: University of California Press, 1991), 39.

26. Alice Friedman, *Women and the Making of the Modern House: A Social and Architectural History* (New York: Harry Abrams, 1998).

27. Nancy Stieber, *Housing Design and Society in Amsterdam: Reconfiguring Urban Order and Identity, 1900–1920* (Chicago: University of Chicago Press, 1998), 3.

28. Ibid., 4.

29. Annabel Jane Wharton, *Building the Cold War: Hilton International Hotels and Modern Architecture* (Chicago: University of Chicago Press, 2001), 7.

30. Ibid., 8.

31. Henry-Russell Hitchcock and Arthur Drexler, eds., *Built in the USA: Post-War Architecture* (New York: Simon and Schuster, 1952), 10.

32. Wharton, *Building the Cold War*, 11.

Chapter 1. Building, Money, and Power

Epigraph: Announcement in *Architectural Record* (February 1932): 38.

1. Louis Sullivan, "The Tall Office Building Artistically Considered," March 1896, in Sullivan, *Kindergarten Chats and Other Writings* (New York: Wittenborn, Schultz, 1947).

2. Sarah Bradford Landau and Carl Condit, *Rise of the New York Skyscraper, 1865–1913* (New Haven, Conn.: Yale University Press, 1996). On the history of tall office buildings and skyscrapers in the Unites States, see Rosemarie Haag Bletter, "The Invention of the Skyscraper: Notes on Its Diverse Histories," *Assemblage* 2 (February 1987); Daniel Bluestone, *Constructing Chicago* (New Haven, Conn.: Yale University Press, 1991); Daniel Bluestone, "Preservation and Renewal in Postwar Chicago," *Journal of the Society of Architectural Historians* 47 (May 1994): 210–23; Carl Condit, *The Rise of the Skyscraper* (Chicago: University of Chicago Press, 1952); Gunter Gad and Deryck Holdsworth, "Corporate Capitalism and the Emergence of the High-Rise Office Building," *Urban Geography* 8, 3 (1987); Paul Goldberger, *The Skyscraper* (New York: Knopf, 1981); Ada Louise Huxtable, *The Tall Building Artistically Reconsidered* (New York: Pantheon, 1984); Thomas A. P. van Leeuwen, *The Skyward Trend of Thought: The Metaphysics of the American Skyscraper* (Cambridge, Mass.: MIT Press, 1986); Cervin Robinson and Rosemarie Haag Bletter, *Skyscraper Style: Art Deco New York* (New York: Oxford University Press, 1975); Robert A. M. Stern, Gregory Gilmartin, and Thomas Mellins, *New York 1930: Architecture and Urbanism Between the Two World Wars* (New York: Rizzoli, 1987); Robert A. M. Stern, Thomas Mellins, and David Fishman, *New York 1960: Architecture and Urbanism Between the Second World War and the Bicentennial* (New York: Rizzoli, 1995); Urban Land Institute, *Tall Office Buildings in the United States* (Washington, D.C.: Urban Land Institute, 1984); David Ward and Oliver Zunz, *The Landscape of Modernity* (New York: Russell Sage, 1992); Carol Willis, *Form Follows Finance: Skyscrapers and Skylines in New York and Chicago* (New York: Princeton Architectural Press, 1995). Recent works elaborating on the role

of money, ambition, and the desire for power along with civic ideals and political influence in shaping the urban skyline include Mona Domosh, *Invented Cities: The Creation of Landscape in Nineteenth-Century New York and Boston* (New Haven, Conn.: Yale University Press, 1996); Max Page, *The Creative Destruction of Manhattan, 1900–1940* (Chicago: University of Chicago Press, 1999); Katherine Solomonson, *The Chicago Tribune Tower Competition: Skyscraper Design and Cultural Change in the 1920s* (Cambridge: Cambridge University Press, 2001); John Stamper, *Chicago's North Michigan Avenue: Planning and Development, 1900–1930* (Chicago: University of Chicago Press, 1991); Lawrence Vale, *Architecture, Power, and National Identity* (New Haven, Conn.: Yale University Press, 1992).

3. Solomonson, *The Chicago Tribune Tower Competition*, 233.

4. Cass Gilbert, "The Financial Importance of Rapid Building," *Engineering Record* 41 (30 June 1900): 624.

5. William R. Taylor, *In Pursuit of Gotham: Culture and Commerce in New York* (Oxford: Oxford University Press, 1992), 12.

6. Stern et al., *New York 1930*, 510.

7. Ibid., 589.

8. Ibid.

9. Deborah Pokinski, *The Development of the American Modern Style* (Ann Arbor, Mich.: UMI Research Press, 1984), 58.

10. Ibid. In particular, Sigfried Giedion, *Space, Time, and Architecture: The Growth of a New Tradition* (Cambridge, Mass.: Harvard University Press, 1941) advanced the view that American architecture was in essence stifled between 1893 (the Columbian Exposition) and the early 1930s (when the Modern Architecture: International Exhibition opened at MoMA).

11. "Everybody Ought to Be Rich: An Interview with John J. Raskob," *Ladies Home Journal* (August 1929): 9, 36.

12. Richard Slotkin, *Gunfighter Nation: The Myth of the Frontier in Twentieth-Century America* (New York: HarperCollins, 1992), 22.

13. The details of the landmark battle over the Empire State Building that involved Donald Trump, Leona Helmsley, a billionaire reputedly from the Japanese underworld, and a host of other shady characters are laid out in Mitchell Pacelle's *Empire: A Tale of Obsession, Betrayal, and the Battle for an American Icon* (New York: Wiley, 2001). The Jack Brod quotation is from 308.

14. David Scobey, *Empire City: The Making and Meaning of the New York City Landscape* (Philadelphia: Temple University Press, 2002), 11.

15. Pokinski, *The Development of the American Modern Style*, 58.

16. The Empire State Building was known far and wide. Architectural historian Jean-Louis Cohen writes of its influence as far away as Stalin's Soviet Union: "[Boris] Iofan's Palace of the Soviets project clearly invoked the Empire State Building"; see *Scenes from the World to Come: European Architecture and the American Challenge, 1893–1960* (Paris: Flammarion/ Montreal: Canadian Centre for Architecture, 1995), 151. Other historians have focused on narrower aspects of the building. William J. R. Curtis restricts his analysis to noting that while the building "enclosed a vertical city of functions . . . the visual solution lacked the subtlety of the Chrysler Building"; see Curtis, *Modern Architecture Since 1900* (London: Phaidon, 1996), 227. Leland Roth, in his history of American architecture, states that the importance of the Empire State "lies in the solution to hundreds of logistical problems created in raising a building of eighty-five stories"; see Roth, *A Concise History of American Architecture* (New York: Harper and Row, 1980), 246. Kenneth Frampton, in his history of modern architecture, ignores the Empire State Building entirely, also choosing instead to write about the "remarkable" Chrysler Building; see Frampton, *Modern Architecture: A Critical History* (London: Thames and Hudson, 1992), 222–23.

17. Stern et al., *New York 1930*, 610–15.

18. Dell Upton, *Architecture in the United States* (Oxford: Oxford University Press, 1998), 215.

19. Willis, *Form Follows Finance*.

20. Ibid., 10.

21. Ibid., 95.

22. Pacelle, *Empire*, 2.

23. "Letter from Pierre S. du Pont to Hugh Drum, May 21, 1948," LMSS 229-15, Box 186, Hagley Museum and Library, Wilmington, Delaware.

24. See Upton, *Architecture in the United States*, 264–65.

25. According to Robert Caro, during Smith's terms as governor he "persuaded the state's voters to pass referenda allocating not only $15,000,000 for parks and $50,000,000 for hospitals but also $300,000,000 for grade-crossing elimination and $100,000,000 for prisons, mental institutions, and other public works"; see Caro, *The Power Broker: Robert Moses and the Fall of New York* (New York: Vintage, 1974), 265.

26. John J. Raskob was a man of wealth, an influential financier who managed both General Motors and Du Pont company investments, and a powerful political figure who led the Democratic party. Yet there is relatively little historical and biographical material available about him. The definitive account of his life and business activities remains to be written. The best biography available is Roy H. Lopata, "John J. Raskob: A Conservative Businessman in the Age of Roosevelt" (Ph.D. dissertation, University of Delaware, 1975); see also Henry F. Pringle, "John J. Raskob: A Portrait," *Outlook* (22 August 1928): 645–49, 678.

27. Alfred Chandler, Jr., and Stephen Salsbury, *Pierre S. du Pont and the Making of the Modern Corporation* (New York: Harper and Row, 1971), 39.

28. Joseph Frazier Wall, *Alfred I. du Pont: The Man and His Family* (New York: Oxford University Press, 1990), 546.

29. Douglas Craig, *After Wilson: The Struggle for the Democratic Party, 1920–1934* (Chapel Hill: University of North Carolina Press, 1992), 136–37.

30. Ibid.

31. It was on Raskob's advice that du Pont purchased 2,000 shares of General Motors common stock (at $82/share) in February 1914. Raskob had bought 500 shares himself and convinced du Pont that the shares of the young corporation would double in value in a year's time. He wasn't quite right: by December 1915, GM shares were selling at $558; see Chandler and Salsbury, *Pierre S. du Pont and the Making of the Modern Corporation*, 433–36.

32. Chandler refers to Raskob as "a brilliant financier"; see Chandler and Salsbury, *Pierre S. du Pont and the Making of the Modern Corporation*, 490.

33. Raskob was by the mid-1920s a power-broker in the New York Irish community. His deposit in 1926 of over $3 million in Du Pont and GM money in the Irish-dominated New York County Trust Company (run by James J. Riordan, a friend of Al Smith's), for instance, made Raskob "a major force in the Irish-Catholic Community in New York City." See John Tauranac, *The Empire State Building: The Making of a Landmark* (New York: Scribner, 1995), 91–92.

34. The Association was founded in 1919 by William H. Stayton, a former officer in the Navy. In addition to Raskob, Pierre S., and his brother Irénée, prominent business figures associated with the Association included Charles Sabin, chairman of the New York Guarantee Company; James Wadsworth, New York State Republican senator; and Major Henry H. Curran, Democratic politician and associate of Al Smith.

35. Chandler and Salsbury, *Pierre S. du Pont and the Making of the Modern Corporation*, 584–85.

36. Ibid.

37. Ibid.

38. See Robert F. Burk, *The Corporate State and the Broker State: The Du Ponts and American National Politics, 1925–1940* (Cambridge, Mass.: Harvard University Press, 1990), 9.

39. Quoted in Tauranac, *The Empire State Building*, 92–93.

40. The DuPont Company is capitalized, the family name du Pont is not.

41. See Gerard Colby, *Du Pont Dynasty* (Secaucus, N.J.: Lyle Stuart, 1984), 106.

42. Burk, *The Corporate State and the Broker State*, 5.

43. Chandler and Salsbury, *Pierre S. du Pont and the Making of the Modern Corporation*, 54–56.

44. Ibid., ix–xx.

45. William H. Carr, *The du Ponts of Delaware* (New York: Dodd, Mead, 1964), 127.

46. Chandler and Salsbury, *Pierre S. du Pont and the Making of the Modern Corporation*, 430.

47. See Graham D. Taylor and Patricia Sudnik, *Du Pont and the International Chemical Industry* (Boston: Twayne, 1984), 30–34 and Burk, *The Corporate State and the Broker State*, 21.

48. Chandler and Salsbury, *Pierre S. du Pont and the Making of the Modern Corporation*, 430 and Table 5, Appendix.

49. See Carr, *The du Ponts of Delaware*, 298–302. This move toward purchasing interests in other industries continued for several decades. Steel, aviation, rubber, pigments, and dyes were all among the holdings acquired by the DuPont corporation throughout the 1920s and 1930s.

50. Pierre purchased the estate in 1906. The park, originally named Peirce's Park, had traditionally been open to the public, a tradition Pierre continued. Now officially Longwood Gardens, It is located near Kennett Square, Pennsylvania, only a short distance from the Delaware border.

51. Craig, *After Wilson*, 134.

52. John K. Winkler, *The Du Pont Dynasty* (Baltimore: Reynal and Hitchcock, 1935), 133.

53. Colby, *Du Pont Dynasty*, 104.

54. Alfred Chandler describes Raskob as an "industrial imperialist" in *Strategy and Structure: Chapters in the History of Industrial Enterprise* (Cambridge, Mass.: MIT Press, 1962), 124; Craig describes the "industrial federalism" of the Du Pont company in *After Wilson*, 134.

55. Robert A. Slayton, *Empire Statesman: The Rise and Redemption of Al Smith* (New York: Free Press, 2001), xv.

56. Some examples of Smith's political writings from the later years of his life are collected in *The Citizen and His Government* (New York: Harper and Row, 1935).

57. Slayton, *Empire Statesman*, ix.

58. James A. Foley, former president of the Society of the Friendly Sons of St. Patrick, eulogized Smith at the November 20, 1944, meeting of the Society. His speech and the addresses of Al Smith to the Society are reprinted in *Addresses of Alfred E. Smith Delivered at the Meetings of the Society of the Friendly Sons of St. Patrick, 1922–1944* (New York: Society of the Friendly Sons of St. Patrick, 1945).

59. Slayton, *Empire Statesman*, 11. Slayton notes that Smith's paternal ancestors were most likely German and Italian. The Irish ancestry was all on his mother's side of the family.

60. See Caro, *The Power Broker*, 116–18.

61. See Oscar Handlin, *Al Smith and His America* (Boston: Little, Brown, 1958), 18–26.

62. See Slayton, *Empire Statesman*, 50–69.

63. A less favorable account of Smith's rise to power in politics can be found in William H. Allen, *Al Smith's Tammany Hall: Champion Political Vampire* (New York: Institute for Public Service, 1928).

64. Slayton, *Empire Statesman*, 80.

65. The Triangle Shirtwaist Company occupied the top three floors of the ten-story (and prophetically named) Asch Building at 22 Washington Place.

66. For a more complete history of the Triangle Shirtwaist Company and the fire, see Corinne Naden, *The Triangle Shirtwaist Fire, March 25, 1911* (New York: Harper and Row, 1971) and Leon Stein, *The Triangle Fire* (Philadelphia: Lippincott, 1962).

67. Slayton, *Empire Statesman*, 94.

68. Ibid., 95.

69. Smith took part in the impeachment of Governor Al Sulzer, a Tammany-backed candidate for the office who became (against the wishes of the Hall) a reformer once he gained office. See Slayton, *Empire Statesman*, 101–4.

70. Over 70 percent of Irish, 63 percent of Jewish, and 52 percent of Italian voters cast their ballots for Smith, testifying to his broad appeal among immigrant communities in the city. See Slayton, *Empire Statesman*, 114.

71. See Henry Pringle, *Alfred E. Smith* (New York: Macy-Massius, 1927), 227 and Slayton, *Empire Statesman*, 112.

72. See Paula Eldot, *Governor Alfred E. Smith: The Politician as Reformer* (New York: Garland, 1983); Slayton, *Empire Statesman*, 116–21; Alfred E. Smith, *Up to Now* (New York: Viking, 1929). Women gained the right to vote in New York State in 1917.

73. See Caro, *The Power Broker*, 5.

74. A more detailed analysis of Smith's political career throughout the 1920s can be found in Donn C. Neal, *The World Beyond the Hudson: Alfred E. Smith and National Politics, 1918–1928* (New York: Garland, 1983).

75. Emily Smith Warner with Hawthorne Daniel, *The Happy Warrior: A Biography of My Father* (New York: Doubleday, 1956), 209–10.

76. Craig, *After Wilson*, 131–32.

77. The speech is reprinted in Franklin D. Roosevelt, *The Happy Warrior, Alfred E. Smith: A Study of a Public Servant* (New York: Houghton Mifflin, 1928).

78. Craig, *After Wilson*, 157.

79. The story of the 1928 presidential campaign and the role bigotry played in it, via the KKK and other organizations, is far more detailed than can be done justice to here. It merits study in its own right. Discussion of the effects of anti-Catholic and anti-immigrant attitudes on the 1928 election can be found in Craig, *After Wilson*, 168–73; Handlin, *Al Smith and His America*, 112–36; Slayton, *Empire Statesman*, 299–317.

80. Slayton, *Empire Statesman*, x.

81. Ibid.

82. Donn Neal offers a slightly more optimistic assessment, noting that Smith's campaign shored up the Democrats' status as a national party. See *The World Beyond the Hudson*, 282.

83. Robert Slayton writes: "The League's origin typical of its later role in public life. R. R. M Carpenter, a retired Du Pont executive, started having problems with his hired help, a fact he blamed on those new-fangled federal programs. 'Five negroes on my place in South Carolina refused work this spring . . . saying they had jobs with the government,' Mr. Carpenter complained to his friend John Raskob; to make matters worse, the cook he employed on his Florida houseboat also quit, because he could now make a dollar an hour as a painter on a national project. Carpenter asked his friend if there was something Raskob could do . . . about FDR's radical initiatives." Raskob could not, as he was not a member of Roosevelt's circle; instead he formed the American Liberty League to promote his vision of social and economic progress. See *Empire Statesman*, 379–80. See also Burk, *The Corporate State and the Broker State*, 147–91; Craig, *After Wilson*, 274–95; Colby, *Du Pont Dynasty*, 348–57; Chandler and Salsbury, *Pierre S. du Pont and the Making of the Modern Corporation*, 589; Wall, *Alfred I. du Pont*, 545–48.

84. Slayton, *Empire Statesman*, 380.

85. One critic at the time suggested the League should have been called "the American Cellophane League," because "first, it's a DuPont product and second, you can see right through it." Quoted in Slayton, *Empire Statesman*, 381.

86. Wall, *Alfred I. du Pont*, 546.

87. On the history of the League, see George Wolfskill, *The Revolt of the Conservatives: The History of the American Liberty League, 1934–1940* (Boston: Houghton Mifflin, 1962).

88. Slayton, *Empire Statesman*, 382.

89. Burk, *The Corporate State and the Broker State*, x.

90. Slotkin, *Gunfighter Nation*, 22.

91. Ibid.

92. Letter from W. D. Gray to P. S. du Pont (April 16, 1930), LMSS 229-15, Box 184.

93. Letter from P. S. du Pont to Al Smith (April 28, 1930), LMSS 229-15, Box 184; letter from P.S. du Pont to Shreve, Lamd, and Harmon (April 28, 1930), LMSS 229-15, Box 184.

94. The Notes on the Construction of the Empire State Building are reprinted in Carol Willis, ed., *Building the Empire State* (New York: Norton, 1998). For the marble used, see 65.

95. Frederick Jackson Turner, "The Significance of the Frontier in American History," address to 41st Annual Meeting of the State Historical Society of Wisconsin, December 14, 1893.

96. Solomonson, *The Tribune Tower Competition*, 197.

97. Alan Brinkley, *Voices of Protest: Huey Long, Father Coughlin, and the Great Depression* (New York: Vintage, 1983), 148–49.

98. See Brinkley, *Voices of Protest*, 151.

99. See "Letter from Robert Brown to Pierre S. du Pont, December 27, 1934," LMSS 229-15, Box 184.

Chapter 2. Setback Skyscrapers and American Architectural Development

1. On the history of real estate in New York, see Elizabeth Blackmar, *Manhattan for Rent, 1785–1850* (Ithaca, N.Y.: Cornell University Press, 1989); Eugene Rachlis and John E. Marqusee, *The Land Lords* (New York: Random House, 1963); Joel Schwartz, *The New York Approach: Robert Moses, Urban Liberals, and the Redevelopment of the Inner City* (Columbus: Ohio State University Press, 1993); and Tom Shactman, *Skyscraper Dreams: The Great Real Estate Dynasties of New York* (Boston: Little Brown, 1991).

2. Mona Domosh, *Invented Cities: The Creation of Landscape in Nineteenth-Century New York and Boston* (New Haven, Conn.: Yale University Press, 1996), 1. Domosh also quotes Christine Boyer's description of New York as the "quintessential bourgeois society."

3. A thorough history of the development of Fifth Avenue falls outside the scope of my task here, readers instead should consult M. Christine Boyer, *Manhattan Manners: Architecture and Style, 1850–1900* (New York: Rizzoli, 1985); Theodore James, Jr., *Fifth Avenue* (New York: Walker, 1971); Bernard Levin, *A Walk Up Fifth Avenue* (London: Sceptre, 1991); Charles Lockwood, *Manhattan Moves Uptown* (Boston: Houghton Mifflin, 1976); Jerry Patterson, *Fifth Avenue: The Best Address* (New York: Rizzoli, 1998); Kate Simon, *Fifth Avenue: A Very Social History* (New York: Harcourt Brace, 1978); and Ronda Wist, *On Fifth Avenue: Then and Now* (New York: Carol Publishing Group, 1992).

4. John Tauranac, *The Empire State Building: The Making of a Landmark* (New York: Scribner, 1995), 111.

5. John Jacob Astor also bought land cheaply by "foreclosing on mortgages and buying up property during the panic of 1837 when many other landowners could not afford to hold onto distressed property until it regained value." See Kenneth Jackson, ed., *The Encyclopedia of New York City* (New Haven, Conn.: Yale University Press, 1995), 989–90; John Haeger, *John J. Astor: Business and Finance in the Early American Republic* (Detroit: Wayne State University Press, 1991); Axel Madsen, *John J. Astor, America's First Multimillionaire* (New York: Wiley, 2001); Kenneth Porter, *John J. Astor, Business Man* (Cambridge, Mass.: Harvard University Press, 1931); Rachlis and Marqusee, *The Land Lords*; and Shactman, *Skyscraper Dreams*.

6. Mark Girouard's comments on the development of Fifth Avenue are worth noting: "The speed at which it moved was remarkable, and can be accurately charted by following the peregrinations of the Astor family. . . . The shops moved up Broadway, then Fifth and Sixth Avenues, following the fashionable people." Girouard, *Cities and People: A Social and Architectural History* (New Haven, Conn.: Yale University Press, 1985), 314.

7. See Jerry Patterson, *The First Four Hundred: Mrs. Astor's New York in the Gilded Age* (New York: Rizzoli, 2000). The "four hundred" was comprised of three hundred regulars and one hundred or so rotating guests (mostly the visiting rich of other cities and nations), and soon "Four Hundred became the magical number for New York Society with a capital S. If you were on the list, you were in Society." See Tauranac, *The Empire State Building*, 113.

8. The future site was now within the nightclub district known as the Tenderloin. Within a decade the fashionable rich had moved farther uptown; the houses they left behind were often taken over by shops and retailers, or in some cases, turned into clubs. By 1890 when William Waldorf Astor inherited his father's house on Thirty-Third Street, the nature of the area had declined so precipitously to his mind that he refused to live there. He moved to England instead, where presumably

more genteel society remained firmly entrenched. In addition to the perceived decline of the area, William Waldorf Astor was moved by a family feud with his cousin Caroline to leave his father's house and in its place erect a hotel, the Waldorf. The hotel, finished in 1893, was designed by Henry J. Hardenbergh, and at thirteen stories it cast shadows over the home of Caroline Astor. Within the year she had also decided to move on, and had a house built at Fifth Avenue and Sixty-Fifth Street. Her home at Thirty-Fourth Street was demolished, and in 1897 the hotel built by her son John Jacob Astor IV and also designed by Hardenbergh, the Astoria, rose in its place.

9. William Waldorf Astor hired George C. Boldt, former manager of the Bellevue Hotel in Philadelphia, to manage the Waldorf. It was a fortuitous move, as Boldt's skill at negotiating family battles and his desire to be in charge of the finest hotel in New York led to the merger of the Waldorf and Astoria Hotels. The emergence of the new Waldorf-Astoria in 1897 was the result of Boldt's careful planning with Hardenbergh. The buildings were joined by demolishing the wall that separated them, creating the elite and grand hotel of Boldt's dreams. Hardenbergh's design, which seemed clumsy and wasteful from the perspective of a free-standing Waldorf or Astoria Hotel alone, had from the beginning taken into account the possibility of joining the two structures. See Tauranac, *The Empire State Building*, 114–15.

10. See Edward Hungerford, *The Story of the Waldorf-Astoria* (New York: Putnam's, 1925) and James R. McCarthy, *Peacock Alley: The Romance of the Waldorf-Astoria Hotel* (New York: Harper Brothers, 1931).

11. Tauranac, *The Empire State Building*, 116.

12. Domosh, *Invented Cities*, 22.

13. Ibid. Domosh also notes the work of Kenneth Scherzer, *The Unbounded Community: Neighborhood Structure and Social Life in New York City, 1830–1875* (Durham, N.C.: Duke University Press, 1992).

14. See William H. Carr, *The du Ponts of Delaware* (New York: Dodd, Mead, 1964), 277; Robert A. M. Stern, Gregory Gilmartin, and Thomas Mellins, *New York 1930: Architecture and Urbanism Between the Two World Wars* (New York: Rizzoli, 1987), 203; and Tauranac, *The Empire State Building*, 116–17.

15. Max Page, *The Creative Destruction of Manhattan, 1900–1940* (Chicago: University of Chicago Press, 1999), 5.

16. See Carol Willis, *Form Follows Finance: Skyscrapers and Skylines in New York and Chicago* (New York: Princeton Architectural Press, 1995), 180.

17. Tauranac, *The Empire State Building*, 119. The Chanin Building was a fairly grand project containing more commercial space than the Woolworth Building. For a short period of time after its completion and prior to the topping off of the Chrysler Building it was the tallest building north of Wall Street. The Chanin Building, at 122 East Forty-Second Street, was designed by Sloan and Robertson and built between 1926 and 1929.

18. Page, *The Creative Destruction of Manhattan*, 21.

19. Ibid., 22.

20. Ibid.

21. Paul Starrett describes Brown's successful skyscraper-building venture in *Changing the Skyline: An Autobiography* (New York: McGraw-Hill, 1938), 285.

22. The spelling of the bank is indeed Phenix, although it is often erroneously spelled Phoenix in articles and books about the Empire State Building. In 1929 its offices were located at 149 Broadway.

23. Ibid., see also Stern et al., *New York 1930*, 612; Tauranac, *The Empire State Building*, 119–21; Willis, *Form Follows Finance*, 90.

24. See Starrett, *Changing the Skyline*, 286.

25. Letter from John J. Raskob to Louis G. Kaufman (28 August 1929), LMSS 229-15, Box 183.

26. Ibid.

27. Letter from Louis G. Kaufman to John Raksob (August 28, 1929), LMSS 229-15, Box 183.

28. The corporation that became Empire State, Inc. was formed on April 30, 1929, and was originally called the Enyan Corporation. Its board of directors was composed of employees of Chatham Phenix Bank. On May 29, 1929, the corporation filed a certificate of change of name to Waldorf-Astoria Building, Inc. Documents relating to the various stages in the corporation's creation, naming, and renaming are in LMSS 229-15, Box 187.

29. Meeting Minutes, Special Meeting of Directors (September 9, 1929), LMSS 229-15, Box 187.

30. Letter from Robert C. Brown to Pierre S. du Pont (September 10, 1929), LMSS 229-15, Box 187.

31. Ibid. The letter closed by noting that payment for "the full subscription price" should be made "in New York funds."

32. The builders were actually called Starrett Brothers and Eken; the minutes of the meeting, however, refer to them only as Starrett Brothers, Incorporated.

33. Meeting Minutes, Special Meeting of the Board of Directors (September 20, 1929), LMSS 229-15, Box 187.

34. Agreement between Empire State, Inc., and Shreve, Lamb and Harmon (September 20, 1929), LMSS 229-15, Box 187.

35. Domosh, *Invented Cities*, 119.

36. The same is true for its contemporary the Chrysler Building. While it remains one of the most recognized New York skyscrapers, its architect, William Van Allen, is spoken of rarely.

37. Carrere was killed in 1911 in an automobile accident. By 1920 Hastings had retired from active duty, thus leading to the change in the firm's name.

38. *The WPA Guide to New York City: The Federal Writers' Project Guide to 1930s New York* (New York: Pantheon, 1938), 180.

39. Tauranac, *The Empire State Building*, 101.

40. Willis, *Form Follows Finance*, 95.

41. Sheldon Cheney, *The New World Architecture* (New York: Longmans, Green, 1930), 120; quoted in Stern et al., *New York 1930*, 507.

42. Deborah Pokinski, *The Development of the American Modern Style* (Ann Arbor, Mich.: UMI Research Press, 1984), 63.

43. See ibid., 58; and Stern et al., *New York 1930*, 508–12.

44. Pokinski, *The Development of the American Modern Style*, 58.

45. Haskell, quoted in Stern et al., *New York 1930*, 510.

46. Hamlin, quoted in Pokinski, *The Development of the American Modern Style*, 58.

47. Talbot Hamlin, quoted in ibid., 59.

48. Ibid., 59, 72.

49. Sheldon Cheney, quoted in ibid., 70.

50. Starrett, quoted in Stern et al., *New York 1930*, 508.

51. Stern et al., *New York 1930*, 612.

52. Pokinski, *The Development of the American Modern Style*, 59; Talbot Hamlin, "The Prizewinning Buildings of 1931," *Architectural Record* 71 (January 1932): 11–26.

53. Hamlin, "The Prizewinning Buildings of 1931," 20.

54. Chappell, quoted in Stern et al., *New York 1930*, 612.

55. Lamb, quoted in ibid., 612.

56. Hood, quoted in ibid., 515.

57. Carol Willis, ed., *Building the Empire State* (New York: Norton, 1998), 20.

Chapter 3. Capital Nightmares

Epigraph: Robert Caro, *The Power Broker: Robert Moses and the Fall of New York* (New York: Vintage, 1975), 323.

1. Letter from H. Hamilton Weber to Robert C. Brown, LMSS 229-15, Box 183.

2. John Kenneth Galbraith, *The Great Crash, 1929* (Boston: Houghton Mifflin, 1997), xi.

3. Michael D. Bordo, Claudia Golding, and Eugene N. White, eds., *The Defining Moment: The Great Depression and the American Economy in the Twentieth Century* (Chicago: University of Chicago Press/National Bureau of Economic Research, 1998).

4. Michael Bernstein, *The Great Depression: Delayed Recovery and Economic Change in America, 1929–1939* (Cambridge: Cambridge University Press, 1987), 21.

5. Caro, *The Power Broker*, 328.

6. Joseph Stiglitz, *Globalization and Its Discontents* (New York: Norton, 2002).

7. See John Tauranac, *The Empire State Building: The Making of a Landmark* (New York: Scribner, 1995), 205–7.

8. Carol Willis, ed., *Building the Empire State* (New York: Norton, 1998), 11–12.

9. Quoted in Robert A. M. Stern, Gregory Gilmartin, and Thomas Mellins, *New York 1930: Architecture and Urbanism Between the Two World Wars* (New York: Rizzoli, 1987), 514.

10. Hine died suddenly in 1940. His family tried to donate his papers and photographs to the Museum of Modern Art, but MoMA refused them. They are now archived at the George Eastman House in Rochester, New York.

11. Daile Kaplan, *Photo Story: Selected Letters and Photographs of Lewis W. Hine* (Washington, D.C.: Smithsonian Institution Press, 1992), 34.

12. Scott Nearing, *Poverty and Riches: A Study of the Industrial Regime* (Philadelphia: J.C. Winston, 1916).

13. Charles Frederick Weller and Eugenia Winston Weller, *Neglected Neighbors: Stories of Life in the Alleys, Tenements, and Shanties of the Nation's Capital* (Philadelphia: J.C. Winston, 1909).

14. Kaplan, *Photo Story*, 34.

15. In the late 1990s a print of workers on the Empire State Building signed by Hine sold at Christie's, New York, for $28,200.

16. Jacquline Salerno, "Zone of Uncomfortable Beauty: Lewis Hine's Window on the World and the Empire State Building," M.A. thesis, Syracuse University, 1998, 45.

17. The adjustment for inflation is calculated according to the Minneapolis Federal Reserve Consumer Price Index calculator, http://minneapolisfed.org/economy/calc/cpihome.html.

18. Report to Stockholders of Empire State, Inc., for the fiscal year ending April 30th, 1932, LMSS 229-15, Box 183.

19. Report to Stockholders of Empire State, Inc., for the fiscal year ending April 30th, 1933, LMSS 229-15, Box 184. The report for the previous fiscal year had merely noted, "In our endeavor to secure tenants we have not loaded your treasury with unexpired leases in other buildings although we have had to assume several, but only for tenants who took a large volume of space and where we benefitted to a considerable extent."

20. Report to Stockholders, 1932.

21. Report to Stockholders, 1933.

22. Stern et al., *New York 1930*, 665.

23. Ibid.

24. "A Phenomenon of Exploitation," *Architectural Forum* (October 1934): 292–98.

25. Report to Stockholders of Empire State, Inc., for the fiscal year ending April 30th, 1934, LMSS 229-15, Box 184.

26. Ibid. Approximately 116,000 square feet of space were rented at the Empire State that fiscal year, compared to 23,000 at the Chrysler Building, 20,000 at the New York Central Building, and 45,000 at the Equitable Building.

27. Ibid.

28. Report to Stockholders for the fiscal year ending April 30th, 1935, LMSS 229-15, Box 185.

29. Report to Stockholders for the fiscal year ending April 30th, 1936, LMSS 229-15, Box 185.

30. Report to Stockholders for the fiscal year ending April 30th, 1938, LMSS 229-15, Box 186.

31. Mitchell Pacelle, *Empire: A Tale of Obsession, Betrayal, and the Battle for an American Icon* (New York: Wiley, 2001), 42.

32. The annual taxes at 2.7 percent would be $1,134,000 on a property worth $42,000,000, and $749,250 for a property worth $27,750,000. By 1937 the rate had crept up to 2.76 percent.

33. Report to Stockholders, 1934.

34. Report to Stockholders, 1935.

35. Report to Stockholders, 1934, 1935.

36. Letter from P. S. du Pont to Al Smith (October 27, 1938), LMSS 229-15, Box 186. In contrast to the familial tone of so much previous correspondence between these two men, Pierre's letter of resignation reads: "Dear Sir: Will you please place before the Board of Directors of Empire State, Incorporated my resignation as Director, to take effect immediately on its acceptance?"

37. Willis, *Building the Empire State*, 13.

38. Ibid.

Chapter 4. The Politics of American Architecture in the 1930s

Epigraph: Paul Starrett, *Changing the Skyline: An Autobiography* (New York: McGraw-Hill, 1938), 284.

1. Immanuel Wallerstein, *Historical Capitalism* (London: Verso, 1999), 14.

2. Katherine Solomonson, *The Chicago Tribune Tower Competition: Skyscraper Design and Cultural Change in the 1920s* (Cambridge: Cambridge University Press, 2001), 200.

3. Letter from John J. Raskob to Louis G. Kaufman (August 28, 1929), LMSS 229-15, Box 183.

4. "Drawing Closer to an Old Friend," *New York Times* (October 11, 2001), F5.

5. Ibid.

6. Letter from Al Smith to the Board of Commissioners, Department of Taxes and Assessments (January 5, 1933), LMSS 229-15, Box 184.

7. After all, as the former governor, Smith would know as well as anyone that tax breaks, since they reduce the amount of revenue available for spending on services, are in effect a form of government spending. If a tax break were granted to the Empire State Building because the owners were charitable enough to give out free office space (in a building that was less than a third occupied at the time anyway), then those charities would indeed have paid rent in the form of savings earned from a reduction in taxes for the building. Now, however, that rent would not be paid by the charities themselves, or by the owners of the Empire State Building, but by all the citizens of the City of New York.

8. *New York Times* (May 1, 1931), clipping in Publicity Associates File, LMSS 229-15, Group 10/A.

9. New York Sun (April 30, 1931), clipping in Publicity Associates File, LMSS 229-15, Group 10/A.

10. New York Times (May 2, 1931), clipping in Publicity Associates File, LMSS 229-15, Group 10/A.

11. *New York World-Telegram* (May 2, 1931), clipping in Publicity Associates File, LMSS 229-15, Group 10/A.

12. Wall Street Journal and New York Daily News (May 1, 1931), clipping in Publicity Associates File, LMSS 229-15, Group 10/A.

13. *New York Times* (May 1, 1931).

14. Ibid.

15. *New Yorker* (January 9, 1932): 14.

16. *New Masses* (June 1931): 9.

17. Minutes of the Regular Meeting of Board of Directors, Empire State, Inc., November 13, 1929, LMSS 229-15, Box 183.

18. Carol Willis, ed., *Building the Empire State* (New York: Norton, 1998), 75.

19. Ibid.

20. Foreword to Hugo Gellert, *Captial in Lithographs* (New York: Long & Smith, 1934).

21. Russell Lynes, *Good Old Modern: An Intimate Portrait of the Museum of Modern Art* (New York: Atheneum, 1973), 4.

22. Ibid., 33.

23. The description of Barr was given by René D'Harnoncourt, MoMA director, at a 1954 party celebrating the Museum's twenty-fifth birthday; quoted in Lynes, *Good Old Modern*, 351.

24. Terence Riley, *The International Style: Exhibition 15 and the Museum of Modern Art* (New York: Rizzoli, 1992), 213.

25. This comment is made in the preface to Henry-Russell Hitchcock and Philip Johnson's famous text, *The International Style: Architecture Since 1922* (New York: Norton, 1932). This quotation is taken from the reprint with a new introduction by Philip Johnson, *The International Style* (New York: Norton, 1995), 30.

26. Hitchcock and Johnson, *The International Style* (1932); later editions were titled simply *The International Style*.

27. Alfred H. Barr, Jr., Foreword, *Modern Architecture: International Exhibition* (New York: Museum of Modern Art, 1932), 12.

28. Franz Schulze's comments are taken from *Philip Johnson: Life and Work* (New York: Knopf, 1994), 80. Edward Durell Stone is quoted in Lynes, *Good Old Modern*, 189, and Franz Schulze, *Mies van der Rohe: A Critical Biography* (Chicago: University of Chicago Press, 1985), 183.

29. See M. Christine Boyer, *Dreaming the Rational City: The Myth of American City Planning* (Cambridge, Mass.: MIT Press, 1983), 285. For Stern see Robert A. M. Stern, Gregory Gilmartin, and Thomas Mellins, *New York 1930: Architecture and Urbanism Between the Two World Wars* (New York: Rizzoli, 1987), 28; for Frampton see Kenneth Frampton, *Modern Architecture: A Critical History* (New York: Oxford University Press, 1980), 249. The article about Philip Johnson is "'I am a whore': Philip Johnson at Eighty," *New Criterion* (December 1986): 57–64.

30. Lewis Mumford, "The Sky Line: Organic Architecture," *New Yorker* (February 27, 1932): 45–46.

31. Ibid., 46.

32. John Irwin Bright, "An 'International' Architecture," *American Magazine of Art* (August 1932): 105–12.

33. William Williams, "A la Mode Horizontale," *Pencil Points* (April 1932): 271–72.

34. "Bauhaus Closed by Nazis," *Architectural Record* (September 1932): 16.

35. William Orr Ludlow, "Let Us Discourage the Materialistic Modern," *American Architect* (April 1932): 24.

36. "Architecture Styled 'International,'" *New York Times* (February 7, 1932): V, 11.

37. Ibid.

38. William Curtis, *Modern Architecture Since 1900* (London: Phaidon, 1996), 15.

39. Mumford, "The Sky Line," 45.

40. Edward Alden Jewell, "Review," *New York Times* (February 14, 1932): VII, 10.

41. Catherine Bauer, "Exhibition of Modern Architecture: Museum of Modern Art," *Creative Art* (March 1932): 201–6.

42. Douglas Haskell, "What the Man About Town Will Build," *Nation* (April 13, 1932): 441–43.

43. Talbot Hamlin, "The International Style Lacks the Essence of Great Architecture," *American Architect* (January 1933): 12–16.

44. *The Masses* was published from 1911 until 1917, when the postmaster general revoked the magazine's mailing license under the Espionage Act of 1917; *The Liberator*, its immediate successor, was published from 1918 to 1924.

45. "Let It Be Really New!" *New Masses* (June 1926): 20. Also quoted in Daniel Aaron, *Writers on the Left: Episodes in American Literary Communism* (New York: Harcourt, Brace, 1961), 201.

46. *U.S. Military Intelligence Reports: Surveillance of Radicals in the United States, 1917–1941*, microfilm series, accessed; quotations from "Estimate of the Subversive Situation as of January 1, 1932."

47. Paul Buhle and Mary Buhle, eds., *Encyclopedia of the American Left* (New York: Garland, 1990), 527. The House Committee on Un-American Activities still listed the *New Masses* in its *Guide to Subversive Organizations and Publications* (Washington, D.C.: the Committee, 1961) thirteen years after it had ceased publication.

48. Paul Buhle, *Marxism in the United States: Remapping the History of the American Left* (London: Verso, 1991), 175. Other chroniclers of the left in the United States less sympathetic to the cause describe the *New Masses* simply as "the Communist weekly magazine." See Philip Jaffe, *The Rise and Fall of American Communism* (New York: Horizon, 1975), 49.

49. John Kwait, "The New Architecture," *New Masses* (May 1932): 23.

50. In his preface to the 1995 edition of *The International Style* (New York: Norton, 1995). Philip Johnson notes that the text and exhibit raised the ire of both those "interested in the social side of architecture," and architects "who resented the emphasis on the slick, oversimplified boxiness of modern architecture." Looking back at the years of the exhibit, Johnson describes Alfred Barr as "the resident ideologue," and recalls that he was himself "five times as enthusiastic and propagandistic." According to Johnson, the formal impulse of the text was the result of Barr, who "shaped our thinking" with his demand for "strict principles" (13–15). Henry-Russell Hitchcock offers a slightly different take, suggesting instead that it was the reception of the exhibit and book which was narrow and formal: "Contrary to our intentions, it would seem that what we merely described was, to some extent, followed like a prescription"; Preface to 1966 edition of *The International Style*, reprinted in 1995 edition, 22.

51. Dolores Hayden, *Seven American Utopias: The Architecture of Communitarian Socialism, 1790–1975* (Cambridge, Mass.: MIT Press, 1976), p. 3.

52. R. E. Somol, "Statement of Editorial Withdrawal," in Somol, ed., *Autonomy and Ideology: Positioning an Avant-Garde in America* (New York: Monacelli Press, 1997), 20, 26.

53. For instance, Charles Jencks writes: "Mies, like so many other architects, was so confused about politics as to be completely apolitical," in *Modern Movements in Architecture* (London: Penguin, 1985), 40. Or, read what Tom Wolfe writes about Gropius: "Gropius' interest in 'the proletariat' or 'socialism' turned out to be no more than aesthetic or fashionable," in *From Bauhaus to Our House* (New York: Farrar, Straus, 1981), 15. Richard Pommer's work on the political ideology of Mies and modern architecture takes a more complex view but, nevertheless, treats the question of political meaning as one of intention rather than reception. See "Mies van der Rohe and the Political Ideology of the Modern Movement in Architecture," in *Mies van der Rohe: Critical Essays*, ed. Franze Schulze (New York: Museum of Modern Art, 1989).

54. Joan Ockman, "The Road Not Taken: Alexander Dorner's Way Beyond Art," in Somol, ed., *Autonomy and Ideology*, 107.

55. Kwait, "The New Architecture," 23.

56. Ibid.

57. See, for instance, Mary McLeod's introduction to Joan Ockman, ed., *Architecture, Criticism, Ideology* (Princeton, N.J.: Princeton Architectural Press, 1985), 8.

58. John Kwait, "Architecture Under Capitalism," *New Masses* (December 1932): 10–13.

59. Kwait, "The New Architecture."

60. Kwait, "Architecture Under Capitalism," 10. Buckminster Fuller and those associated with *Shelter* in turn referred to Kwait (Schapiro) and *New Masses* as: "A small coterie . . . whose weakness is its dominance by vituperant [sic] iconoclasm, with no scientific substitute for the object of its passion, and a complete lack of empirical knowledge of the mechanics-of-evolution of the human phenomenon in its essential economic trends in the North American continent." See *Shelter* (November 1932): 16.

61. Hayden, *Seven American Utopias*, 5.

62. Ibid.

Chapter 5. Architecture Culture into the 1950s

1. "Socialist Cities Arise," *Soviet Russia Today* (June 1932): 6–9.

2. James Sloan Allen, *The Romance of Commerce and Culture: Capitalism, Modernism, and the Chicago-Aspen Crusade for Cultural Reform* (Chicago: University of Chicago Press, 1983), 6.

3. Elaine Hochman, *Architects of Fortune: Mies van der Rohe and the Third Reich* (New York: Weidenfeld and Nicolson, 1989), 73. Hochman's text lays out the trajectory of the Nazis' opposition to modern architecture and art. Her argument that Mies's "formalistic style" implied "social irresponsibility," however, is far less grounded.

4. Ibid., 98–101.

5. Barbara Miller Lane's study of German architecture and politics is indispensable when considering this era; see Lane, *Architecture and Politics in Germany, 1918–1945* (Cambridge, Mass.: Harvard University Press, 1968). See also Peter Adam, *The Arts of the Third Reich* (London: Thames and Hudson, 1992); William J. R. Curtis, *Modern Architecture Since 1900* (London: Phaidon, 1996), 350–69; Leon Krier, ed., *Albert Speer: Architecture, 1932–1942* (Brussels: Archives d'Architecture Moderne, 1985); and Robert R. Taylor, *The Word in Stone: The Role of Architecture in the Third Reich* (Berkeley: University of California Press, 1974).

6. Richard Weston, *Modernism* (London: Phaidon, 1996), 162; see also Curtis, *Modern Architecture Since 1900*, 350–69.

7. Curtis, *Modern Architecture Since 1900*, 359.

8. Ibid., 239.

9. For further details on the nature and design of the curricula established by Mies and Gropius at IIT and Harvard respectively, see Cammie D. McAtee, "Mies van der Rohe and Architectural Education: The Curriculum at the Illinois Institute of Technology, Student Projects, and Built Work," Master's Thesis, Queen's University, 1996; Anthony Alfonsin, *The Struggle for Modernism: Architecture, Landscape Architecture, and City Planning at Harvard* (New York: Norton, 2002); and Klaus Herdeg, *The Decorated Diagram: Harvard Architecture and the Failure of the Bauhaus Legacy* (Cambridge, Mass.: MIT Press, 1983).

10. Serge Guilbaut, *How New York Stole the Idea of Modern Art: Abstract* (Chicago: University of Chicago Press, 1985).

11. Dell Upton, *Architecture in the United States* (New York: Oxford University Press, 1998), 168.

12. "A Noted Architect Dissects Our Cities," *New York Times* (January 3, 1932): V10.

13. Ayn Rand, *The Fountainhead* (New York: Bobbs-Merrill, 1943, reprinted New York: Signet, 1993).

14. Nancy Levinson, "Tall Buildings, Tall Tales," in *Architecture on Film*, ed. Mark Lamster (New York: Princeton Architectural Press, 2000), 24.

15. Ayn Rand, *The Fountainhead* (New York: Signet, 1993), 708.

16. Book review, *New York Times* (March 16, 1943): 7.

17. Book review, *The Nation* (June 12, 1943).

18. Publications that discuss *The Fountainhead* include "Fountainhead at 50," *Architecture* (May 1993); "Fountainhead Film at Fifty," *RIBA Journal* (November 1998): 24–25; "Film," *Interior Design* (August 1994): 64–69; "From Fallingwater to Fountainhead," *Journal of the Taliesin Fellows* (Spring 1997); "On Being Roarkian," *Oculus* (March 1993); "Fountainheadache," *Design Book Review* (Winter 1996–97). Nancy Levinson mentions a 1992 panel of architects and historians in Boston addressing the influence of the novel; see "Tall Buildings, Tall Tales," 28.

19. Rand, *The Fountainhead*, 708.

20. Ibid., 529.

21. Levinson, "Tall Buildings, Tall Tales," 24.

22. Ibid., 31.

23. Lary May, *The Big Tomorrow: Hollywood and the Politics of the American Way* (Chicago: University of Chicago Press, 2000), 180.

24. Ibid., 205.

25. Peter Blake, *No Place like Utopia: Modern Architecture and the Company We Kept* (New York: Knopf, 1993), 9.

26. Katherine Solomonson, *The Chicago Tribune Tower Competition: Skyscraper Design and Cultural Change in the 1920s* (Cambridge: Cambridge University Press, 2001), 100–101.

27. Ibid., 103.

28. Allen, *The Romance of Commerce and Culture*, 12.

29. Advertisement, "Telephone Wire Coming Up," *Newsweek* (February 1, 1943).

30. "After Total War Can Come Total Living," *Revere's Part in Better Living* 10 (1943); reprinted in Upton, *Architecture in the United States*, 235.

31. Advertisements, "Forecasting by Bohn," "Future Housing Developments," and "New Designs for Living," *Newsweek* (March, January, October 1943).

32. Advertisement, "Men Who Plan Beyond Tomorrow Like the Lightness of Seagram's V.O.," *Newsweek* (March 29, 1943).

33. See in particular the rendering of his proposal in Le Corbusier, *Towards a New Architecture* (New York: Dover, 1986), 57.

34. Advertisement, "Men Who Plan Beyond Tomorrow Like Canadian Whisky at Its Glorious Best!" *Newsweek* (March 1, 1943).

Chapter 6. Clients and Architect

1. Alfred Barr, Jr., Introduction to Henry-Russell Hitchcock and Philip Johnson, *The International Style: Architecture Since 1922* (New York: Norton, 1932; reprint 1995), 30.

2. The total cost of the Seagram Building is difficult to pin down with precision, in part because of the absence of a mortgage. The corporate documents tracking the building expenses associated with the project, a series of handwritten entries in an accounting ledger, are inconclusive. No mention of total building cost is found in the operating expense summaries for the fiscal years that followed (the only fixed charges listed are taxes and insurance). Corporate records elsewhere show variations in cost assessment as wide as 10 percent. A 1957 internal memo lists the total cost of the building as $40,000,000, with construction accounting for $32,000,000, land $5,000,000, and machinery and equipment $3,000,000; see "Memorandum to H. Fieldsteel, 6.18.57," Seagram Company LTD/Bronfman Family Collection, Hagley Museum and Library, Wilmington, Delaware (hereafter SC/BF Collection, HML), Record Series 2126, Box 195 (hereafter 2126/195), File Correspondence. A memo from September 1958, however, states that Price Waterhouse, who served as accountants for the corporation, had determined that the "revised estimated cost of the new building at 375 Park Avenue, New York, is $44,000,000"; see "Memorandum from H. Fieldsteel to W. Frauenthal," 2126/844, Vertical File Accounting, 1955–1958. A 1958 article in *Time* magazine listed the construction cost as $35,000,000, a figure repeated in other sources at the time and more recently; see "Monument in Bronze," *Time* (March 3, 1958): 52, and Charles Bagli, "On Park Avenue, Another Trophy Changes Hands," *New York Times* (October 12, 2000): B1. Adjusted according to the U.S. Bureau of Labor Statistics Consumer Price Index (a common index for measuring the change in prices over time), $35,000,000 in 1958 would be the equivalent of just under $250,000,000 at the end of 2007; $44,000,000 would be just over a staggering $314,000,000.

3. "Seagram's Bronze Tower," *Architectural Forum* 109 (July 1958): 67. The article gives the total cost as $43,000,000.

4. The organization of the various entities that made up the business known generally simply as Seagram was in the 1950s unnecessarily labyrinthine and redundant. Joseph E. Seagram & Sons, Inc. (which in some publications, confusingly, is also listed as Seagram Company Ltd.), was the parent corporation of the House of Seagram, which in turn was divided into five brands: the major brands Seagram, Calvert, and Four Roses, and the smaller brands Kessler and General Wine and Spirits. In addition, another tier of brands (and companies), Browne Vintners, operated under the direction of Seagram. Here, when I refer to Seagram, I am referring to the corporate entity Joseph E. Seagram & Sons, Inc.

5. Lary May, ed., *Recasting America: Culture and Politics in the Age of Cold War* (Chicago: University of Chicago Press, 1989), 5.

6. Roger Montgomery, "The Goal of Architecture: Why It Should Help Promote a Humane Environment," *St. Louis Dispatch* (April 5, 1959), unpaginated clipping in SC/BF Collection, HML, 2173/797, Seagram Building Activities—Clips, 1959 File.

7. "Seagram House Re-Reassessed," *Progressive Architecture* (June 1959): 140–45, clipping in SC/BF Collection, HML, 2126/845, Vertical File—Publicity, 1956–1959.

8. "Design for a Museum," *New York Herald Tribune* (June 1, 1959), 12, clipping in SC/BF Collection, HML, 2173/797, Seagram Building Activities—Articles, 1956–1986 File.

9. "Shrinking Skyscrapers: High Costs Keep New Ones Below '20s Peaks," *Wall Street Journal* (July 1, 1959), unpaginated clipping in SC/BF Collection, HML, 2173/797, Seagram Building Activities—Articles, 1956–1986 File.

10. Lewis Mumford, "The Skyline: The Lessons of the Master," *New Yorker* (September 13, 1958): 141–52.

11. William J. R. Curtis, *Modern Architecture Since 1900* (London: Phaidon, 1996), 307.

12. Leland Roth, *A Concise History of American Architecture* (New York: Harper and Row, 1980), 284–86.

13. Kenneth Frampton, *Modern Architecture: A Critical History* (London: Thames and Hudson, 1985), 237.

14. Sadly, in the days since September 11, 2001, the lobby of the Seagram Building, like so many others in New York, has been "secured" with cordons of velvet rope and superfluous security guards designed to keep those who have no business to transact out of the building. The spare and pure lobby now resembles the foyer of a bank.

15. Curtis, *Modern Architecture Since 1900*, 409.

16. Carol Willis, *Form Follows Finance: Skyscrapers and Skylines in New York and Chicago* (New York: Princeton Architectural Press, 1995), 141.

17. "Shrinking Skyscrapers."

18. "Modern Living: The City," *Time* (28 September 1962): 56, clipping in SC/BF Collection, HML, 2173/797, Seagram Building Activities—Articles, 1956–1986 File.

19. Curtis, *Modern Architecture Since 1900*, 409.

20. "A Skyscraper Crammed with Innovations," *Engineering News-Record*: 8–9, undated clipping in SC/BF Collection, HML, 2173/797, Seagram Building Activities—Articles, 1956–1986 File.

21. Exactly how old he was when the family came to Canada is a subject of some dispute. Samuel Bronfman usually claimed that he was born in Canada, although most histories of the family state that he came to Canada as a young child.

22. "Lolly Golt Interview with Phyllis Bronfman Lambert (January 8, 1980)," 20, SC/BF Collection, HML, HML, 2173/10.

23. Edgar Bronfman, *The Making of a Jew* (New York: Putnam, 1996), 6.

24. Canadian law during the 1920s and 1930s forbade shipping liquor within provinces but not among them. Ibid., 7.

25. The original company formed after the purchase of the Seagram distillery was known as Distillers Corporation—Seagrams Ltd. Distillers Corporation was a British company that also produced whiskey, and which Samuel Bronfman had convinced to invest in the first distillery the

family built. After Samuel Bronfman's death, his son Edgar (who inherited control of the company), renamed it The Seagram Company Ltd., "to make it easier for investors to find the listing in the newspapers." See Bronfman, *The Making of a Jew,* 9.

26. An extensive account of the various illegal practices employed by the Bronfman family during the 1920s and 1930s can be found in Peter C. Newman, *Bronfman Dynasty: The Rothschilds of the New World* (Toronto: McClelland and Stewart, 1978), 62–131.

27. Bronfman, *The Making of a Jew,* 8.

28. Newman, *Bronfman Dynasty,* 64.

29. Ibid., 65.

30. The U.S. Senate Special Committee to Investigate Organized Crime in Interstate Commerce was headed by Senator Estes Kefauver of Tennessee.

31. Nicholas Faith, *The Bronfmans: The Rise and Fall of the House of Seagram* (New York: St. Martin's, 2006), 1.

32. See ibid., 27, 73–74, 118–19, 127 and Edgar M. Bronfman, *Good Spirits: The Making of a Businessman* (New York: Putman, 1998), 23–42.

33. Quoted in Newman, *Bronfman Dynasty,* 118.

34. Reflecting on the 1920s, one Canadian observed, "it is fair to say that the Bronfman rumrunning was a major factor in the closet anti-Semitism of the United Grain Growers [and] the Women's Christian Temperance Movement, and the overt anti-Semitism of the Ku Klux Klan that provided the drive to elect the Tory administration of 1929." See Newman, *Bronfman Dynasty,* 118. Edgar Bronfman describes the anti-Semitism of Montreal in the 1930s as "palpable," writing that "there were restricted hotels (no dogs or Jews allowed), and Jews were not welcome on the boards of banks or of McGill University. . . the powers-that-be had very little, if any, social contact with Jews, and very little business dealings [with them]." See Bronfman, *The Making of a Jew,* 10.

35. This claim was put forward in 1920 with the warning "Bolshevism flourishes in wet soil, failure to enforce Prohibition in Russia was followed by Bolshevism. Failure to enforce Prohibition here will encourage disrespect for law and invite Industrial disaster. Radical and Bolshevist outbreaks are practically unknown in states where Prohibition has been in effect for years"; Newman, *Bronfman Dynasty,* 82.

36. "Lolly Golt, Interview with Phyllis Bronfman Lambert," 13.

37. Ibid., 16.

38. Newman, *Bronfman Dynasty,* 161–67.

39. There are a variety of stories about exactly how Phyllis found out about the original Pereira & Luckman design. The story her mother tells is found in "Lolly Golt, Interview with Saidye Bronfman (August 8, 1978)," 227, SC/BF Collection, HML, 2173/10. Robert A. M. Stern's history of New York architecture offers an alternative tale: "Lambert was living in Paris when she saw a picture of the Luckman scheme in the international edition of the *Herald Tribune*"; see Stern, Thomas Mellins, and David Fishman, *New York 1960: Architecture and Urbanism Between the Second World War and the Bicentennial* (New York: Monacelli, 1995), 342. In an article about the construction of the Seagram Building written for the Vassar alumnae magazine, Phyllis writes, "I was living in Europe when Seagram's intent to build reached me in Paris in July through a rendering of a very mediocre building." Phyllis Bronfman Lambert, "How a Building Gets Built," *Vassar Alumnae Magazine* 44 (February 1959): 13–19. I have decided here to side with Saidye Bronfman on the details of how Phyllis Lambert first discovered the P & L design.

40. "Press Release," SC/BF Collection, HML, 2126/797.

41. Many in the world of business and architecture at the time thought incorrectly that Charles Luckman had been fired from Lever Brothers because of Lever House's daring design. See Stern et al., *New York 1960,* 339.

42. The length of the letter and its topic are discussed in Newman, *Bronfman Dynasty,* 165 and Robert Fulford, "Joan of Architecture," *Imperial Oil Review* (Winter 1989): 9–12.

43. Newman, *Bronfman Dynasty*, 165.

44. "Lolly Golt Interview with Saidye Bronfman," 227.

45. Ibid., 227–28.

46. Ibid., 227.

47. Ibid., 228.

48. Newman, *Bronfman Dynasty*, 165–66.

49. "Lolly Golt Interview with Phyllis Bronfman," 10.

50. Schulze, *Philip Johnson*, 240.

51. Stern et al., *New York 1960*, 344.

52. Meredith Clausen, *Pietro Belluschi: Modern American Architect* (Cambridge, Mass.: MIT Press, 1994), 271.

53. Franz Schulze, *Philip Johnson: Life and Work* (New York: Knopf, 1994), 243.

54. Phyllis Bronfman Lambert quoted in Peter Blake, *The Master Builders: Le Corbusier, Mies van der Rohe, Frank Lloyd Wright* (New York: Norton, 1976), 264; Schulze, *Philip Johnson*, 243.

55. "Memorandum (March 11, 1952)," SC/BF Collection, HML, 2126/844, File "Skytop," Ellis D. Slater file, 1952–1954.

56. "Lolly Golt Interview with Saidye Bronfman," 228.

57. Newman, *Bronfman Dynasty*, 166.

58. Thomas Ennis, "Building Is Designer's Testament," *New York Times* (November 10, 1957), unpaginated clipping in SC/BF Collection, HML, 2126/797, Seagram Building Activities (1957)—Clippings, A. A. Schecter File.

59. Francis Bello, "Architecture's New Technology," *Fortune* (March 1956): 128–30, clipping in SC/BF Collection, HML, 2126/ 797, Seagram Building Activities—Articles (1958–1986) File.

60. Quoted in a "Seagram Overseas Corporation House Organ Memo" dated January 2, 1964, SC/BF Collection, HML, 2126/797, Seagram Building Activities—Articles (1958–1986) File.

61. "Slenderella in the Sky," *Playboy*, undated, unpaginated clipping in SC/BF Collection, HML, 2126/797, Seagram Building Activities—Clips (1958) File.

62. "Confidential Building Bulletin," December 1954, SC/BF Collection, HML, 2126/798, Seagram Building Activities—Press Releases (1954–1958) File.

63. "Monument in Bronze," *Time* (March 3, 1958): 52–55.

64. Rand, *The Fountainhead*, 196, 309.

65. "Monument in Bronze."

66. William Norwich, "Sex and Real Estate," *New York Times Magazine* (June 1, 2003): 70–75.

67. Terence Riley and Barry Bergdoll, eds., *Mies in Berlin* (New York: Museum of Modern Art, 2001).

68. For more on Rand's antipathy toward architects who worked as part of a team, see her attack on Raymond Hood and his work as "the ugliest, flattest, most conventional, meaningless, unimaginative, and uninspiring in the book." Quote from Rand's notes published in *The Fountainhead*, 702.

69. Lewis Mumford, "The Sky Line: The Lesson of the Master," *New Yorker* (September 13, 1958): 141–52.

70. On the production of the public image of Jackson Pollock, see Erika Doss, *Benton, Pollock, and the Politics of Modernism: From Regionalism to Abstract Expressionism* (Chicago: University of Chicago Press, 1991); on Mies see Ricardo Daza, *Looking for Mies* (Barcelona: ACTAR, 2000).

71. For details about the sober, well-organized, and decidedly unromantic operations in the design offices of Shreve, Lamb & Harmon, see William F. Lamb, "The Empire State Building. VII: The General Design," *Architectural Forum* 54 (1931): 1–9; R. H. Shreve, "The Empire State Building Organization," *Architectural Forum* 52 (1930): 770–74; R. H. Shreve, "The Economic Design of Office Buildings," *Architectural Record* 67 (1930): 352; John Tauranac, *The Empire State Building: The Making of a Landmark* (New York: Scribner, 1995), 99–110; and Carol Willis, ed., *Building the Empire State* (New York: Norton, 1998).

72. This pithy assessment of the relative anonymity of Shreve, Lamb & Harmon was pointed out to me by Katherine Solomonson. *The Oxford Dictionary of Architecture*, ed. James Stevens Curl (Oxford: Oxford University Press, 1998), lacks an entry for Shreve, Lamb & Harmon or the individual architects who composed the firm.

Chapter 7. Gangland's Grip on Business

1. "Memorandum: Suggested Outline of Program for Development of Building to House the Seagram Companies, July 16, 1951," SC/BF Collection, HML, 2126/844, File Ellis Slater, 1952–1954.

2. "Project 'Skytop,' March 24, 1952," SC/BF Collection, HML, 2126/196, Building Proposal File; "Memorandum: Re-Building, March 11, 1952," SC/BF Collection, HML, 2126/844, File Ellis Slater, 1952–1954.

3. "Memorandum: Suggested Outline."

4. "Minutes of the Meeting of the Advisory Committee, May 27, 1952," SC/BF Collection, HML, 2126/376, Advisory Committee Minutes Book 1 of 4.

5. "Report from Cross & Brown to Lou R. Crandall, President George A. Fuller Company, May 8, 1952," SC/BF Collection, HML, 2126/844, File Ellis D. Slater, 1952–1954.

6. "Project 'Skytop,' Studies of various schemes showing allowable building size and comparable financial set up, March 24, 1952," unpaginated document, SC/BF Collection, HML, 2126/196, File Project "Skytop," building proposal.

7. Ibid. Scheme 3A was a seven-story building with two basement levels designed to be occupied solely by the Seagram Company; Scheme 4C was a fifty-story tower set back 100 feet from Park Avenue.

8. Ibid. Scheme 3A was the least expensive at $14 million; Scheme 1C, a fairly traditional office building design with a 32-story tower rising from an 18-story base made up of multiple setbacks was the most expensive at $34 million.

9. Ibid. Scheme 3B featured a tower oriented perpendicular to Park Avenue atop a base parallel to the street. While the renderings at this early stage lack much of the detailing of Lever House, the broad outlines of the design are clearly influenced by Gordon Bunshaft's building. Scheme 4B, a 43-story tower that cut into a smaller six-story rectangular building, was designed to allow for a large setback along Park Avenue to create "advertising space."

10. This was in fact how Seagram's own corporate memos phrased the issue; see "Memorandum: Suggested Outline."

11. "Gangland's Grip on Business," *Business Week* (May 12, 1951): 22, clipping in SC/BF Collection, HML, 2167/797, File Public Relations Department, Kefauver Investigation, 1951.

12. See Charles Fontenay, *Estes Kefauver: A Biography* (Knoxville: University of Tennessee Press, 1980), 180–85; Estes Kefauver, *Crime in America* (Garden City, N.Y.: Doubleday, 1951), 313; William Howard Moore, *The Kefauver Crime Committee and the Politics of Crime* (Columbia: University of Missouri Press, 1974), 184–85. According to James L. Baughman, local broadcasts of the hearings in New York were aired on WPIX; see "Television," in Kenneth T. Jackson, ed., *The Encyclopedia of New York* (New Haven, Conn.: Yale University Press, 1995), 1159.

13. Fontenay, *Estes Kefauver*, 164–65.

14. Fontenay refers to the traveling hearings as a "road show"; ibid., 168.

15. Estes Kefauver, quoted in ibid., 171–72.

16. News clipping, SC/BF Collection, HML, 2126/797, File Public Relations Department, Kefauver Investigation, 1951. Details of Lansky's exploits can be found in Robert Lacey, *Little Man: Meyer Lansky and the Gangster Life* (Boston: Little Brown, 1991) and Hank Messick, *Lansky* (New York: Putnam, 1971); the life and career of Frank Costello are dealt with in George Walsh, *Public Enemies: The Mayor, the Mob, and the Crime That Was* (New York: Norton, 1991).

17. "Letter from Harry Bulow to Elliott Bell, Editor *Business Week*," SC/BF Collection, HML, 2126/797, File Public Relations Department, Kefauver Investigation, 1951. The letter continued: "In Kansas City, Missouri, where Seagram's has several distributors, one firm subsequently was found to be controlled by a nefarious character and its license was revoked, at which time Seagram's revoked its franchise with that firm. Just for the record, it is Seagram's policy to choose its distributors on the basis of business policy consistent with all available information about their character. Seagram's does not give licenses to known hoodlums. The company believes that the state liquor authorities are responsible for determining whether or not a person is fit to operate with a license. Once such a license is granted, we presume that the character of the licensee is satisfactory."

18. "Confidential" undated, unsigned, unpaginated report, SC/BF Collection, HML, 2126/797, File Public Relations Department, Kefauver, 1951

19. According to his biographer, Kefauver received telephone death threats and had his phone tapped at various points during the hearings; the FBI also learned of a failed plot by a professional gambler to kill Kefauver. See Fontenay, *Estes Kefauver*, 178–85.

20. William J. R. Curtis, *Modern Architecture Since 1900* (London: Phaidon, 1996), 409; Robert A. M. Stern, Thomas Mellins, and David Fishman, *New York 1960: Architecture and Urbanism Between the Second World War and the Bicentennial* (New York: Monacelli, 1995), 345.

21. William Jordy, *American Buildings and Their Architects: The Impact of European Modernism in the Mid-Twentieth Century* (New York: Oxford University Press, 1972), 262.

22. "Letter from Irving Green to President, Seagram Corporation," SC/BF Collection, HML, 2126/797, File Seagram Building—Correspondence, 1955–1959.

23. "Text of Broadcast, Bill Leonard, New York Story, at 6:30 p.m. over WCBS (NY), January 13, 1959," SC/BF Collection, HML, 2126/798, File Radio Reports, 1954–1969.

24. Jack Sterling on WCBS seems to have made a habit of cracking jokes about the "booze building," much to the chagrin of Seagram executives. This quote is from "Text of Broadcast, Jack Sterling at 6 a.m. over WCBS (October 13, 1959)," SC/BF Collection, HML, 2126/798, File Radio Reports, 1954–1969.

25. "Text of Broadcast, Jack Sterling at 6 a.m. over WCBS (March 13, 1958)" SC/BF Collection, HML. 2126/798, File Radio Reports, 1954–1969.

26. "Text of Broadcast, Jack Sterling at 6 a.m. over WCBS (October 13, 1959)."

27. "Text of Broadcast, Jack Sterling at 6 a.m. over WCBS (December 8, 1958)," SC/BF Collection, HML, 2126/798, File Radio Reports, 1954–1969.

28. "Text of Broadcast, Dorothy and Dick Kollmar at 8:15 a.m. over WOR (NY), October 3, 1957," SC/BF Collection, HML, 2126/798, File Radio Reports, 1954–1969.

29. "Undated Draft of Letter to William Paley from Edgar Bronfman," SC/BF Collection, HML, 2126/797, File Correspondence, Seagram Building, 1955–1959. Edgar, Samuel Bronfman's oldest son, was then president of Seagram-Distillers Corporation. It is not known whether the letter was ever sent to William Paley.

30. "Advertising's Million $ Avenue," *The Advertiser* (November 1956), unpaginated clipping in SC/BF Collection, HML, 2126/797, File Seagram Building Activities—Clips, 1957.

Chapter 8. Modern Architecture and Corporate America in the 1950s

Epigraph: Bernard Tschumi, *Architecture and Disjunction* (Cambridge, Mass.: MIT Press, 1994), 21.

1. Carol Herselle Krinsky, *Gordon Bunshaft of Skidmore, Owings & Merrill* (Cambridge, Mass.: MIT Press, 1988), 24.

2. Ibid., 18.

3. Katherine Solomonson, *The Chicago Tribune Tower Competition: Skyscrapers and Cultural Change in the 1920s* (Cambridge: Cambridge University Press, 2001), 233.

4. Paul Goldberger, *The City Observed, New York: A Guide to the Architecture of Manhattan* (New York: Penguin, 1979), 156.

5. Krinsky, *Gordon Bunshaft of Skidmore, Owings & Merrill*, 49–50.

6. Ibid., 49.

7. Francis Conroy Saunders, *The Cultural Cold War: The CIA and the World of Arts and Letters* (New York: New Press, 1999), 344.

8. Carol Willis, *Form Follows Finance: Skyscrapers and Skylines in Chicago and New York* (New York: Princeton Architectural Press, 1995), 134–35.

9. Saidye Bronfman recalls that Phyllis told her father "Daddy you should have a modern building." "Lolly Golt Interview with Saidye Bronfman (August 8, 1978)," SC/BF Collection, HML, 2173/10, 227.

10. Franz Schulze, *Philip Johnson: Life and Work* (New York: Knopf, 1994), 242. The Seagram Company headquarters in Montreal, built in 1928 at 1430 Peele Street, was a miniature castle mixing, as one biographer of the family puts it, "Gothic and Tudor elements with early Disneyland"; Peter C. Newman, *Bronfman Dynasty: The Rothschilds of the New World* (Toronto: McClelland and Stewart, 1978), 26.

11. According to my survey of the hundreds of pages of clippings in the SC/BF Collection, HML.

12. "Memo from A. A. Schechter Associates to Harry Bulow, July 7, 1958," SC/BF Collection, HML, 2126/798, File Seagram Building Dedication, 1958.

13. The clippings related to the Seagram Building collected by Schechter for 1956 alone number in the hundreds. Part of this has to do with multiple papers picking up the same AP or UPI story, but it also is a reflection of the tremendous interest new buildings, in particular modern ones, circulating in the general public at this time. See SC/BF Collection, HML 2126/797, File Seagram Building Activities—Clips, 1956.

14. "Portholes for Sidewalk Superintendents," *Sunday News* (August 12, 1956), clipping in SC/BF Collection, HML, 2126/797, File Seagram Building Activities—Clips, 1956.

15. "New Building Has Finished Model," *Troy Record* (October 5, 1956), clipping in SC/BF Collection, HML, 2126/797, File Seagram Building Activities—Clips, 1956. The same release was printed in the *El Paso Times*, *Troy Times Record*, *Peoria Journal Star*, and *Allentown Chronicle*, among others.

16. "'Super' Art," *Jacksonville* (Illinois) *Journal* (June 24, 1956), clipping in SC/BF Collection, HML, 2126/797, File Seagram Building Activities—Clips, 1956; "Public Informed on Seagram Building," *Philadelphia Observer* (March 25, 1957), clipping in SC/BF Collection, HML, 2126/797, File Seagram Building Activities—Clips, 1957.

17. "Press Release, October 23, 1958," in SC/BF Collection, HML, 2126/798, File Seagram Building Activities—Press Releases, 1954–1958.

18. "Lobby Light Matches Sun," *New York Journal American* (June 16, 1957), unpaginated clipping in SC/BF Collection, HML, 2126/797, File Seagram Building Activities—Clips.

19. Mel Heimer, "My New York," clippings from various newspapers dated June 25, 1956, in SC/BF Collection, HML, 2126/797, File Seagram Building Activities—Clips, 1956.

20. "Seagram First with 'Forty-Niner,'" *New Mexico Beverage Journal* (March 1959), clipping in SC/BF Collection, HML, 2126/797, File Seagram Building Activities—Clips, 1959. Similar stories were printed in newspapers across the U.S.

21. "First for Seagram," *Missouri Beverage Journal* (April 1957), clipping in SC/BF Collection, HML, 2126/797, File Seagram Building Activities—Clips, 1957; "Midtown, N.Y., by Robert Williams," *New York Post* (April 17, 1957), clipping in SC/BF Collection, HML, 2126/797, File Seagram Building Activities—Clips, 1957.

22. "Fact Sheet," written by A. A. Schechter Associates and sent to Harry Bulow, SC/BF Collection, HML, 2126/196, File Special Operating Procedures, 1958.

23. "Talk of the Town," *New Yorker* (May 25, 1963), unpaginated clipping in SC/BF Collection, HML, 2126/797, File Seagram Building Activities—Articles, 1958–1986.

24. William H. Whyte, *City: Rediscovering the Center* (New York: Doubleday, 1988; reprint Philadelphia: University of Pennsylvania Press, 2009), 104.

25. Whyte, *City*, 31.

26. Quoted in Robert A. M. Stern, Thomas Mellins, and David Fishman, *New York 1960: Architecture and Urbanism Between the Second World War and the Bicentennial* (New York: Monacelli, 1995), 348.

27. "Chile Praises Seagram for Use of Bronze in Building," *Daily Metal Reporter* (October 11, 1956), unpaginated clipping in SC/BF Collection, HML, 2126/797, File Seagram Building Activities—Clips, 1956.

28. *National Jewish Post* (May 17, 1957), clipping in SC/BF Collection, HML, 2126/797, File Seagram Building Activities—Clips, 1954–1988.

29. *Centralizer* 30, 6 (August 1958): 2, clipping in SC/BF Collection, 2126/797, File Seagram Building Activities—Ads, 1957–1964. For the history of the H-bomb, see Richard Rhodes, *Dark Sun: The Making of the Hydrogen Bomb* (New York: Simon and Schuster, 1995) and Herbert York, *The Advisors: Oppenheimer, Teller, and the Superbomb* (Stanford, Calif.: Stanford University Press, 1989).

30. *Centralizer* 30, 6 (August 1958), 2.

31. *Beverage Retailer Weekly* (May 21, 1962), clipping in SC/BF Collection, 2126/797, File Seagram Building Activities—Clips, 1960. Information on the Polaris missile, a submarine-launched nuclear-armed ballistic missile, can be found in James Baar, *Polaris!* (New York: Harcourt Brace, 1960) and Harvey Sapolsky, *The Polaris System Development: Bureaucratic and Programmatic Success in Government* (Cambridge, Mass.: Harvard University Press, 1972).

32. *Playboy* (August 1958), unpaginated clipping in SC/BF Collection, 2126/797, File Seagram Building Activities—Clips, 1958.

33. "Famous Park Avenue Beauty Enjoys Flexalum Light Control," *Architectural Forum* (February 1960), unpaginated clipping in SC/BF Collection, 2126/797, File Seagram Building Activities—Clips, 1960. A number of magazines in the late 1950s and early 1960s, including *Town and Country*, *New York Times Magazine*, and others, used the Seagram Building as a location for fashion shoots as well. They generally employed the ground floor and plaza for the shoots, and the accompanying text identified the Seagram Building by name, suggesting that the building had quickly attained a fashionable cachet.

34. "Memorandum: Suggested Outline of Program for Development of Building to House the Seagram Companies, July 16, 1951," SC/BF Collection, 2126/844, File Ellis Slater, 1952–1954.

35. Letter from Major General Robert E. Condon to General Frank R. Schwengel, November 18, 1955, SC/BF Collection, 2126/844, Vertical File Civil Defense.

36. Memo from F. M. Kramer to Ellis Slater, November 21, 1955, SC/BF Collection, 2126/844, Vertical File Civil Defense.

37. Fred N. Severud and Anthony F. Merrill, *The Bomb, Survival, and You: Protection for People, Buildings, Equipment* (New York: Reinhold, 1954).

38. "Report from Severud, Elstad, and Krueger to Mies van der Rohe and Philip Johnson, February 1, 1956," SC/BF Collection, 2126/844, Vertical File Civil Defense.

39. Ibid.

40. Letter from Richard Foster to Fred Kramer, February 24, 1956, SC/BF Collection, 2126/844, Vertical File Civil Defense.

41. "Architecture's New Technology," *Fortune* (March 1956): 128, clipping in SC/BF Collection, HML, 2126/797, File Seagram Building Activities—Articles, 1956–1986.

42. "A Skyscraper Crammed with Innovations," *Engineering News-Record*, undated and unpaginated clipping in SC/BF Collection, HML, 2126/797, File Seagram Building Activities—Articles, 1956–1986.

43. "Values Stressed for Nuclear Age," *New York Times* (September 30, 1959).

44. "Symposium Dedicates a Building," *Spirits* (November 1959), unpaginated clipping in SC/BF Collection, HML, 2126/797, File Seagram Building Activities—Clips, 1960.

45. "Selling a Vintage Building," *New York Times* (16 May 1979), unpaginated clipping in SC/BF Collection, HML, 2126/797, File Seagram Building Activities—Clips, 1954–1958. The building was sold to the TIAA pension fund for $85 million in 1979.

46. Michael Robert Marrus, *Samuel Bronfman: The Life and Times of Seagram's Mr. Sam* (Hanover, N.H. University Press of New England for Brandeis University Press, 1991), 388–94.

47. "Our New Home . . . 375 Park Avenue," Seagram Company Employee Guide, SC/BF Collection, HML, 2126/760, File Miscellany, ca. 1957–1958.

48. Edgar M. Bronfman, *Good Spirits: The Making of a Businessman* (New York: Putnam, 1998), 81.

Chapter 9. Regeneration Through Violence

1. Michael Sorkin and Sharon Zukin, Introduction to *After the World Trade Center: Rethinking New York City*, ed. Sorkin and Zukin (New York: Routledge, 2002), ix.

2. Edwin G. Burrows, "Manhattan at War," in Sorkin and Zukin, eds., *After the World Trade Center*, 23.

3. Pete Hamill, quoted in *New York: A Documentary Film*, Steeplechase Films production in association with WGBH Boston, Thirteen/WNET New York, New York Historical Society ; producers, Lisa Ades, Ric Burns; director, Ric Burns, DVD, (2001).

4. Ann Buttenwieser, "'Fore and Aft: The Waterfront and Downtown's Future," in *The Lower Manhattan Plan: The 1966 Vision for Downtown New York*, ed. Carol Willis (New York: Princeton Architectural Press, 2002), 21.

5. Paul Willen and James Rossant, "In Retrospect," in Willis, ed., *The Lower Manhattan Plan*, 29.

6. Russell Shorto, *The Island at the Center of the World: The Epic Story of Dutch Manhattan and the Forgotten Colony That Shaped America* (New York: Doubleday, 2004), 3.

7. Richard Slotkin, *The Fatal Environment: The Myth of the Frontier in the Age of Industrialization, 1800–1890* (New York: HarperPerennial, 1985), 16.

8. Richard Slotkin, *Regeneration Through Violence: The Mythology of the American Frontier, 1600–1860* (Middletown, Conn.: Wesleyan University Press, 1973), 7.

9. Burrows, "Manhattan at War," 32.

10. Ibid.

11. Sorkin and Zukin, Introduction, *After the World Trade Center*, xi.

12. Slotkin, *Regeneration Through Violence*, 5.

13. Richard Slotkin, *Gunfighter Nation: The Myth of the Frontier in Twentieth-Century America* (New York: HarperPerennial, 1992), 13.

14. Leslie M. Harris, *In the Shadow of Slavery: African Americans in New York City, 1626–1863* (Chicago: University of Chicago Press, 2003), 13.

15. On the conflicts between the Dutch and Native Americans, see Burroughs, "Manhattan at War, 23–31 and Edwin G. Burrows and Mike Wallace, *Gotham: A History of New York City to 1898* (New York: Oxford University Press, 2000), 3–57.

16. Harris, *In the Shadow of Slavery*, 14.

17. Ibid., 15.

18. Ibid., 26–27.

19. Ibid., 27.

20. Ibid.

21. On the history of slavery in New York City, see Ira Berlin, *Many Thousands Gone: The First Two Centuries of Slavery in North America* (Cambridge, Mass.: Belknap Press of Harvard University Press 1998), David Brion Davis, *The Problem of Slavery in the Age of Revolution, 1770–1823* (Ithaca, N.Y.:

Cornell University Press, 1975), Phyllis Field, *The Politics of Race in New York: The Struggle for Black Suffrage in the Civil War Era* (Ithaca, N.Y.: Cornell University Press, 1982); Philip Foner, *Business and Slavery: The New York Merchants and the Irrepressible Conflict* (Chapel Hill: University of North Carolina Press, 1941); Harris, *In the Shadow of Slavery;* Anthony Gronowicz, *Race and Class Politics in New York City Before the Civil War* (Boston: Northeastern University Press, 1998); Graham Russell Hodges, *Root and Branch: African Americans in New York and East Jersey, 1613–1863* (Chapel Hill: University of North Carolina Press, 1999), Jill Lepore, *New York Burning: Liberty, Slavery, and Conspiracy in Eighteenth Century Manhattan* (New York: Vintage, 2006), Edgar McManus, *A History of Negro Slavery in New York* (Syracuse, N.Y.: Syracuse University Press, 1966); and Shane White, *Somewhat More Independent: The End of Slavery in New York City, 1770–1810* (Athens: University of Georgia Press, 1995).

22. Ira Berlin and Leslie Harris, "Digging in New York's Slave Past Beyond the African Burial Ground," *The New-York Journal of American History* 66, 2 (Fall/Winter 2005): 23–33.

23. Harris, *In the Shadow of Slavery,* 27.

24. Berlin and Harris, "Digging in New York's Slave Past."

25. David Quigley, "Southern Slavery in a Free City: Economy, Politics, and Culture," in *Slavery in New York,* ed. Ira Berlin and Leslie M. Harris (New York: New Press, 2005), 267–69.

26. Ibid., 269.

27. Ibid., 269, 272.

28. A brief but perceptive look at the way the built environment accommodated slavery and vice versa is John Michael Vlach's "Slave Housing in Manhattan," in Berlin and Harris, eds., *Slavery in New York.*

29. See Beverly Gage, *The Day Wall Street Exploded: A Story of America in Its First Age of Terror* (Oxford: Oxford University Press, 2008).

30. Mike Davis, *Ecology of Fear: Los Angeles and the Imagination of Disaster* (New York: Metropolitan Books, 1998), 287.

31. Slotkin, *Gunfighter Nation,* 213.

32. On the history of New York in movies, see James Saunders, *Celluloid Skyline: New York and the Movies* (New York: Knopf, 2001).

33. Ada Louise Huxtable, "Ode to Manhattan's Spires and Shards," *New York Times* (December 6, 1970).

34. Ada Louise Huxtable, "Who's Afraid of the Big Bad Buildings?," *New York Times* (May 29, 1966).

35. Martin Arnold, "High Court Plea Is Lost by Foes of Trade Center," *New York Times* (November 13, 1963).

36. Huxtable, "Who's Afraid of the Big Bad Buildings?"

37. Glenn Fowler, "32 More Stores Give Way to Trade Center Site," *New York Times* (March 2, 1966).

38. Edith Evans Asbury, "Downtown Merchants Parade to Protest World Trade Center," *New York Times* (July 14, 1962).

39. Quoted in Eric Darton, *Divided We Stand: A Biography of New York's World Trade Center* (New York: Basic Books, 1999), 92.

40. Huxtable, "Who's Afraid of the Big Bad Buildings?"

41. Ada Louise Huxtable, "The Planning Vacuum," *Wall Street Journal* (June 22, 2005).

42. Quoted in Philip Nobel, *Sixteen Acres: Architecture and the Outrageous Struggle for the Future of Ground Zero* (New York: Metropolitan Books, 2005), 177, 204.

43. Quoted in Angus Kress Gillespie, *Twin Towers: The Life of New York City's World Trade Center* (New York: New American Library, 2002), 183.

44. Nobel, *Sixteen Acres,* 16.

45. Wolf von Eckardt, quoted in Gillespie, *Twin Towers,* 181.

46. Quoted in Gillespie, *Twin Towers,* 185.

47. See Norval White and Elliot Willensky, *AIA Guide to New York City*, 4th ed. (New York: Three Rivers Press, 2000).

48. Nobel, *Sixteen Acres*, 4.

Chapter 10. The Rhetoric and Reality of Urban Renewal

Epigraph: Robert Moses, "Significance: What the City Means to Me," *New York Times* (April 29, 1956).

1. David Rockefeller, *Memoirs* (New York: Random House, 2003), 51.

2. Ibid., 383–85.

3. Ibid., 384–86.

4. Ibid., 387.

5. Roger Cohen, "Casting Giant Shadows: The Politics of Building the World Trade Center," *Portfolio: A Quarterly Review of Trade and Transportation* (Winter 1990/91).

6. M. Christine Boyer, "Meditations on a Wounded Skyline and Its Stratigraphies of Pain," in *After the World Trade Center: Rethinking New York City*, ed. Michael Sorkin and Sharon Zukin (New York: Routledge, 2002), 113–14.

7. Cohen, "Casting Giant Shadows."

8. Joseph Schumpeter, *Capitalism, Socialism and Democracy* (1942; New York: Harper, 1975).

9. Boyer, "Meditations on a Wounded Skyline," 114.

10. Cohen, "Casting Giant Shadows."

11. On the history of the Port Authority, see Robert Caro, *The Power Broker: Robert Moses and the Fall of New York* (New York: Vintage Books, 1974); Jameson W. Doig, *Empire on the Hudson: Entrepreneurial Vision and Political Power at the Port of New York Authority* (New York: Columbia University Press, 2001); and Joe Mysak, *Perpetual Motion: The Illustrated History of the Port Authority of New York and New Jersey* (Los Angeles: General Publishing Group, 1997).

12. Angus Kress Gillespie, *Twin Towers: The Life of New York City's World Trade Center* (New York: New American Library, 2002), 39; Rockefeller, *Memoirs*, 389.

13. Gillespie, *Twin Towers*, 52.

14. Rockefeller, *Memoirs*, 386; Cohen, "Casting Giant Shadows."

15. Rockefeller, *Memoirs*, 388.

16. Ibid.

17. "High Court Plea Is Lost by Foes of Trade Center," *New York Times* (November 13, 1963).

18. Gillespie, *Twin Towers*, 49.

19. "Downtown Merchants Parade to Protest World Trade Center," *New York Times* (July 14, 1962).

20. "Downtown Merchants Parade to Protest World Trade Center," *New York Times* (July 14, 1962).

21. Eric Darton, *Divided We Stand: A Biography of New York's World Trade Center* (New York: Basic Books, 1999), 92.

22. Gillespie, *Twin Towers*, 50.

23. Cohen, "Casting Giant Shadows."

24. "High Court Plea Is Lost."

25. "Pickets to Follow Governor on Tour," *New York Times* (January 4, 1964).

26. "Biggest Buildings in World to Rise at Trade Center," *New York Times* (January 19, 1964).

27. "Trade Center Foe Broadens Attack," *New York Times* (June 26, 1964)

28. "Thirty-Two More Stores Give Way to Trade Center Site," *New York Times* (March 2, 1966).

29. "160 Claims on File over Trade Center," *New York Times* (August 27, 1978).

30. James Glanz and Eric Lipton, "The Height of Ambition," *New York Times Magazine* (September 8, 2002), 36.

31. Ad for Asbestos Corporation, *Asbestos Magazine* (November 1981).

32. Port Authority Advertisement for World Trade Center, 1984.

33. Boyer, "Meditations on a Wounded Skyline," 109–10.

34. Carol Krinsky, *Rockefeller Center* (Oxford: Oxford University Press, 1978), 196.

Chapter 11. Cathedrals of Commerce: Minoru Yamasaki, Skyscraper Design, and the Rise of Postmodernism

1. Eric Darton, *Divided We Stand: A Biography of New York's World Trade Center* (New York: Basic Books, 1999), 114.

2. David Rockefeller, *Memoirs* (New York: Random House, 2003), 163. As Rockefeller notes, Harrison "could well have assumed that he was the best architect for the job. In any case, he graciously accepted my explanation that since we were such good friends, I wanted to select someone to avoid the appearance of favoritism. Wally unhesitatingly recommended the firm of Skidmore, Owings & Merrill." While Bunshaft and Harrison make repeat appearances in his memoirs, Rockefeller never mentions Minoru Yamasaki in his discussion of the World Trade Center (or anywhere else, for that matter), a curious omission.

3. On the dollar value of Stone's projects in the mid-1960s, see Christopher Gray, "Streetscapes: Edward Durrell Stone and the Gallery of Modern Art," *New York Times* (October 27, 2002): 11, 9.

4. Darton, *Divided We Stand*, 114–16.

5. Ibid., 116.

6. Minoru Yamasaki, *A Life in Architecture* (New York: Weatherhill, 1979), 9–11.

7. Ibid., 12.

8. Ibid., 12.

9. Ibid.

10. Ibid., 18.

11. Ibid., 20; Darton, *Twin Towers*, 114.

12. Yamasaki, *A Life in Architecture*, 112–14; Philip Nobel, *Sixteen Acres: Architecture and the Outrageous Struggle for the Future of Ground Zero* (New York: Metropolitan Books, 2005), 25.

13. "Now 100% Small Parts for Victory," advertisement in *Architectural Record* (January 1943).

14. "In Defense," advertisement in *Architectural Record* (January 1943).

15. "Buzzards Brushed Off like Flies," advertisement in *Architectural Record* (May 1943).

16. John Dower, *War Without Mercy: Race and Power in the Pacific War* (New York: Pantheon, 1987), 4.

17. "Jap-Killing Machine," advertisement in *Newsweek* (1943).

18. Richard Slotkin, *Gunfighter Nation: The Myth of the Frontier in Twentieth Century America* (New York: HarperPerennial, 1992), 318–19.

19. Yamasaki, *A Life in Architecture*, 23.

20. Ibid., 39.

21. Ibid., 17, Nobel, *Sixteen Acres*, 24.

22. Nobel, *Sixteen Acres*, 24.

23. James Glanz and Eric Lipton, "The Height of Ambition," *New York Times Magazine* (September 8, 2002), 36; Nobel, *Sixteen Acres*, 17–18.

24. Darton, *Divided We Stand*, 117.

25. Yamasaki, *A Life in Architecture*, 115.

26. Angus Kress Gillespie, *Twin Towers: The Life of New York City's World Trade Center* (New York: New American Library, 2002), 170.

27. Austin Tobin quoted in Darton, *Divided We Stand*, 109.

28. In a late edition of *Space, Time, and Architecture: The Growth of a New Tradition* (Cambridge, Mass: Harvard University Press, 1970), Sigfried Giedion called the Twin Towers a "distortion" of the Lake Shore Drive apartments.

29. For these and other reactions to the Twin Towers, see Nobel, *Sixteen Acres*, 24–25.

30. David Rockefeller quoted in Darton, *Divided We Stand*, 76.

31. Glanz and Lipton, "The Height of Ambition," 38.

32. Minoru Yamasaki quoted in Gillespie, *Twin Towers*, 241.

33. Quoted in Nobel, *Sixteen Acres*, 24–25.

34. Minoru Yamasaki, "Minoru Yamasaki," *Art in America* 50, 4 (Winter 1962): 50, quoted in Nobel, *Sixteen Acres*, 34.

Conclusion: Into the Future

1. Philippe de Montebello, "The Iconic Power of an Artifact," *New York Times* (September 25, 2001).

2. Quoted in Philip Nobel, *Sixteen Acres: Architecture and the Outrageous Struggle for the Future of Ground Zero* (New York: Metropolitan Books, 2005), 26.

3. John Allman/David Zane Mairowitz, "Letters," in *September 11, 2001: American Writers Respond*, ed. William Heynan (Silver Spring, Md.: Etruscan Press, 2002), 13.

4. Quoted in Nobel, *Sixteen Acres*, 42.

5. Quoted in Nobel, *Sixteen Acres*, 138.

6. Sharon Zukin, "Our World Trade Center," in *After the World Trade Center: Rethinking New York City*, ed. Michael Sorkin and Sharon Zukin (New York: Routledge, 2002), 15.

7. Fred Bernstein, "Drawing Closer to an Old Friend," *New York Times* (October 11, 2001): F5.

8. Max Page, "New Angles of Vision: Reflections on New York History After September 11," *New-York Journal of American History* (Spring 2003): 12–18.

9. Richard Slotkin, *Regeneration Through Violence: The Mythology of the American Frontier, 1600–1860* (Middletown, Conn.: Wesleyan University Press, 1973), 5.

Epilogue

1. "Rebuilding at 9/11 Site Runs Late, Report Says," *New York Times* (July 1, 2008).

2. "The Human Toll of a Building Binge," *New York Times* (May 31, 2008).

3. "To Name Towers in the Sky, Many Look There for Inspiration," *New York Times* (July 8, 2008).

4. "From Cracks to Falling Cranes, a Big Job for Building Inspectors," *New York Times* (May 20, 2008).

5. "Top City Inspector Accused of Taking Bribes," *New York Times* (June 7, 2008), "Inspector is Charged with Filing False Report Before Crane Collapse," *New York Times* (March 21, 2008).

6. "Engineer Is Charged in Fatal Wall Collapse," *New York Times* (June 20, 2008); "Manslaughter Charge in Trench Collapse," *New York Times* (June 12, 2008).

7. "Editorial: A Far Too Dangerous Business," *New York Times* (June 11, 2008).

8. "Fire Dept. Did Not Inspect Pipe in Doomed Building," *New York Times* (August 23, 2007); "Two New Deaths, Same Old Questions," *New York Times* (August 25, 2007).

9. "Abu Dhabi Buys 90% Stake in Chrysler Building," *New York Times* (July 10, 2008).

10. E-mail communication with author, June 6, 2008.

11. Richard Lacayo, "The Architecture of Autocracy," *Foreign Policy* (May/June 2008): 53–57.

12. "I'm the Designer. My Client's the Autocrat," *New York Times* (June 22, 2008).

INDEX

Italics indicate illustrations.

ACKNOWLEDGMENTS

This book, like any such project, benefited from the advice and assistance of many individuals and institutions. At the University of Minnesota Katherine Solomonson and Lary May offered encouragement and trenchant criticism, along with polite but forceful (and I would add, necessary) requests for revision, and then revision again. Likewise John Archer pushed me to clarify and refine my thinking about the forces that shape the built environment. David Roediger, David Noble, and Roger Miller brought their vast reserves of knowledge about history and geography to bear on my thinking and writing, all for the better. My fellow travelers Steven Garabedian, Deirdre Murphy, Bill Anthes, Karen Connely-Lane, and David Monteyne kindly read early versions of this book and supportively sat through I don't know how many conference presentations. At Wesleyan University my studies with Richard Slotkin, Joseph Siry, and Joel Pfister launched me on the intellectual journey that led to this book. Portions of this book were presented in early form at a number of conferences and benefited from the thoughtful comments of Gregor Kalas, Dorothy Habel, Wallis Miller, and Sandy Isenstadt. At the 2001 Dissertation Colloquium at the Temple Hoyne Buell Center for the Study of American Architecture at Columbia University Gwendolyn Wright and Kevin Harrington, among others, suggested important and useful avenues of inquiry. My colleagues at the Georgia Institute of Technology, especially Sabir Khan, George Johnston, and Robert Craig, offered thoughtful advice and support. At the University of Pennsylvania Press, my editor Robert Lockhart guided this project from infancy to maturity. He was and remains a calm and thoughtful guide to the world of scholarly publishing.

Financial support for this project came at critical junctures from many sources. A Harold Leonard Memorial Fellowship and Harold Leonard Grant from the University of Minnesota supported a year of research and writing. A generous grant from the Hagley Museum and Library's Center for the History of Business, Technology, and Society allowed me to spend weeks perusing their holdings related to corporate patronage of architecture. The Society of Architectural Historians kindly funded my travel to present at their annual conference. The Georgia Tech Foundation supported costs associated with the production of illustrations for the book.

Many friends outside the academy played important roles in the research for this project. Brendan O'Toole, Derek Nelsen, Eric and Natasha Schnabel, Jeremy Tennis, Kara Alfonso, and Joanna Clark all housed and fed me in New York City many, many times. They also very nicely never told me that they really had heard quite enough about the obscure details of the financing of the Empire State Building. When I was a resource-starved grad student Brendan bought me lunch at the Brasserie in the Seagram Building; Eric and Natasha spotted me dinner upstairs at the Four Seasons a few years later. Their companionship was a wonderful compliment to Mies' luxurious minimalism.

George and Norie Flowers always encouraged my scholarly pursuits with great affection. Donald and Linda Clark did likewise. Scooter sat in my lap while I wrote and re-wrote the manuscript. Most important of all is all the love, support, and, of course, patience shown to me by Jennifer Clark. This project has been part of her life for as many years as it has mine, and although she had ample reason many times to throw her hands up about both this book and its author, she never did. For that reason, and many more, I am grateful.